William Allingham

Nightingale Valley

A collection of choice lyrics and short poems from the time of Shakespeare to the present day

William Allingham

Nightingale Valley
A collection of choice lyrics and short poems from the time of Shakespeare to the present day

ISBN/EAN: 9783744780230

Printed in Europe, USA, Canada, Australia, Japan

Cover: Foto ©Thomas Meinert / pixelio.de

More available books at **www.hansebooks.com**

NIGHTINGALE VALLEY.

NIGHTINGALE VALLEY;

A COLLECTION OF CHOICE LYRICS

AND SHORT POEMS.

FROM THE TIME OF SHAKESPEARE TO

THE PRESENT DAY.

EDITED BY

WILLIAM ALLINGHAM.

LONDON:
BELL AND DALDY, 186, FLEET STREET.
1862.

PREFACE.

THE intention of this book simply is to delight the lover of poetry. Specimens critical and chronological have their own worth; we desire to present a jewel, aptly arranged of many stones, various in colour and value, but all precious. Nothing personal or circumstantial, nothing below a pure and loving loyalty to the Muse, has been wittingly suffered to interfere betwixt the idea and its realization. Much, it is true, is perforce omitted; but should the brotherly reader and the judicious critic haply find the little volume, *per se*, a good thing, they will scarcely complain that it does but its part. Do we curse the cup of refreshing handed us from the well because it is not twice as large — when the well itself, too, remains? Those who best know of such things will the most readily see that a collection in any sense complete or exhaustive has not been thought of here, but an arrangement of a limited number of short poems, with some eye to grouping and general effect, and to the end (as said) of delight.

But of delight—noble and fruitful. The grand word " Poetry" has its mean associations, —as " organ" may suggest a solemn cathedral, or a Savoyard and monkey. True Poetry, however, is *not*, as some suppose, a kind of verbal confectionery, with cramp fantastic laws that impose great labour to little purpose.

If one has anything to express in words, why go thus roundabout? asks our sternly prosaic friend. The relations of the human mind with the world are not so simple as he takes for granted. Men are not only intellectual and moral, but emotional and imaginative. Sorrow and joy are very real, yet often very illogical; and so also, and oftener, are those faint rapid shadows and gleams that pass continually over the mind, composing the multiplex hue of life. The moods of the sagest, are they never submissive to the wind in a keyhole, the crackling of the flame, a vernal odour, or the casual brightness or gloom upon a landscape? At the least touch of any sense gates to Infinity are ready to fly open.

Such is man's nature; and since he further finds himself urged to regulate what belongs to him, without and within, and mutually to control the one by the other, so, as he gains industrial, scientific, religious development, he also becomes an Artist—in picture, in sculpture, in architecture, in music, in verse.

Language *has music in it;* from this Poetry (Verse-Poetry is always meant) derives its form and quality. It is the most melodious arrangement of language. The *proportionality* necessary for this end excites mystically a desire for proportionality in all other respects, reaching inward to the very spirit of the thought which is to be expressed. The stimulated and thoroughly alert Imagination requires its pure insight to be shapen forth in the most perfect possible diction—judging all by a fine rapid-glancing logic, peculiar, airy, genuine. In short, Musical Proportionality is the life-principle of Poetry, and the product Poetic Beauty. As for the *use* of Poetry—I will tell you this accurately, when you can put me Love into a crucible, and Faith into a balance.

Such an attempt being too difficult, let us agree to abide by matter-of-fact. And matter-of-fact shows us that Verse-Poetry (daughter of Language and Music, born at a time of the world whereto History stretches not backward) has been cherished and beloved amongst all the nations, ancient and modern, barbarous and civilized. Babes love the sound of it, youth passionately delights in it, age remembers it gladly; it helps memory, purifies and steadies language, guards elocution; it gives wings to thought, touches hidden verities, can soothe grief, heighten joy, beautify the common world, and blend with the divinest aspirations.

Poetry and Science (rank them as you please) are equally founded on the nature of man in mystic relation with the Universe.

How Poetry manages to evince itself in material form would be hard or impossible to explain; even if possible, still doubtless the secrets ought to be kept, like those of love. The profane, when they suppose themselves to comprehend either, have but lost the degree of sympathetic knowledge—of instinctive and genuine feeling, which they inherited as men. It is difficult indeed to become a critic and remain a man. Fitly, therefore, to examine even the shortest genuine Poem is the rarest success of literary judgment. Perhaps it is not venturing too far to say that a true Poem is always conceived by a sort of happy chance—descending, as it were, out of the sky; but, as a finished whole, is the fruit of a most actively attentive condition (yet with ease—not strained) of the rarest natural endowment.

Every Poet is not a great one; but, whatever his rank in the guild, he is a *maker*, creator in little, and his successful work fine and true of its kind, possessing (however simple and modest) a secure, determinate, dignified aspect, standing firm with good hold upon the ground, and proving its direct right to exist as much as a healthy human being when he looks into your eye. Every true Poet is such by the same peculiar and inimitable fire that so splendidly beams from the greatest; and is born capable to discover the art of poetry, had it been thitherto unknown. Some poems have soul in a bad body, and are by nature soon for death; many things under the name are only puppets, dolls, mere wax and wood,—finer and prettier, sometimes, and, for a little, more admired than what is alive.

Our Book hopes to please best the most unsectarian worshipper of Song,—one who can equally enjoy the floating charm of " Claribel," or "Tell me, thou Star," a thing of close-wrought gold like "My Last Duchess" or "Ulysses," the work-a-day vigour of Scott's lyrics, the sympathies of Wordsworth in their pensive and deliberate movement, the celestial-infantine fancies of William Blake, and the unconscious pathos and picturesqueness of an Old Ballad. He will perhaps compare Shelley's "Fugitives" with Campbell's more realistic treatment of a similar theme in "Lord Ullin's Daughter," finding himself in the midst of either storm — with the lovers pushing off from shore, where

"In the scowl of Heaven each face
Grew dark as they were speaking,"

and with the other two, murmuring proud pleasure,

"While, around, the lash'd ocean,
Like mountains in motion,
Is withdrawn and uplifted,
Sunk, shatter'd, and shifted
To and fro."

He will love Herrick (naturally and always a true lyrist), and taste, almost with a kind of awe, the delicately delicious lighter movements of our grand Master, like those of Philomel herself to the Faëry Queen—

"Philomel with melody
Sing in our sweet lullaby;
Lulla, lulla, lullaby:"

and then admire how one little Song (such a one is "Go, lovely Rose,") can save a sinking Poet, like a solitary plank in the shipwreck of his fame. He will bring fit audience to the subtle, romantic vibrations of Coleridge's too often despondingly-introspective mind, or to the winged rush of Shelley's most eager spirit, leaving air alive with billows of melody, or to the rich and dreamful tones of that even younger voice which too soon fell silent. He will gladly claim America for blood-relation in intellect and poetry, on account of her one Great Writer (as yet), whose prose is so royally precious as to outvalue even his own verse, fine as that is. Nor will he fail to recognize the sad fantastic tune of the few weird notes, sounding as from a cave, which belong to the poet of " the Raven;" or the firm and trustworthy tone of Bryant, the transatlantic Campbell. He will be one who can appreciate the emphatic swing of " Ye Mariners," and the mysterious modulation in such words as " *Wild roses and ivy serpentine*." And he will greatly rejoice to remember that of the men who have enriched these pages and the world, some are still living, " to brighten the sunshine."

CONTENTS.

		Page
SONNET. To the Nightingale	Milton	1
Wake, Lady	Joanna Baillie	2
Inscription for a Fountain on a Heath	Coleridge	2
Fair Ines	Hood	3
Sic Vita		5
A Sonnet upon Sonnets	Wordsworth	5
Jock o' Hazeldean	Scott	6
The Passionate Shepheard to his Love	Chr. Marlowe	7
To-day	T. Carlyle	8
The Seven Sisters	Wordsworth	9
Song. From "The Miller's Daughter"	Tennyson	11
Autumn. A Dirge	Shelley	12
The Amulet	Emerson	13
The Character of a Happy Life	Sir H. Wotton	13
Want of Sleep	Wordsworth	14
Abou Ben Adhem and the Angel	Leigh Hunt	15
Lucy Ashton's Song	Scott	16
A Dream	W. Allingham	16
Ode to the Cuckoo	John Logan	18
Coronach. From "The Lady of the Lake"	Scott	19
It is not beautie I demand		20
The Question	Shelley	21
Barthram's Dirge		23
The World's Wanderers	Shelley	24
My Last Duchess	R. Browning	25
Song. The Season for Wooing	W. C. Bryant	27
Sonnet. Composed by Grasmere Lake	Wordsworth	28
Hohenlinden	Campbell	29
Sonnet. From the Portuguese	E. B. Browning	30
Clerk Saunders	Old Ballad	31
Invocation of Silence	R. Flecknoe	35

xii   CONTENTS.

		Page
Claribel. A Melody	*Tennyson*	36
France seen from the Coast of England	*Wordsworth*	37
The Sower's Song	*T. Carlyle*	37
Song. Why so pale and wan	*Sir J. Suckling*	38
I remember, I remember	*Hood*	39
Sonnet. The Idle Voyager	*Hart. Coleridge*	40
The Lover of Music to his Piano-Forte	*Leigh Hunt*	41
The Fairies. A Child's Song	*W. Allingham*	42
The Last Day of Autumn		44
Ballad. Sigh on, sad heart	*Hood*	44
To Dianeme	*Herrick*	46
The Bells	*Edgar A. Poe*	46
To Mary in Heaven	*Burns*	50
The Northern Star		51
To Lucasta, going to the Warres	*R. Lovelace*	52
A Farewell	*Tennyson*	53
Sonnet. Twilight among Mountains	*Wordsworth*	54
Introduction to "Songs of Innocence"	*W. Blake*	54
Song. The Owl	*Tennyson*	55
Sonnet. To Mr. Lawrence	*Milton*	56
The Dream of Eugene Aram	*Hood*	56
To the Virgins, to make much of Time	*Herrick*	63
Protus	*R. Browning*	64
Song. I wander'd by the brook-side	*R. M. Milnes*	66
The Nightingale	*Coleridge*	67
The Haunted Palace	*Edgar A. Poe*	71
Evening Song of the Priest of Pan	*John Fletcher*	72
The Fugitives	*Shelley*	74
To a Departed Friend	*In Memoriam*	76
Song. From "As you like it"	*Shakespeare*	77
Sonnet. On first looking into Chapman's Homer	*Keats*	78
The Apology	*Emerson*	78
Tibbie	*Burns*	79
Choral Song of Illyrian Peasants	*Coleridge*	81
The Raven	*Edgar A. Poe*	81
Flowers	*Hood*	88
Fable	*Emerson*	89
As I lay a-thinking	*R. H. Barham*	89
A Man's Requirements	*E. B. Browning*	91

CONTENTS. xiii

		Page
Mea Culpa		93
Break, break, break	Tennyson	94
Sonnet. Absence	Shakespeare	95
The Tiger	W. Blake	95
Song. From the Spanish of Iglesias	W. C. Bryant	96
Yarrow unvisited	Wordsworth	97
Adieu	T. Carlyle	99
To a Sky-Lark	Wordsworth	101
The Twa Corbies	Bor. Minstrelsy	101
Dirge for the Year	Shelley	102
Song of Ariel	Shakespeare	103
Sonnet. On his Blindness	Milton	104
Song on May Morning	Milton	104
Ulysses	Tennyson	105
Song of Ariel	Shakespeare	107
To Autumn	Keats	107
I do confesse thou'rt smooth and faire		109
Ned Bolton	W. Kennedy	110
Goodbye	Emerson	113
The Caique	W. Thackeray	114
To ——	Shelley	115
Therania	W. Allingham	115
The Blossom	W. Blake	116
Sonnet. Love's Slave	Shakespeare	117
Song. Go, lovely rose	E. Waller	118
Tam Glen	Burns	119
Ode to Evening	W. Collins	120
Loss	In Memoriam	122
The Lady's Yes	E. B. Browning	123
A Lament	Shelley	124
The Forging of the Anchor	Sam. Ferguson	125
To Daffodils	Herrick	129
An Angel in the House	Leigh Hunt	130
Bonnie George Campbell		131
The Humble-Bee	Emerson	132
Disdain returned	Thomas Carew	134
Auld Robin Gray	Lady Lindsay	134
Song. From "Zapolya"	Coleridge	136
Sonnet. Mary Queen of Scots	Wordsworth	137
Lines composed in a Concert Room	Coleridge	137
Over hill, over dale	Shakespeare	138
Circumstance	Tennyson	139
The Sands o' Dee	C. Kingsley	139
Ode to a Nightingale	Keats	140

CONTENTS.

		Page
The Laboratory	R. Browning	143
Inscription for a Fountain	Barry Cornwall	146
The Rose that deck'd her Breast	W. Barnes	146
Fitz-Eustace's Song	Scott	148
The Exile	Hood	149
Sonnet. Love's Consolation	Shakespeare	150
O'Brien of Arra	Thomas Davis	151
Lord Amiens' Song, in the Forest of Arden	Shakespeare	152
Sonnet. September	Hart. Coleridge	153
The Two April Mornings	Wordsworth	154
Lord Ullin's Daughter	Campbell	156
The Arrow and the Song	H. Longfellow	158
O whistle, and I'll come to you, my lad	Burns	158
Sonnet. Absence and Presence	Shakespeare	159
Kubla Khan; or, a Vision in a Dream	Coleridge	160
She dwelt among the untrodden ways	Wordsworth	162
Up at a Villa—down in the City	R. Browning	163
Forbearance	Emerson	167
The Brook	Tennyson	167
La belle Dame sans Mercy	Keats	169
Sonnet. The Sense of Loss	Wordsworth	171
The Hour of Prayer	Felicia Hemans	172
Sonnet. Love's Silence	Sir P. Sidney	173
Song. From "The Princess"	Tennyson	173
To my Sister	Wordsworth	174
Ye Mariners of England	Campbell	176
Sonnet. To Cyriack Skinner	Milton	177
Fairy Song		178
Sonnet. A Parting	M. Drayton	179
Nose versus Eyes	Cowper	180
Cupid's Curse	George Peele	181
Song. From "The Lady of the Lake"	Scott	183
The Lady's Grave	M. Boddington	184
To the Cuckoo	Wordsworth	185
In the stillness o' the Night	W. Barnes	186
Song. A spirit haunts the year's last hours	Tennyson	187
Herrick's Litany	Herrick	188
Sonnet. From "Michael Angelo"	Hart. Coleridge	189
Spring and Sorrow	In Memoriam	189

CONTENTS.

		Page
Chorus of the Flowers	*Leigh Hunt*	190
An End	*Chris. Rossetti*	194
To a Water-Fowl	*W. C. Bryant*	195
Venus of the Needle	*W. Allingham*	196
Song of Ariel	*Shakespeare*	198
To a cold Beauty	*Hood*	198
I cannot see the features right	*In Memoriam*	199
Ulalume	*Edgar A. Poe*	200
Lines. Written in Early Spring	*Wordsworth*	203
The Maid's Lament	*W. S. Landor*	204
Fairy Song. From "The Maid's Metamorphosis"	*John Lyly*	205
Evening	*Tennyson*	205
Edom o' Gordon	*Old Ballad*	206
Phillida and Corydon	*N. Breton*	211
Lord Randal	*Bor. Minstrelsy*	212
Evening	*In Memoriam*	213
The Bridge of Sighs	*Hood*	214
Song. At a Lady's Window	*Shakespeare*	217
Song. False friend, wilt thou smile or weep	*Shelley*	218
The Wife of Usher's Well	*Old Ballad*	218
The Knight's Tomb	*Coleridge*	220
The Shadow of Night	*Cov. Patmore*	221
The Fairy Thorn	*Sam. Ferguson*	223
The House	*Emerson*	226
His Wish to Privacy	*Herrick*	227
Love	*Coleridge*	227
Song for August	*H. Martineau*	231
Lullaby for Titania	*Shakespeare*	232
Upon the Image of Death	*R. Southwell*	233
The Angel	*W. Blake*	235
Lovely Mary Donnelly	*W. Allingham*	235
Waly, Waly	*Old Ballad*	238
Hymn to Diana	*Ben Jonson*	239
Sonnet. Eagles	*Wordsworth*	240
The Reverie of poor Susan	*Wordsworth*	241
The Pains of Sleep	*Coleridge*	242
The Skylark	*James Hogg*	243
Edward, Edward	*Old Ballad*	244
Ode on Melancholy	*Keats*	246
Sonnet. The Trosachs	*Wordsworth*	247
Ballad. She's up and gone	*Hood*	248
Incantation. From "Remorse"	*Coleridge*	249
Song. From "Rokeby"	*Scott*	249

		Page
Now the hungry lion roars	*Shakespeare*	250
What Pleasure have great Princes	*Byrd*	251
Fair Helen of Kirkconnell	*Bor. Minstrelsy*	252
Down on the Shore	*W. Allingham*	254
The Jovial Beggar	*Playford*	255
Love for no less than Love	*George Wither*	256
The Soldier's Dream	*Campbell*	258
A Lyke-Wake Dirge		259
Where he would have his Verses read	*Herrick*	260
Young Lochinvar	*Scott*	261
When the World is burning	*Ebenezer Jones*	263
May and Death	*R. Browning*	264
Lines to an Indian Air	*Shelley*	265
The Death of the Old Year	*Tennyson*	266
Lyrics for Legacies	*Herrick*	268
Notes		269
Index of First Lines		283

NIGHTINGALE VALLEY.

NIGHTINGALE VALLEY.

A COLLECTION,

INCLUDING A GREAT NUMBER

OF THE CHOICEST LYRICS

AND

SHORT POEMS

IN

THE ENGLISH LANGUAGE.

EDITED BY GIRALDUS.

Sul lito un bosco era di querce ombrose.
Dove ognor par che Filomena piagna;
Ch' in mezzo avea un pratel con una fonte,
E quinci e quindi un solitario monte.
                ARIOSTO, *Orl. Fur.* X. 113.

LONDON:
BELL AND DALDY, 186, FLEET STREET.
1860.

NIGHTINGALE VALLEY.

TO THE NIGHTINGALE.

  NIGHTINGALE, that on yon
   bloomy spray
  Warblest at eve, when all the
   woods are still,
  Thou with fresh hopes the lover's
 heart dost fill,
While the jolly hours lead on propitious May.
The liquid notes that close the eye of day,
 First heard before the shallow cuckoo's bill,
 Portend success in love. O! if Jove's will
Have link'd that amorous power to thy soft lay,
Now timely sing, ere the rude bird of hate
 Foretell my hapless doom in some grove nigh,
As thou from year to year hast sung too late
 For my relief, yet hadst no reason why.
Whether the Muse, or Love call thee his mate,
 Both them I serve, and of their train am I.

MILTON.

[WAKE, LADY!]

UP! quit thy bower, late wears the hour,
    Long have the rooks caw'd round the tower;
O'er flower and tree loud hums the bee,
And the wild kid sports merrily.
The sun is bright, the sky is clear,
Wake, lady! wake, and hasten here.

Up! maiden fair, and bind thy hair,
And rouse thee in the breezy air:
The lulling stream that soothed thy dream
Is dancing in the sunny beam.
Waste not these hours, so fresh, so gay,
Leave thy soft couch, and haste away.

Up! time will tell the morning bell
Its service-sound has chimed well:
The aged crone keeps house alone,
The reapers to the fields are gone;
Lose not these hours, so cool, so gay,
Lo! while thou sleep'st they haste away!

                JOANNA BAILLIE.

INSCRIPTION

FOR A FOUNTAIN ON A HEATH.

THIS Sycamore, oft musical with bees,—
    Such tents the Patriarchs loved! O long
        unharm'd
May all its aged boughs o'er-canopy

The small round basin, which this jutting stone
Keeps pure from falling leaves! Long may the
    Spring,
Quietly as a sleeping infant's breath,
Send up cold waters to the traveller
With soft and even pulse! Nor ever cease
Yon tiny cone of sand its soundless dance,
Which at the bottom, like a Fairy's page,
As merry and no taller, dances still,
Nor wrinkles the smooth surface of the Fount.
Here twilight is and coolness: here is moss,
A soft seat, and a deep and ample shade.
Thou mayst toil far and find no second tree.
Drink, Pilgrim, here; here, rest! and if thy heart
Be innocent, here too shalt thou refresh
Thy spirit, listening to some gentle sound,
Or passing gale or hum of murmuring bees!
                        COLERIDGE.

FAIR INES.

O SAW ye not fair Ines?
    She's gone into the West,
To dazzle when the sun is down,
    And rob the world of rest:
She took our daylight with her,
    The smiles that we love best,
With morning blushes on her cheek,
    And pearls upon her breast.

O turn again, fair Ines,
    Before the fall of night,
For fear the moon should shine alone,
    And stars unrivall'd bright;

And blessed will the lover be
  That walks beneath their light,
And breathes the love against thy cheek
  I dare not even write!

Would I had been, fair Ines,
  That gallant cavalier,
Who rode so gaily by thy side,
  And whisper'd thee so near!
Were there no bonny dames at home,
  Or no true lovers here,
That he should cross the seas to win
  The dearest of the dear?

I saw thee, lovely Ines,
  Descend along the shore
With bands of noble gentlemen,
  And banners waved before;
And gentle youth and maidens gay,
  And snowy plumes they wore;—
It would have been a beauteous dream,—
  If it had been no more!

Alas, alas, fair Ines,
  She went away with song,
With music waiting on her steps,
  And shoutings of the throng;
But some were sad and felt no mirth,
  But only music's wrong,
In sounds that sang farewell, farewell,
  To her you've loved so long.

Farewell, farewell, fair Ines,
  That vessel never bore
So fair a lady on its deck,
  Nor danced so light before,—

>   Alas, for pleasure on the sea,
>   And sorrow on the shore!
>   The smile that blest one lover's heart
>   Has broken many more!
>   HOOD.

SIC VITA.

LIKE to the falling of a star,
  Or as the flightes of eagles are,
Or like the fresh Spring's gaudie hue,
Or silver drops of morning dewe,
Or like a wind that chafes the flood,
Or bubbles which on water stood,—
E'en such is man—whose borrow'd light
Is straight call'd in and paid to-night.
The wind blows out, the bubble dies,
The Spring entomb'd in Autumn lies,
The dewe's dried up, the star is shot,
The flight is past—and man forgot.

[A SONNET UPON SONNETS.]

NUNS fret not at their convent's narrow
          room;
And hermits are contented with their cells;
And students with their pensive citadels;
Maids at the wheel, the weaver at his loom,
Sit blithe and happy; bees that soar for bloom,
High as the highest Peak of Furness-fells,
Will murmur by the hour in foxglove bells:

In truth, the prison, unto which we doom
Ourselves, no prison is: and hence to me,
In sundry moods, 'twas pastime to be bound
Within the sonnet's scanty plot of ground:
Pleased if some souls (for such there needs must be)
Who have felt the weight of too much liberty,
Should find brief solace there, as I have found.
WORDSWORTH.

JOCK O' HAZELDEAN.

"WHY weep ye by the tide, ladye?
    Why weep ye by the tide?
I'll wed you to my youngest son,
    And ye shall be his bride.
And ye shall be his bride, ladye,
    Sae comely to be seen"—
But aye she loot the tears doon fa'
    For Jock o' Hazeldean.

"Now let this wilfu' grief be done,
    And dry that cheek so pale:
Young Frank is chief of Errington,
    And lord of Langley-dale;
His step is first in peaceful ha',
    His sword in battle keen,"—
But aye she loot the tears doon fa'
    For Jock o' Hazeldean.

"A chain of gold ye shall not lack,
    Nor braid to bind your hair;
Nor mettled hound, nor managed hawk,
    Nor palfrey fresh and fair:

And you, the foremost o' them a',
    Shall ride our forest queen"—
But aye she loot the tears doon fa'
    For Jock o' Hazeldean.

The kirk was deck'd at morning-tide,
    The tapers glimmer'd fair;
The priest and bridegroom wait the bride,
    And dame and knight were there.
They sought her baith by bower and ha';
    The lady was not seen:
She's o'er the border and awa'
    Wi' Jock o' Hazeldean!
                  SCOTT.

THE PASSIONATE SHEPHEARD TO HIS LOVE.

COME live with me, and be my Love,
    And we will all the pleasures prove
That vallies, groves, hills, and fields,
Woods or steepie mountaines yields.

And we will sit upon the rockes
Seeing the shepheards feede their flockes
By shallow rivers, to whose falls
Melodious birds sing madrigalls.

And I will make thee beds of roses,
And a thousand fragrant posies,
A cap of flowers, and a kirtle
Imbroydered all with leaves of myrtle:

A gowne made of the finest wooll
Which from our pretty lambs we pull;
Fair linèd slippers for the cold,
With buckles of the purest gold:

A belt of straw, and ivie buds,
With corall clasps and amber studs:
And if these pleasures may thee move,
Come live with me, and be my Love.

The Shepheard swaines shall dance and sing
For thy delights each May-morning:
If these delights thy mind may move,
Then live with me, and be my Love.
CHRISTOPHER MARLOWE.

TO-DAY.

SO here hath been dawning
    Another blue day:
Think wilt thou let it
    Slip useless away.

Out of Eternity
    This new Day is born;
Into Eternity,
    At night, will return.

Behold it aforetime
    No eye ever did;
So soon it for ever
    From all eyes is hid.

Here hath been dawning
Another blue Day :
Think wilt thou let it
Slip useless away.
   T. Carlyle.

THE SEVEN SISTERS ;

OR, THE SOLITUDE OF BINNORIE.

I.

SEVEN daughters had Lord Archibald,
 All children of one mother :
You could not say in one short day
What love they bore each other.
A garland, of seven lilies wrought !
Seven sisters that together dwell ;
But he, bold Knight as ever fought,
Their Father, took of them no thought,
He loved the wars so well.
Sing, mournfully, oh ! mournfully,
The solitude of Binnorie !

II.

Fresh blows the wind, a western wind,
And from the shores of Erin,
Across the wave a Rover brave
To Binnorie is steering :
Right onward to the Scottish strand
The gallant ship is borne ;
The warriors leap upon the land,
And hark ! the Leader of the band
Hath blown his bugle horn.
Sing, mournfully, oh ! mournfully,
The solitude of Binnorie !

III.

Beside a grotto of their own,
With boughs above them closing,
The seven are laid, and in the shade
They lie like fawns reposing.
But now, upstarting with affright
At noise of man and steed,
Away they fly to left, to right—
Of your fair household, Father-knight,
Methinks you take small heed!
Sing, mournfully, oh! mournfully,
The solitude of Binnorie!

IV.

Away the seven fair Campbells fly,
And, over hill and hollow,
With menace proud, and insult loud,
The youthful Rovers follow.
Cried they, " Your Father loves to roam :
Enough for him to find
The empty house when he comes home ;
For us your yellow ringlets comb,
For us be fair and kind !"
Sing, mournfully, oh! mournfully,
The solitude of Binnorie!

V.

Some close behind, some side by side,
Like clouds in stormy weather,
They run, and cry, " Nay, let us die,
And let us die together."
A lake was near ; the shore was steep ;
There never foot had been ;
They ran, and with a desperate leap
Together plunged into the deep,
Nor ever more were seen.

Sing, mournfully, oh! mournfully,
The solitude of Binnorie!

VI.

The stream that flows out of the lake,
As through the glen it rambles,
Repeats a moan o'er moss and stone
For those seven lovely Campbells.
Seven little Islands, green and bare,
Have risen from out the deep:
The fishers say, those sisters fair
By fairies are all buried there,
And there together sleep.
Sing, mournfully, oh! mournfully,
The solitude of Binnorie!

WORDSWORTH.

[SONG.]

(FROM "THE MILLER'S DAUGHTER.")

IT is the miller's daughter,
   And she is grown so dear, so dear,
That I would be the jewel
   That trembles at her ear:
For hid in ringlets day and night,
I'd touch her neck so warm and white.

And I would be the girdle
   About her dainty, dainty waist,
And her heart would beat against me,
   In sorrow and in rest:
And I should know if it beat right,
I'd clasp it round so close and tight.

And I would be the necklace,
   And all day long to fall and rise
Upon her balmy bosom,
   With her laughter or her sighs;
And I would lie so light, so light,
I scarce should be unclasp'd at night.
                TENNYSON.

AUTUMN.

A DIRGE.

THE warm sun is failing, the bleak wind is wailing,
The bare boughs are sighing, the pale flowers are dying;
        And the year
On the earth her death-bed, in a shroud of leaves dead
        Is lying.
    Come, months, come away,
    From November to May,
    In your saddest array,—
    Follow the bier
    Of the dead cold year,
And like dim shadows watch by her sepulchre.

The chill rain is falling, the nipt worm is crawling,
The rivers are swelling, the thunder is knelling
        For the year;
The blithe swallows are flown, and the lizards each gone
        To his dwelling.
    Come, months, come away;
    Put on white, black, and grey;

Let your light sisters play;
Ye, follow the bier
Of the dead cold year,
And make her grave green with tear on tear.
SHELLEY.

THE AMULET.

YOUR picture smiles as first it smiled,
　　The ring you gave is still the same,
Your letter tells, O changing child,
　　No tidings *since* it came.

Give me an amulet that keeps
　　Intelligence with you,
Red when you love, and rosier red,
　　And when you love not, pale and blue.

Alas, that neither bonds nor vows
　　Can certify possession;
Torments me still the fear that love
　　Died in its last expression.
EMERSON.

THE CHARACTER OF A HAPPY LIFE.

HOW happy is he born and taught,
　　That serveth not another's will;
Whose armour is his honest thought,
　　And simple truth his utmost skill!

Whose passions not his masters are;
    Whose soul is still prepared for death;
Untied unto the worldly care
    Of publick fame or private breath:

Who envies none that chance doth raise,
    Or vice; who never understood
How deepest wounds are given by praise;
    Nor rules of state, but rules of good:

Who hath his life from humours freed;
    Whose conscience is his strong retreat;
Whose state can neither flatterers feed,
    Nor ruin make accusers great:

Who late and early doth God pray
    More of his grace than gifts to lend;
And entertains the harmless day
    With a well-chosen book or friend:

This man is freed from servile bands
    Of hope to rise, or fear to fall;
Lord of himself, though not of lands;
    And having nothing, yet hath all.

                SIR HENRY WOTTON.

[WANT OF SLEEP.]

A FLOCK of sheep that leisurely pass by,
    One after one; the sound of rain, and trees
Murmuring; the fall of rivers, winds and seas,
Smooth fields, white sheets of water, and pure sky;

I thought of all by turns, and yet I lie
Sleepless! and soon the small birds' melodies
Must hear, first utter'd from my orchard trees;
And the first cuckoo's melancholy cry.
Even thus last night, and two nights more, I lay,
And could not win thee, Sleep! by any stealth:
So do not let me wear to-night away:
Without Thee what is all the morning's wealth?
Come, blessed barrier between day and day,
Dear mother of fresh thoughts and joyous health!

      WORDSWORTH.

ABOU BEN ADHEM AND THE ANGEL.

(D'HERBELOT—BIBLIOTHEQUE ORIENTALE,

1781, TOM. I. P. 161.)

ABOU Ben Adhem (may his tribe increase)
 Awoke one night from a deep dream of peace,
And saw, within the moonlight in his room,
Making it rich, and like a lily in bloom,
An angel writing in a book of gold:—
Exceeding peace had made Ben Adhem bold,
And to the presence in the room he said,
" What writest thou?"—The vision raised its
  head,
And with a look made of all sweet accord,
Answer'd, " The names of those who love the
  Lord."
" And is mine one?" said Abou. " Nay, not so,"
Replied the Angel. Abou spoke more low,

But cheerly still; and said, "I pray thee then,
Write me as one that loves his fellow-men."

The angel wrote, and vanish'd. The next night
It came again with a great wakening light,
And show'd the names whom love of God had
    bless'd,
And lo! Ben Adhem's name led all the rest.

LEIGH HUNT.

LUCY ASHTON'S SONG.

[FROM "THE BRIDE OF LAMMERMOOR."]

LOOK not thou on beauty's charming;
  Sit thou still when kings are arming;
Taste not when the wine cup glistens;
Speak not when the people listens;
Stop thine ear against the singer;
From the red gold keep thy finger;
Vacant heart and hand and eye,
Easy live and quiet die.

SCOTT.

A DREAM.

I HEARD the dogs howl in the moonlight night,
  And I went to the window to see the sight;
All the dead that ever I knew
Going one by one and two by two.

On they pass'd, and on they pass'd;
Townsfellows all from first to last;

Born in the moonlight of the lane,
And quench'd in the heavy shadow again.

Schoolmates, marching as when we play'd
At soldiers once—but now more staid;
Those were the strangest sight to me
Who were drown'd, I knew, in the awful sea.

Straight and handsome folk; bent and weak too;
And some that I loved, and gasp'd to speak to;
Some but a day in their churchyard bed;
And some that I had not known were dead.

A long, long crowd—where each seem'd lonely.
And yet of them all there was one, one only,
That raised a head, or look'd my way;
And she seem'd to linger, but might not stay.

How long since I saw that fair pale face!
Ah, mother dear, might I only place
My head on thy breast, a moment to rest,
While thy hand on my tearful cheek were prest!

On, on, a moving bridge they made
Across the moon-stream, from shade to shade:
Young and old, women and men;
Many long-forgot, but remember'd then.

And first there came a bitter laughter;
And a sound of tears a moment after;
And then a music so lofty and gay,
That every morning, day by day,
I strive to recal it if I may.

W. ALLINGHAM.

ODE TO THE CUCKOO.

Hail, beauteous stranger of the grove!
   Thou messenger of Spring!
Now Heaven repairs thy rural seat,
   And woods thy welcome sing.

What time the daisy decks the green,
   Thy certain voice we hear:
Hast thou a star to guide thy path,
   Or mark the rolling year?

Delightful visitant! with thee
   I hail the time of flowers,
And hear the sound of music sweet
   From birds among the bowers.

The schoolboy, wandering in the wood
   To pull the primrose gay,
Starts, the new voice of Spring to hear,
   And imitates thy lay.

Soon as the pea puts on the bloom,
   Thou fliest thy vocal vale,
An annual guest in other lands,
   Another Spring to hail.

Sweet bird! thy bower is ever green,
   Thy sky is ever clear;
Thou hast no sorrow in thy song,
   No Winter in thy year!

O could I fly, I'd fly with thee!
   We'd make, with joyful wing,
Our annual visit o'er the globe,
   Companions of the Spring.

                    JOHN LOGAN.

CORONACH.[1]

[FROM "THE LADY OF THE LAKE."]

HE is gone on the mountain,
   He is lost to the forest;
Like a summer-dried fountain,
   When our need was the sorest.
The font, reappearing,
   From the rain-drops shall borrow:
But to us comes no cheering,
   No Duncan to-morrow.

The hand of the reaper
   Takes the ears that are hoary;
But the voice of the weeper
   Wails manhood in glory;
The autumn winds rushing
   Waft the leaves that are serest,
But our flower was in flushing
   When blighting was nearest.

Fleet foot on the correi,[2]
   Sage counsel in cumber,
Red hand in the foray,
   How sound is thy slumber!
Like the dew on the mountain,
   Like the foam on the river,
Like the bubble on the fountain,
   Thou art gone, and for ever!

SCOTT.

[1] *Coronach*, funeral song.
[2] *Correi*, the hollow side of the hill.

IT is not beautie I demand,
   A chrystall brow, the moon's despair,
Nor the snow's daughter, a white hand,
   Nor mermaid's yellow pride of hair.

Tell me not of your starrie eyes,
   Your lips, that seem on roses fed,
Your breastes, where Cupid tumbling lies,
   Nor sleeps for kissing of his bed,—

A bloomie pair of vermeil cheeks,
   Like Hebe's in her ruddiest hours,
A breath that softer musick speaks
   Than summer winds a-wooing flow'rs.

These are but gauds: nay, what are lips?
   Corall beneath the ocean-stream,
Whose brink when your adventurer slips,
   Full oft he perisheth on them.

And what are cheeks, but ensigns oft
   That wave hot youth to fields of blood?
Did Helen's breast, though ne'er so soft,
   Do Greece or Ilium any good?

Eyes can with baleful ardour burn;
   Poison can breath, that erst perfum'd;
There's many a white hand holds an urn,
   With lovers' hearts to dust consumed.

For chrystall brows, there's nought within;
   They are but empty cells for pride;
He who the Syren's hair would win,
   Is mostly strangled in the tide.

Give me, instead of Beautie's bust,
   A tender heart, a loyall mind,
Which with temptation I would trust,
   Yet never link'd with error find,—

One in whose gentle bosom I
   Could pour my secret heart of woes,
Like the care-burthen'd honey-flie,
   That hides his murmurs in the rose,—

My earthlie comforter! whose love
   So indefeasible might be,
That, when my spirit wonn'd above,
   Hers could not stay, for sympathy.

THE QUESTION.

I DREAM'D that, as I wander'd by the way,
   Bare Winter suddenly was changed to Spring,
And gentle odours led my steps astray,
   Mix'd with a sound of waters murmuring,
Along a shelving bank of turf, which lay
   Under a copse, and hardly dared to fling
Its green arms round the bosom of the stream,
But kiss'd it, and then fled, as thou mightest in
      dream.

There grew pied wind-flowers and violets;
   Daisies, those pearl'd Arcturi of the earth,
The constellated flower that never sets;
   Faint oxlips; tender bluebells, at whose birth
The sod scarce heaved; and that tall flower that
      wets
Its mother's face with heaven-collected tears,
When the low wind its playmate's voice it hears.

And in the warm hedge grew lush eglantine,
  Green cowbind and the moonlight-colour'd
    may,
And cherry blossoms, and white cups, whose wine
  Was the bright dew yet drain'd not by the day;
And wild roses, and ivy serpentine,
  With its dark buds and leaves, wandering astray;
And flowers azure, black, and streak'd with gold,
Fairer than any waken'd eyes behold.

And nearer to the river's trembling edge
  There grew broad flag-flowers, purple prankt
    with white,
And starry river-buds among the sedge,
  And floating water-lilies, broad and bright,
Which lit the oak that overhung the hedge
  With moonlight beams of their own watery light;
And bulrushes, and reeds of such deep green
As soothed the dazzled eye with sober sheen.

Methought that of these visionary flowers
  I made a nosegay, bound in such a way
That the same hues which in their natural bowers
  Were mingled or opposed, the like array
Kept these imprison'd children of the Hours
  Within my hand,—and then, elate and gay,
I hasten'd to the spot whence I had come,
That I might there present it! Oh! to whom?

                                    SHELLEY.

BARTHRAM'S DIRGE.

(FROM " MINSTRELSY OF THE SCOTTISH BORDER.")

THEY shot him on the Nine-Stane Rig,
 Beside the Headless Cross;
And they left him lying in his blood,
 Upon the muir and moss.

They made a bier of the broken bough,
 The saugh[1] and the aspen grey;
And they bore him to the Lady Chapel,
 And waked him there all day.

A lady came to that lonely bower,
 And threw her robes aside,
She tore her [2]ling-long yellow hair,
 And knelt at Barthram's side.

She bathed him in the Lady-Well,
 His wounds sae deep and sair;
And she plaited a garland for his breast,
 And a garland for his hair.

They row'd him in a lily sheet,
 And bare him to his earth,
And the Grey Friars sung the dead man's mass,
 As they pass'd the Chapel-Garth.

They buried him at the mirk midnight,
 When the dew fell cold and still,
When the aspen grey forgot to play,
 And the mist clung to the hill.

[1] *Saugh*, " sally," willow.   [2] *Ling*, heather.

They dug his grave but a bare foot deep,
  By the edge of the Nine-Stane Burn,
And they cover'd him o'er wi' the heather-flower,
  The moss and the lady-fern.

A Grey Friar stay'd upon the grave,
  And sang till the morning-tide;
And a friar shall sing for Barthram's soul,
  While the Headless Cross shall bide.

THE WORLD'S WANDERERS.

TELL me, thou star whose wings of light
  Speed thee in thy fiery flight,
In what cavern of the night
  Will thy pinions close now?

Tell me, moon, thou pale and grey
Pilgrim of heaven's homeless way,
In what depth of night or day
  Seekest thou repose now?

Weary wind who wanderest
Like the world's rejected guest,
Hast thou still some secret nest
  On the tree or billow?

SHELLEY.

MY LAST DUCHESS.

(FERRARA.)

THAT'S my last Duchess painted on the wall,
    Looking as if she were alive; I call
That piece a wonder, now; Frà Pandolf's hands
Work'd busily a day, and there she stands.
Will't please you sit and look at her? I said
" Frà Pandolf" by design, for never read
Strangers like you that pictured countenance,
The depth and passion of its earnest glance,
But to myself they turn'd (since none puts by
The curtain I have drawn for you, but I)
And seem'd as they would ask me, if they durst,
How such a glance came there: so not the first
Are you to turn and ask thus. Sir, 'twas not
Her husband's presence only, call'd that spot
Of joy into the Duchess' cheek: perhaps
Frà Pandolf chanced to say, " Her mantle laps
Over my Lady's wrist too much," or " Paint
Must never hope to reproduce the faint
Half-flush that dies along her throat;" such stuff
Was courtesy, she thought, and cause enough
For calling up that spot of joy. She had
A heart—how shall I say!—too soon made glad,
Too easily impress'd; she liked whate'er
She look'd on, and her looks went everywhere.
Sir, 'twas all one! My favour at her breast,
The dropping of the daylight in the West,
The bough of cherries some officious fool
Broke in the orchard for her, the white mule
She rode with round the terrace—all and each
Would draw from her alike the approving speech,

Or blush, at least. She thank'd men,—good; but thank'd
Somehow,—I know not how—as if she rank'd
My gift of a nine hundred years old name
With anybody's gift. Who'd stoop to blame
This sort of trifling? Even had you skill
In speech—(which I have not)—to make your will
Quite clear to such an one, and say " Just this
Or that in you disgusts me; here you miss,
Or there exceed the mark"—and if she let
Herself be lesson'd so, nor plainly set
Her wits to yours, forsooth, and made excuse,
—E'en then would be some stooping, and I choose
Never to stoop. Oh Sir, she smiled, no doubt,
Whene'er I pass'd her; but who pass'd without
Much the same smile? This grew; I gave command;
Then all smiles stopp'd together. There she stands
As if alive. Will't please you rise? We'll meet
The company below then. I repeat
The Count your Master's known munificence
Is ample warrant that no just pretence
Of mine for dowry will be disallow'd;
Though his fair daughter's self, as I avow'd
At starting, is my object. Nay, we'll go
Together down, Sir! Notice Neptune, though,
Taming a sea-horse, thought a rarity,
Which Claus of Innsbruck cast in bronze for me.

      ROBERT BROWNING.

SONG.

[THE SEASON FOR WOOING.]

DOST thou idly ask to hear
    At what gentle seasons
Nymphs relent, when lovers near
    Press the tenderest reasons?
Ah, they give their faith too oft
    To the careless wooer;
Maidens' hearts are always soft;
    Would that men's were truer!

Woo the fair one, when around
    Early birds are singing;
When, o'er all the fragrant ground,
    Early herbs are springing:
When the brookside, bank, and grove,
    All with blossoms laden,
Shine with beauty, breathe of love,—
    Woo the timid maiden.

Woo her when, with rosy blush,
    Summer eve is sinking;
When on rills that softly gush
    Stars are softly winking;
When, through boughs that knit the bower,
    Moonlight gleams are stealing;
Woo her, till the gentle hour
    Wake a gentler feeling.

Woo her when autumnal dyes
    Tinge the woody mountain;
When the dropping foliage lies
    In the weedy fountain;

Let the scene, that tells how fast
    Youth is passing over,
Warn her, ere her bloom is past,
    To secure her lover.

Woo her when the north winds call
    At the lattice nightly;
When, within the cheerful hall,
    Blaze the fagots brightly;
While the wintry tempest round
    Sweeps the landscape hoary,
Sweeter in her ear shall sound
    Love's delightful story.

W. C. BRYANT.

SONNET.

COMPOSED BY THE SIDE OF GRASMERE LAKE, 1807.

CLOUDS, lingering yet, extend in solid bars
    Through the grey west; and lo! these waters, steel'd
By breezeless air to smoothest polish, yield
A vivid repetition of the stars;
Jove, Venus, and the ruddy crest of Mars
Amid his fellows beauteously reveal'd,
At happy distance from earth's groaning field,
Where ruthless mortals wage incessant wars.
Is it a mirror?—or the nether Sphere
Opening to view the abyss in which she feeds
Her own calm fires?—But list! a voice is near;
Great Pan himself low-whispering through the
    reeds,
" Be thankful, thou; for, if unholy deeds
Ravage the world, tranquillity is here!"

WORDSWORTH.

HOHENLINDEN.

ON Linden, when the sun was low,
   All bloodless lay th' untrodden snow,
And dark as winter was the flow
   Of Iser, rolling rapidly.

But Linden saw another sight,
When the drum beat, at dead of night,
Commanding fires of death to light
   The darkness of her scenery.

By torch and trumpet fast array'd,
Each horseman drew his battle-blade,
And furious every charger neigh'd,
   To join the dreadful revelry.

Then shook the hills with thunder riven,
Then rush'd the steed to battle driven,
And louder than the bolts of heaven,
   Far flash'd the red artillery.

But redder yet that light shall glow
On Linden's hills of stained snow,
And bloodier yet the torrent flow
   Of Iser, rolling rapidly.

'Tis morn, but scarce yon level sun
Can pierce the war-clouds, rolling dun,
Where furious Frank, and fiery Hun,
   Shout in their sulph'rous canopy.

The combat deepens. On, ye brave,
Who rush to glory, or the grave!

Wave, Munich! all thy banners wave,
  And charge with all thy chivalry!

Few, few, shall part where many meet!
The snow shall be their winding-sheet,
And every turf beneath their feet
  Shall be a soldier's sepulchre.

CAMPBELL.

SONNET.

FROM THE PORTUGUESE.

HOW do I love thee? Let me count the ways.
  I love thee to the depth and breadth and height
My soul can reach, when feeling out of sight
For the ends of Being and Ideal Grace.
I love thee to the level of every day's
Most quiet need, by sun and candlelight.
I love thee freely, as men strive for Right;
I love thee purely, as they turn from Praise;
I love thee with the passion put to use
In my old griefs, and with my childhood's faith;
I love thee with a love I seem'd to lose
With my lost saints,—I love thee with the breath,
Smiles, tears, of all my life!—and, if God choose,
I shall but love thee better after death.

ELIZABETH BARRETT BROWNING.

CLERK SAUNDERS.

[OLD BALLAD.]

CLERK Saunders and may Margaret
    Walk'd ower yon garden green;
And deep and heavy was the love
    That fell thir twa between.

"A bed, a bed," Clerk Saunders said,
    "A bed for you and me!"
"Fye na, fye na," said may Margaret,
    "Till anes we married be."

"Then I'll take the sword frae my scabbard,
    And slowly lift the pin;
And you may swear, and save your aith,
    Ye never let me in.

"Take you a napkin in your hand,
    Tie up your bonnie e'en,
And you may swear and save your aith,
    Ye saw me na since yestreen."

It was about the midnight hour
    When they asleep were laid,
When in and came her seven brothers
    Wi' torches burning red:

When in and came her seven brothers
    Wi' torches burning bright;
They said, "We hae but one sister,
    And behold her lying with a knight!"

Then out and spake the first o' them,
  "We will awa' and let them be."
And out and spake the second o' them,
  "His father has nae mair but he."

And out and spake the third o' them,
  "I wot that they are lovers dear."
And out and spake the fourth o' them,
  "They hae been in love this mony a year."

Then out and spake the fifth o' them,
  "It were great sin true love to twain."
And out and spake the sixth o' them,
  "It were shame to slay a sleeping man."

Then up and gat the seventh o' them,
  And never a word spake he;
But he has striped his bright brown brand
  Out through Clerk Saunders' fair bodye.

Clerk Saunders he started, and Margaret she turn'd
  Into his arms as asleep she lay;
And sad and silent was the night
  That was atween thir twae.

And they lay still and sleepit sound,
  Until the day began to dawe,
And kindly to him she did say,
  "It is time, true love, you were awa'."

But he lay still, and sleepit sound,
  Albeit the sun began to sheen;
She look'd atween her and the wa',
  And dull and drowsie were his e'en.

Then in and came her father dear;
  Said—"Let a' your mourning be;

I'll carry the dead corpse to the clay,
    And I'll come back and comfort thee."

" Comfort weel your seven sons,
    For comforted I will never be.
I trow 'twas neither knave nor loon
    Was in the bower last night wi' me."

The clinking bell gaed through the town,
    And carried the dead corpse to the clay.
Clerk Saunders stood at may Margaret's window,
    I wot, an hour before the day.

" Are ye sleeping, Margaret?" he says,
    " Or are ye waking presentlie?
Give me my faith and troth again,
    I wot, true love, I gied to thee."

" Your faith and troth ye sall never get,
    Nor our true love sall never twin,
Until ye come within my bower,
    And kiss me cheek and chin."

" My mouth it is full cold, Margaret,
    It has the smell, now, of the ground;
And if I kiss thy comely mouth
    Thy days will soon be at an end.

" O, cocks are crowing a merry midnight,
    I wot the wild fowls are boding day;
Give me my faith and troth again,
    And let me fare me on my way."

" Thy faith and troth thou sall na get,
    And our true love sall never twin,
Until ye tell what comes o' women,
    Wot ye, who die in strong traivelling?"

"Their beds are made in the heavens high,
   Down at the foot of our good Lord's knee,
Weel set about wi' gillyflowers;
   I wot, sweet company for to see.

" O, cocks are crowing a merry midnight,
   I wot the wild fowls are boding day;
The psalms of heaven will soon be sung,
   And I, ere now, will be miss'd away."

Then she has taken a chrisom wand,
   And she has stroken her troth thereon;
She has given it to him at the shot-window,
   Wi' mony a sad sigh and heavy groan.

" I thank ye, Marg'ret; I thank ye, Marg'ret;
   Ever I thank ye heartilie;
But gin I were living, as I am dead,
   I'd keep my faith and troth with thee."

It's hosen and shoon, and gown alone,
   She climb'd the wall and follow'd him,
Until she came to the green forest,
   And there she lost the sight o' him.

" Is there ony room at your head, Saunders?
   Is there ony room at your feet?
Is there ony room at your side, Saunders?
   Where fain, fain, I wad sleep."

" There's nae room at my head, Marg'ret,
   There's nae room at my feet;
My bed it is fu' lowly now,
   Amang the hungry worms I sleep.

" Cauld mould it is my covering now,
   But and my winding-sheet;

The dew it falls nae sooner down
　　　Than my resting-place is weet."

　　Then up and crew the red red cock,
　　　And up and crew the gray:
　　" 'Tis time, 'tis time, my dear Marg'ret,
　　　That you were going away.

　　" And fair Marg'ret, and rare Marg'ret,
　　　And Marg'ret, o' veritie,
　　Gin e'er ye love another man,
　　　Ne'er love him as ye did me."

INVOCATION OF SILENCE.

STILL-BORN Silence! thou that art
　　Flood-gate of the deeper heart!
Offspring of a heavenly kind,
Frost o' the mouth, and thaw o' the mind,
Secresy's confidant, and he
Who makes religion mystery,
Admiration's speaking'st tongue,
Leave, thy desert shades among,
Reverend hermits' hallow'd cells,
Where retired Devotion dwells,—
With thy enthusiasms come,
Seize our tongues, and strike us dumb!
　　　　　　　　RICHARD FLECKNOE.

CLARIBEL.

A MELODY.

WHERE Claribel low-lieth
    The breezes pause and die,
  Letting the rose-leaves fall:
But the solemn oak-tree sigheth,
    Thick-leaved, ambrosial,
    With an ancient melody
    Of an inward agony,
Where Claribel low-lieth.

At eve the beetle boometh
  Athwart the thicket lone:
At noon the wild-bee hummeth
  About the moss'd headstone:
At midnight the moon cometh,
  And looketh down alone.

Her song the lintwhite swelleth,
The clear-voiced mavis dwelleth,
  The fledgling throstle lispeth,
The slumbrous wave outwelleth,
  The babbling runnel crispeth,
The hollow grot replieth
Where Claribel low-lieth.
              TENNYSON.

[FRANCE SEEN FROM THE COAST OF ENGLAND.]

SEPTEMBER, 1802.

INLAND, within a hollow vale, I stood;
  And saw, while sea was calm and air was clear,
The coast of France—the coast of France how near!
Drawn almost into frightful neighbourhood.
I shrunk; for verily the barrier flood
Was like a lake, or river bright and fair,
A span of waters; yet what power is there!
What mightiness for evil and for good!
Even so doth God protect us if we be
Virtuous and wise. Winds blow, and waters roll,
Strength to the brave, and Power, and Deity;
Yet in themselves are nothing! One decree
Spake laws to *them*, and said that by the soul
Only, the Nations shall be great and free.
                        WORDSWORTH.

THE SOWER'S SONG.

NOW hands to seed-sheet, boys,
  We step and we cast; old Time's on wing;
And would ye partake of Harvest's joys,
  The corn must be sown in Spring.
    Fall gently and still, good corn,
      Lie warm in thy earthy bed;
    And stand so yellow some morn,
      For beast and man must be fed.

Old Earth is a pleasure to see
　　In sunshiny cloak of red and green;
The furrow lies fresh; this Year will be
　　As Years that are past have been.
　　　　Fall gently, &c.

Old Mother, receive this corn,
　　The son of Six Thousand golden sires:
All these on thy kindly breast were born;
　　One more thy poor child requires.
　　　　Fall gently, &c.

Now steady and sure again,
　　And measure of stroke and step we keep;
Thus up and down we cast our grain:
　　Sow well and you gladly reap.
　　　　Fall gently and still, good corn,
　　　　　　Lie warm in thy earthy bed;
　　　　And stand so yellow some morn,
　　　　　　For beast and man must be fed.

　　　　　　　　　　T. CARLYLE.

SONG.

WHY so pale and wan, fond lover?
　　Prithee, why so pale?
Will, when looking well can't move her,
　　Looking ill prevail?
　　Prithee, why so pale?

Why so dull and mute, young sinner,
　　Prithee, why so mute?
Will, when speaking well can't win her,
　　Saying nothing do't?
　　Prithee, why so mute?

Quit, quit for shame; this will not move,
    This cannot take her:
If of herself she will not love,
    Nothing can make her.
    The devil take her!
            Sir John Suckling.

I REMEMBER, I REMEMBER.

I REMEMBER, I remember,
    The house where I was born,
The little window where the sun
    Came peeping in at morn;
He never came a wink too soon,
    Nor brought too long a day,
But now, I often wish the night
    Had borne my breath away!

I remember, I remember,
    The roses, red and white,
The violets and the lily-cups,
    Those flowers made of light!
The lilacs where the robin built,
    And where my brother set
The laburnum on his birth-day,—
    The tree is living yet,

I remember, I remember,
    Where I was used to swing,
And thought the air must rush as fresh
    To swallows on the wing;
My spirit flew in feathers then,
    That is so heavy now,
And summer pools could hardly cool
    This fever on my brow!

I remember, I remember,
　　The fir-trees dark and high;
I used to think their slender tops,
　　Were close against the sky:
It was a childish ignorance,
　　But now 'tis little joy
To know I'm farther off from heav'n
　　Than when I was a boy.
　　　　　　　　Hood.

SONNET.

[THE IDLE VOYAGER.]

How long I sail'd, and never took a thought
　　To what port I was bound! Secure as sleep,
I dwelt upon the bosom of the deep
And perilous sea. And though my ship was fraught
With rare and precious fancies, jewels brought
From fairy-land, no course I cared to keep,
Nor changeful wind nor tide I heeded aught,
But joy'd to feel the merry billows leap,
And watch the sunbeams dallying with the waves;
Or haply dream what realms beneath may lie,
Where the clear ocean is an emerald sky,
And mermaids warble in their coral caves,
Yet vainly woo me to their secret home:
And sweet it were for ever so to roam!
　　　　　　　　Hartley Coleridge.

THE LOVER OF MUSIC TO HIS PIANO-FORTE.

O H friend, whom glad or grave we seek,
    Heav'n-holding shrine!
I ope thee, touch thee, hear thee speak,
    And peace is mine.
No fairy casket, full of bliss,
    Outvalues thee;
Love only, waken'd with a kiss,
    More sweet may be.

To thee, when our full hearts o'erflow
    In griefs or joys,
Unspeakable emotions owe
    A fitting voice:
Mirth flies to thee, and Love's unrest,
    And Memory dear,
And Sorrow, with his tighten'd breast,
    Comes for a tear.

Oh, since few joys of human mould
    Thus wait us still,
Thrice bless'd be thine, thou gentle fold
    Of peace at will.
No change, no sullenness, no cheat,
    In thee we find;
Thy saddest voice is ever sweet,—
    Thine answer, kind.

                LEIGH HUNT.

THE FAIRIES.

A CHILD'S SONG.

UP the airy mountain,
    Down the rushy glen,
We daren't go a-hunting
    For fear of little men;
Wee folk, good folk,
    Trooping all together;
Green jacket, red cap,
    And white owl's feather!

Down along the rocky shore
    Some make their home,
They live on crispy pancakes
    Of yellow tide-foam;
Some in the reeds
    Of the black mountain-lake,
With frogs for their watch-dogs,
    All night awake.

High on the hill-top
    The old King sits;
He is now so old and gray
    He's nigh lost his wits.
With a bridge of white mist
    Columbkill he crosses,
On his stately journeys
    From Slieveleague to Rosses;
Or going up with music
    On cold starry nights,
To sup with the Queen
    Of the gay Northern Lights.

They stole little Bridget
　For seven years long;
When she came down again
　Her friends were all gone.
They took her lightly back,
　Between the night and morrow,
They thought that she was fast asleep,
　But she was dead with sorrow.
They have kept her ever since
　Deep within the lakes,
On a bed of flag-leaves,
　Watching till she wakes.

By the craggy hill-side,
　Through the mosses bare
They have planted thorn-trees
　For pleasure here and there.
Is any man so daring
　As dig one up in spite,
He shall find the thornies set
　In his bed at night.

Up the airy mountain,
　Down the rushy glen,
We daren't go a-hunting
　For fear of little men;
Wee folk, good folk,
　Trooping all together;
Green jacket, red cap,
　And white owl's feather!

　　　　　WILLIAM ALLINGHAM.

THE LAST DAY OF AUTUMN.

(FROM THE GERMAN.)

THE year lies dying in this evening light;
  The poet, musing in autumnal woods,
      Hears melancholy sighs
      Among the wither'd leaves.

Not so: but like a spirit glorified
The angel of the year departs, lays down
      His robes, once green in spring,
      Or bright with summer's blue;

And, having done his mission on the earth,
Filling ten thousand vales with golden corn,
      Orchards with rosy fruit,
      And scattering flowers around,—

He lingers for a moment in the west,
With the declining sun sheds over all
      A pleasant, farewell smile,
      And so returns to God.

BALLAD.

SIGH on, sad heart, for Love's eclipse
  And Beauty's fairest queen!
Though 'tis not for my peasant lips
  To soil her name between.
A king might lay his sceptre down,
  But I am poor and nought:
The brow should wear a golden crown
  That wears her in its thought!

The diamonds glancing in her hair,
  Whose sudden beams surprise,
Might bid such humble hopes beware
  The glancing of her eyes.
Yet looking once, I look'd too long;
  And if my love is sin,
Death follows on the heels of wrong,
  And kills the crime within.

Her dress seem'd wove of lily-leaves,
  It was so pure and fine;
O lofty wears, and lowly weaves!
  But hoddan grey is mine.
And homely hose must step apart
  Where garter'd princes stand:
But, may he wear my love at heart,
  That wins her lily hand!

Alas! there's far from russet frieze
  To silks and satin gowns;
I doubt if God made like degrees
  In courtly hearts and clowns:
My father wrong'd a maiden's mirth,
  And brought her cheeks to blame,
And all that's lordly of my birth,
  Is my reproach and shame.

'Tis vain to weep, 'tis vain to sigh,
  'Tis vain this idle speech;
For where her happy pearls do lie,
  My tears may never reach.
Yet when I'm gone, e'en lofty pride
  May say of what has been,
His love was nobly born and died,
  Though all the rest was mean.

My speech is rude, but speech is weak
    Such love as mine to tell;
Yet, had I words, I dare not speak:
    So, Lady, fare thee well!
I will not wish thy better state
    Was one of low degree,
But I must weep that partial fate
    Made such a churl of me.
Hood.

TO DIANEME.

SWEET, be not proud of those two eyes,
    Which star-like sparkle in their skies;
Nor be you proud that you can see
All hearts your captives, yours yet free;
Be you not proud of that rich hair
Which wantons with the love-sick air:
Whenas that ruby which you wear,
Sunk from the tip of your soft ear,
Will last to be a precious stone
When all your world of beauty's gone.
Herrick.

THE BELLS.

I.

HEAR the sledges with the bells—
    Silver bells!
What a world of merriment their melody foretells!
    How they tinkle, tinkle, tinkle,
        In the icy air of night!

While the stars that over-sprinkle
All the heavens, seem to twinkle
  With a crystalline delight;
Keeping time, time, time,
In a sort of Runic rhyme,
To the tintinabulation that so musically wells
  From the bells, bells, bells, bells,
    Bells, bells, bells,
From the jingling and the tinkling of the bells.

II.

Hear the mellow wedding bells,
  Golden bells!
What a world of happiness their harmony foretells!
  Through the balmy air of night
  How they ring out their delight!
  From the molten-golden notes,
    And all in tune,
  What a liquid ditty floats
To the turtle-dove that listens, while she gloats
    On the moon!
  Oh, from out the sounding cells,
What a gush of euphony voluminously wells!
    How it swells!
    How it dwells
    On the Future! how it tells
    Of the rapture that impels
    To the swinging and the ringing
      Of the bells, bells, bells,
      Of the bells, bells, bells, bells,
        Bells, bells, bells,—
To the rhyming and the chiming of the bells!

III.

Hear the loud alarum bells—
  Brazen bells!

What a tale of terror, now, their turbulency tells!
    In the startled ear of night
    How they scream out their affright!
    Too much horrified to speak,
    They can only shriek, shriek,
      Out of tune,
In a clamourous appealing to the mercy of the fire,
In a mad expostulation with the deaf and frantic
    fire
    Leaping higher, higher, higher,
    With a resolute endeavour
    Now—now to sit, or never,
    By the side of the pale-faced moon.
      Oh, the bells, bells, bells!
    What a tale their terror tells
      Of Despair!
    How they clang, and clash, and roar!
    What a horror they outpour
On the bosom of the palpitating air!
    Yet the ear it fully knows,
      By the twanging,
      And the clanging,
    How the danger ebbs and flows;
    Yet the ear distinctly tells,
      In the jangling,
      And the wrangling,
    How the danger sinks and swells,
By the sinking or the swelling in the anger of the
    bells—
      Of the bells—
    Of the bells, bells, bells, bells,
      Bells, bells, bells—
In the clamor and the clangor of the bells!

        IV.
    Hear the tolling of the bells—
      Iron bells!

What a world of solemn thought their monody
    compels!
      In the silence of the night,
      How we shiver with affright
At the melancholy menace of their tone!
    For every sound that floats
    From the rust within their throats
      Is a groan.
    And the people—ah, the people—
    They that dwell up in the steeple,
      All alone;
    And who, tolling, tolling, tolling,
      In that muffled monotone,
    Feel a glory in so rolling
      On the human heart a stone—
    They are neither man nor woman—
    They are neither brute nor human—
      They are Ghouls!
      And their king it is who tolls;
      And he rolls, rolls, rolls,
        Rolls
    A pæan from the bells!
    And his merry bosom swells
      With the pæan of the bells!
    And he dances and he yells;
    Keeping time, time, time,
    In a sort of Runic rhyme,
    To the pæan of the bells—
      Of the bells:
    Keeping time, time, time,
    In a sort of Runic rhyme,
      To the throbbing of the bells—
      Of the bells, bells, bells,—
      To the sobbing of the bells;
    Keeping time, time, time,
      As he knells, knells, knells,

In a happy Runic rhyme,
  To the rolling of the bells—
Of the bells, bells, bells,—
  To the tolling of the bells,
Of the bells, bells, bells, bells—
    Bells, bells, bells—
To the moaning and the groaning of the bells.

EDGAR A. POE.

TO MARY IN HEAVEN.

THOU lingering star with lessening ray,
  That lov'st to greet the early morn,
Again thou usherest in the day
  My Mary from my soul was torn.
Oh Mary! dear departed shade!
  Where is thy place of blissful rest?
See'st thou thy lover lowly laid?
  Hear'st thou the groans that rend his breast?

That sacred hour can I forget!—
  Can I forget the hallow'd grove,
Where by the winding Ayr we met
  To live one day of parting love!
Eternity will not efface
  Those records dear of transports past!
Thy image at our last embrace—
  Ah! little thought we 'twas our last!

Ayr, gurgling, kiss'd his pebbled shore,
  O'erhung with wild woods, thickening green;
The fragrant birch, and hawthorn hoar,
  Twined amorous round the raptured scene.

The flowers sprung wanton to be press'd,
　　The birds sung love on every spray,
Till too, too soon, the glowing west
　　Proclaim'd the speed of winged day.

Still o'er these scenes my memory wakes,
　　And fondly broods, with miser care,
Time but the impression deeper makes,
　　As streams their channels deeper wear.
My Mary! dear departed shade!
　　Where is thy place of blissful rest?
See'st thou thy lover lowly laid?
　　Hear'st thou the groans that rend his breast?

　　　　　　　　　　BURNS.

"THE NORTHERN STAR."

[A TYNEMOUTH SHIP.]

THE *Northern Star*
　　Sail'd over the bar,
Bound to the Baltic Sea—
In the morning grey
She stretch'd away,—
　　'Twas a weary day to me.

For many an hour,
In sleet and shower,
　　By the lighthouse rock I stray:
And watch till dark
For the winged barque
　　Of him that is far away.

The castle's bound[1]
I wander round
   Amidst the grassy graves,
But all I hear
Is the north wind drear,
   And all I see are the waves.

The *Northern Star*
Is set afar
   Set in the Baltic Sea;
And the waves have spread
The sandy bed
   That holds my love from me.

TO LUCASTA,

GOING TO THE WARRES.

[PUBLISHED 1649.]

I.

TELL me not, Sweet, I am unkinde,
   That from the Nunnerie
Of thy chaste breast and quiet minde,
   To Warre and Armes I flie.

II.

True, a new Mistresse now I chase,
   The first Foe in the Field;
And with a stronger faith imbrace
   A Sword, a Horse, a Shield.

---

[1] *The castle's bound*—Tynemouth castle, the grounds of which are used as a cemetery, or were when this was written.

III.

 Yet this inconstancy is such
  As you too shall adore;
 I could not love thee, Deare, so much,
  Loved I not Honour more.
RICHARD LOVELACE.

A FAREWELL.

FLOW down, cold rivulet, to the sea,
 Thy tribute wave deliver:
No more by thee my steps shall be,
 For ever and for ever.

Flow, softly flow, by lawn and lea,
 A rivulet then a river:
No where by thee my steps shall be,
 For ever and for ever.

But here will sigh thine alder tree,
 And here thine aspen shiver;
And here by thee will hum the bee,
 For ever and for ever.

A thousand suns will stream on thee,
 A thousand moons will quiver;
But not by thee my steps shall be,
 For ever and for ever.
TENNYSON.

SONNET.

[TWILIGHT AMONG MOUNTAINS.]

HAIL, Twilight, sovereign of one peaceful hour!
Not dull art Thou as undiscerning Night;
But studious only to remove from sight
Day's mutable distinctions.—Ancient Power!
Thus did the waters gleam, the mountains lower,
To the rude Briton, when, in wolf-skin vest
Here roving wild, he laid him down to rest
On the bare rock, or through a leafy bower
Look'd ere his eyes were closed. By him was seen
The self-same Vision which we now behold,
At thy meek bidding, shadowy Power! brought forth;
These mighty barriers, and the gulf between;
The flood, the stars,—a spectacle as old
As the beginning of the heavens and earth!

WORDSWORTH.

[INTRODUCTION TO "SONGS OF INNOCENCE."]

PIPING down the valleys wild,
    Piping songs of pleasant glee,
On a cloud I saw a child,
    And he, laughing, said to me,

" Pipe a song about a lamb,"
    So I piped with merry cheer;

"Piper, pipe that song again,"
  So I piped, he wept to hear.

"Drop thy pipe, thy happy pipe,
  Sing thy songs of happy cheer;"
So I sung the same again,
  While he wept with joy to hear.

"Piper, sit thee down and write
  In a book, that all may read."
So he vanish'd from my sight;
  And I pluck'd a hollow reed;

And I made a rural pen,
  And I stain'd the water clear,
And I wrote my happy songs,
  Every child may joy to hear.
                    WILLIAM BLAKE.

SONG.

THE OWL.

WHEN cats run home and light is come,
      And dew is cold upon the ground,
And the far-off stream is dumb,
  And the whirring sail goes round,
  And the whirring sail goes round;
    Alone, and warming his five wits,
    The white owl in the belfry sits.

When merry milkmaids click the latch,
  And rarely smells the new-mown hay,
And the cock hath sung beneath the thatch
  Twice or thrice his roundelay,

Twice or thrice his roundelay:
Alone, and warming his five wits,
The white owl in the belfry sits.

TENNYSON.

SONNET.

TO MR. LAWRENCE.

LAWRENCE, of virtuous father virtuous son,
   Now that the fields are dank and ways are
    mire,
Where shall we sometimes meet, and by the fire
Help waste a sullen day, what may be won
From the hard season gaining? Time will run
   On smoother, till Favonius re-inspire
   The frozen earth, and clothe in fresh attire
The lily and rose that neither sow'd nor spun.
What neat repast shall feast us, light and choice,
   Of Attic taste, with wine, whence we may rise
To hear the lute well touch'd, or artful voice
   Warble immortal notes and Tuscan air?
   He who of these delights can judge, and spare
To interpose them oft, is not unwise.

MILTON.

THE DREAM OF EUGENE ARAM.

'TWAS in the prime of summer time,
   An evening calm and cool,
And four-and-twenty happy boys
   Came bounding out of school:

There were some that ran, and some that leapt,
    Like troutlets in a pool.

Away they sped with gamesome minds,
    And souls untouch'd by sin;
To a level mead they came, and there
    They drave the wickets in:
Pleasantly shone the setting sun
    Over the town of Lynn.

Like sportive deer they coursed about,
    And shouted as they ran—
Turning to mirth all things of earth,
    As only boyhood can:
But the usher sat remote from all,
    A melancholy man!

His hat was off, his vest apart,
    To catch heaven's blessed breeze;
For a burning thought was in his brow,
    And his bosom ill at ease:
So he lean'd his head on his hands, and read
    The book between his knees!

Leaf after leaf he turn'd it o'er,
    Nor ever glanced aside;
For the peace of his soul he read that book
    In the golden eventide:
Much study had made him very lean,
    And pale, and leaden-eyed.

At last he shut the ponderous tome;
    With a fast and fervent grasp
He strain'd the dusky covers close,
    And fix'd the brazen hasp:
" O God, could I so close my mind,
    And clasp it with a clasp!"

Then leaping on his feet upright,
    Some moody turns he took;
Now up the mead, then down the mead,
    And past a shady nook:
And lo! he saw a little boy
    That pored upon a book!

" My gentle lad, what is't you read—
    Romance or fairy fable?
Or is it some historic page,
    Of kings and crowns unstable?"
The young boy gave an upward glance—
    " It is the Death of Abel."

The usher took six hasty strides,
    As smit with sudden pain;
Six hasty strides beyond the place,
    Then slowly back again:
And down he sat beside the lad,
    And talk'd with him of Cain;

And, long since then, of bloody men,
    Whose deeds tradition saves;
Of lonely folk cut off unseen,
    And hid in sudden graves;
Of horrid stabs, in groves forlorn,
    And murders done in caves;

And how the sprites of injured men
    Shriek upward from the sod—
Aye, how the ghostly hand will point
    To show the burial clod;
And unknown facts of guilty acts
    Are seen in dreams from God!

He told how murderers walk'd the earth
    Beneath the curse of Cain—

With crimson clouds before their eyes,
   And flames about their brain:
For blood has left upon their souls
   Its everlasting stain!

" And well," quoth he, " I know, for truth,
   Their pangs must be extreme—
Wo, wo, unutterable wo—
   Who spill life's sacred stream!
For why? Methought last night I wrought
   A murder in a dream!

" One that had never done me wrong—
   A feeble man, and old;
I led him to a lonely field,
   The moon shone clear and cold:
Now here, said I, this man shall die,
   And I will have his gold!

" Two sudden blows with a ragged stick,
   And one with a heavy stone,
One hurried gash with a hasty knife—
   And then the deed was done:
There was nothing lying at my foot,
   But lifeless flesh and bone!

" Nothing but lifeless flesh and bone,
   That could not do me ill;
And yet I fear'd him all the more,
   For lying there so still:
There was a manhood in his look,
   That murder could not kill!

" And lo! the universal air
   Seem'd lit with ghastly flame—
Ten thousand thousand dreadful eyes
   Were looking down in blame:

I took the dead man by the hand,
  And call'd upon his name!

"Oh God, it made me quake to see
  Such sense within the slain!
But when I touch'd the lifeless clay,
  The blood gush'd out amain!
For every clot, a burning spot
  Was scorching in my brain!

"My head was like an ardent coal,
  My heart as solid ice;
My wretched, wretched soul, I knew,
  Was at the devil's price:
A dozen times I groan'd; the dead
  Had never groan'd but twice!

"And now from forth the frowning sky,
  From the heaven's topmost height,
I heard a voice—the awful voice
  Of the blood-avenging sprite:
'Thou guilty man! take up thy dead,
  And hide it from my sight!'

"I took the dreary body up,
  And cast it in a stream—
A sluggish water, black as ink,
  The depth was so extreme.
My gentle boy, remember this
  Is nothing but a dream!

"Down went the corse with a hollow plunge,
  And vanish'd in the pool;
Anon I cleansed my bloody hands,
  And wash'd my forehead cool,
And sat among the urchins young
  That evening in the school!

" O heaven, to think of their white souls,
    And mine so black and grim!
I could not share in childish prayer,
    Nor join in evening hymn:
Like a devil of the pit I seem'd,
    'Mid holy cherubim!

" And peace went with them one and all,
    And each calm pillow spread;
But Guilt was my grim chamberlain
    That lighted me to bed,
And drew my midnight curtains round,
    With fingers bloody red!

" All night I lay in agony,
    In anguish dark and deep;
My fever'd eyes I dared not close,
    But stared aghast at Sleep;
For Sin had render'd unto her
    The keys of hell to keep!

" All night I lay in agony,
    From weary chime to chime,
With one besetting horrid hint,
    That rack'd me all the time—
A mighty yearning, like the first
    Fierce impulse unto crime!

" One stern, tyrannic thought, that made
    All other thoughts its slave;
Stronger and stronger every pulse
    Did that temptation crave—
Still urging me to go and see
    The dead man in his grave!

" Heavily I rose up—as soon
    As light was in the sky—

And sought the black accursed pool
  With a wild misgiving eye;
And I saw the dead in the river bed,
  For the faithless stream was dry!

" Merrily rose the lark, and shook
  The dewdrop from its wing;
But I never mark'd its morning flight,
  I never heard it sing:
For I was stooping once again
  Under the horrid thing.

" With breathless speed, like a soul in chase,
  I took him up and ran—
There was no time to dig a grave
  Before the day began:
In a lonesome wood, with heaps of leaves,
  I hid the murder'd man!

" And all that day I read in school,
  But my thought was other where!
As soon as the mid-day task was done,
  In secret I was there:
And a mighty wind had swept the leaves,
  And still the corse was bare!

" Then down I cast me on my face,
  And first began to weep,
For I knew my secret then was one
  That earth refused to keep;
Or land or sea, though he should be
  Ten thousand fathoms deep!

" So wills the fierce avenging sprite,
  Till blood for blood atones!
Aye, though he's buried in a cave,
  And trodden down with stones,

And years have rotted off his flesh—
    The world shall see his bones!

" Oh God, that horrid, horrid dream
    Besets me now awake!
Again—again, with a dizzy brain,
    The human life I take;
And my red right hand grows raging hot
    Like Cranmer's at the stake.

" And still no peace for the restless clay
    Will wave or mould allow:
The horrid thing pursues my soul—
    It stands before me now!"
The fearful boy look'd up, and saw
    Huge drops upon his brow!

That very night, while gentle sleep
    The urchin eyelids kiss'd,
Two stern-faced men set out from Lynn,
    Through the cold and heavy mist;
And Eugene Aram walk'd between,
    With gyves upon his wrist.

                      HOOD.

TO THE VIRGINS, TO MAKE MUCH OF TIME.

GATHER ye rosebuds while ye may!
    Old Time is still a-flying:
And this same flower, that smiles to-day,
    To-morrow will be dying.

The glorious lamp of heaven, the sun,
    The higher he's a-getting,

The sooner will his race be run,
   And nearer he's to setting.

That age is best which is the first,
   When youth and blood are warmer;
But, being spent, the worse and worst
   Times still succeed the former.

Then be not coy, but use your time;
   And while ye may, go marry;
For, having lost but once your prime,
   You may for ever tarry.

                HERRICK.

PROTUS.

AMONG these latter busts we count by scores,
   Half-emperors and quarter-emperors,
Each with his bay-leaf fillet, loose-thong'd vest,
Loric and low-brow'd Gorgon on the breast;
One loves a baby face, with violets there,
Violets instead of laurel in the hair,
As those were all the little locks could bear.

Now read here. " Protus ends a period
Of empery beginning with a god:
Born in the porphyry chamber at Byzant;
Queens by his cradle, proud and ministrant.
And if he quicken'd breath there, 'twould like fire
Pantingly through the dim vast realm transpire.
A fame that he was missing, spread afar—
The world, from its four corners, rose in war,

Till he was borne out on a balcony
To pacify the world when it should see.
The captains ranged before him, one, his hand
Made baby points at, gain'd the chief command.
And day by day more beautiful he grew
In shape, all said, in feature and in hue,
While young Greek sculptors gazing on the child
Were, so, with old Greek sculpture reconciled.
Already sages labour'd to condense
In easy tomes a life's experience:
And artists took grave counsel to impart
In one breath and one hand-sweep, all their art—
To make his graces prompt as blossoming
Of plentifully-water'd palms in spring;
Since well beseems it, whoso mounts the throne,
For beauty, knowledge, strength, should stand
    alone,
And mortals love the letters of his name."

  Stop! Have you turn'd two pages? Still the same.
New reign, same date. The scribe goes on to say
How that same year, on such a month and day,
" John the Pannonian, groundedly believed
A blacksmith's bastard, whose hard hand reprieved
The Empire from its fate the year before,—
Came, had a mind to take the crown, and wore
The same for six years, (during which the Huns
Kept off their fingers from us) till his sons
Put something in his liquor"—and so forth.
Then a new reign. Stay—" Take at its just worth"
(Subjoins an annotator) " what I give
As hearsay. Some think John let Protus live
And slip away. 'Tis said, he reach'd man's age
At some blind northern court; made first a page,
Then, tutor to the children—last, of use
About the hunting-stables. I deduce

F

He wrote the little tract ' On worming dogs,'
Whereof the name in sundry catalogues
Is extant yet. A Protus of the Race
Is rumour'd to have died a monk in Thrace,—
And if the same, he reach'd senility."

 Here's John the smith's rough-hammer'd head.
  Great eye,
Gross jaw and griped lips do what granite can
To give you the crown-grasper. What a man!
   ROBERT BROWNING.

SONG.

I WANDER'D by the brook-side,
 I wander'd by the mill,—
I could not hear the brook flow,
 The noisy wheel was still;
There was no burr of grasshopper,
 No chirp of any bird;
But the beating of my own heart
 Was all the sound I heard.

I sat beneath the elm-tree,
 I watch'd the long, long shade,
And as it grew still longer
 I did not feel afraid;
For I listen'd for a footfall,
 I listen'd for a word,—
But the beating of my own heart
 Was all the sound I heard.

He came not,—no, he came not;
 The night came on alone;
The little stars sat one by one
 Each on his golden throne;

The evening air pass'd by my cheek,
   The leaves above were stirr'd,—
But the beating of my own heart
   Was all the sound I heard.

Fast silent tears were flowing,
   When some one stood behind;
A hand was on my shoulder,
   I knew its touch was kind:
It drew me nearer—nearer;
   We did not speak a word,—
For the beating of our own hearts
   Was all the sound we heard.
             R. M. MILNES.

THE NIGHTINGALE.

A CONVERSATION POEM.

NO cloud, no relique of the sunken day
   Distinguishes the West, no long thin slip
Of sullen light, no obscure trembling hues.
Come, we will rest on this old mossy bridge!
You see the glimmer of the stream beneath,
But hear no murmuring: it flows silently,
O'er its soft bed of verdure. All is still,
A balmy night! and though the stars be dim,
Yet let us think upon the vernal showers
That gladden the green earth, and we shall find
A pleasure in the dimness of the stars.
And hark! the Nightingale begins its song,
" Most musical, most melancholy" bird![1]

---

[1] *Most musical, most melancholy.*—This passage in Milton possesses an excellence far superior to that of mere description. It is spoken in the character of the melancholy

A melancholy bird! Oh! idle thought!
In nature there is nothing melancholy.
But some night-wandering man whose heart was
    pierced
With the remembrance of a grievous wrong,
Or slow distemper, or neglected love,
(And so, poor wretch! fill'd all things with himself,
And made all gentle sounds tell back the tale
Of his own sorrow) he, and such as he,
First named these notes a melancholy strain,
And many a poet echoes the conceit;
Poet who hath been building up the rhyme
When he had better far have stretch'd his limbs
Beside a brook in mossy forest-dell,
By sun or moon-light, to the influxes
Of shapes and sounds and shifting elements
Surrendering his whole spirit, of his song
And of his fame forgetful! so his fame
Should share in Nature's immortality,
A venerable thing! and so his song
Should make all Nature lovelier, and itself
Be loved like Nature! But 'twill not be so;
And youths and maidens most poetical,
Who lose the deepening twilights of the spring
In ball-rooms and hot theatres, they still
Full of meek sympathy must heave their sighs
O'er Philomela's pity-pleading strains.

My Friend, and thou, our Sister! we have learnt
A different lore: we may not thus profane
Nature's sweet voices, always full of love
And joyance! 'Tis the merry Nightingale
That crowds, and hurries, and precipitates

---

man, and has therefore a dramatic propriety. The author makes this remark, to rescue himself from the charge of having alluded with levity to a line in Milton.

With fast thick warble his delicious notes,
As he were fearful that an April night
Would be too short for him to utter forth
His love-chant, and disburthen his full soul
Of all its music!

    And I know a grove
Of large extent, hard by a castle huge,
Which the great lord inhabits not; and so
This grove is wild with tangling underwood,
And the trim walks are broken up, and grass,
Thin grass and king-cups grow within the paths,
But never elsewhere in one place I knew
So many nightingales; and far and near,
In wood and thicket, over the wide grove,
They answer and provoke each other's song,
With skirmish and capricious passagings,
And murmurs musical and swift jug, jug,
And one low-piping sound more sweet than all—
Stirring the air with such a harmony,
That should you close your eyes, you might almost
Forget it was not day! On moon-lit bushes,
Whose dewy leaflets are but half disclosed,
You may perchance behold them on the twigs,
Their bright, bright eyes, their eyes both bright
   and full,
Glistening, while many a glow-worm in the shade
Lights up her love-torch.

      A most gentle Maid,
Who dwelleth in her hospitable home
Hard by the castle, and at latest eve
(Even like a Lady vow'd and dedicate
To something more than Nature in the grove)
Glides through the pathways; she knows all their
   notes,
That gentle Maid! and oft a moment's space,

What time the moon was lost behind a cloud,
Hath heard a pause of silence; till the moon
Emerging, hath awaken'd earth and sky
With one sensation, and these wakeful birds
Have all burst forth in choral minstrelsy,
As if some sudden gale had swept at once
A hundred airy harps! And she hath watch'd
Many a nightingale perch'd giddily
On blossomy twig still swinging from the breeze,
And to that motion tune his wanton song
Like tipsy joy that reels with tossing head.

   Farewell, O Warbler! till to-morrow eve,
And you, my friends! farewell, a short farewell!
We have been loitering long and pleasantly,
And now for our dear homes.—That strain again!
Full fain it would delay me! My dear babe,
Who, capable of no articulate sound,
Mars all things with his imitative lisp,
How he would place his hand beside his ear,
His little hand, the small forefinger up,
And bid us listen! And I deem it wise
To make him Nature's playmate. He knows well
The evening-star; and once, when he awoke
In most distressful mood (some inward pain
Had made up that strange thing, an infant's dream)
I hurried with him to our orchard-plot,
And he beheld the moon, and, hush'd at once,
Suspends his sobs, and laughs most silently,
While his fair eyes, that swam with undropp'd tears,
Did glitter in the yellow moon-beam! Well!—
It is a father's tale: But if that Heaven
Should give me life, his childhood shall grow up
Familiar with these songs, that with the night
He may associate joy.—Once more, farewell,
Sweet Nightingale! Once more, my friends!
      farewell.   COLERIDGE.

THE HAUNTED PALACE.

IN the greenest of our valleys,
    By good angels tenanted,
Once a fair and stately palace—
    Radiant palace—rear'd its head.
In the monarch Thought's dominion—
    It stood there!
Never seraph waved a pinion
    Over fabric half so fair.

Banners yellow, glorious, golden,
    On its roof did float and flow,
(This—all this—was in the olden
    Time long ago,)
And every gentle air that dallied
    In that sweet day,
Along the ramparts plumed and pallid
    A wingèd odour went away.

Wanderers in that happy valley,
    Through two luminous windows, saw
Spirits moving musically,
    To a lute's well-tunèd law,
Round about a throne, where sitting
    (Porphyrogene!)
In state his glory well befitting,
    The ruler of the realm was seen.

And all with pearl and ruby glowing
    Was the fair palace door,
Through which came flowing, flowing, flowing,
    And sparkling evermore,

A troop of Echoes, whose sweet duty
    Was but to sing,
In voices of surpassing beauty,
    The wit and wisdom of their king.

But evil things, in robes of sorrow,
    Assail'd the monarch's high estate.
(Ah, let us mourn!—for never morrow
    Shall dawn upon him desolate!)
And round about his home the glory
    That blush'd and bloom'd,
Is but a dim-remember'd story
    Of the old time entomb'd.

And travellers, now, within that valley,
    Through the red-litten windows see
Vast forms, that move fantastically
    To a discordant melody,
While, like a ghastly rapid river,
    Through the pale door
A hideous throng rush out for ever,
    And laugh—but smile no more.

EDGAR A. POE.

[EVENING SONG OF THE PRIEST OF PAN.]

(FROM " THE FAITHFUL SHEPHERDESS.")

SHEPHERDS all, and maidens fair,
    Fold your flocks up, for the air
'Gins to thicken, and the sun
Already his great course hath run.
See the dew-drops how they kiss
Every little flower that is;

Hanging on their velvet heads
Like a rope of crystal beads;
See the heavy clouds low-falling,
And bright Hesperus down calling
The dead Night from underground,
At whose rising, mists unsound,
Damps and vapours, fly apace
Hovering o'er the wanton face
Of these pastures; where they come
Striking dead both bud and bloom.
Therefore from such danger, lock
Every one his loved flock,
And let your dogs lie loose without,
Lest the wolf come as a scout
From the mountain, and, e'er day,
Bear a lamb or kid away,
Or the crafty thievish fox
Break upon your simple flocks.
To secure yourselves from these,
Be not too secure in ease;
Let one eye his watches keep,
While the other eye doth sleep;
So shall you good shepherds prove,
And for ever hold the love
Of our great God. Sweetest slumbers
And soft silence fall in numbers
On your eyelids: so farewell;
Thus I end my evening's knell.
JOHN FLETCHER.

THE FUGITIVES.

1.

THE waters are flashing,
　The white hail is dashing,
The lightnings are glancing,
The hoar spray is dancing,—
　　Away!

The whirlwind is rolling,
The thunder is tolling,
The forest is swinging,
The minster bells ringing,—
　　Come away!

The Earth is like Ocean,
Wreck-strewn and in motion;
Bird, beast, man, and worm,
Have crept out of the storm—
　　Come away!

II.

" Our boat has one sail,
And the helmsman is pale;—
A bold pilot, I trow,
Who should follow us now,"—
　　Shouted he—

And she cried: " Ply the oar;
Put off gaily from shore!"
As she spoke, bolts of death
Mix'd with hail, speck'd their path
　　O'er the sea.

And from isle, tower, and rock,
The blue beacon-cloud broke,
Though dumb in the blast,
The red cannon flash'd fast
    From the lee.

III.

" And fear'st thou, and fear'st thou?
And see'st thou, and hear'st thou?
And drive we not free
O'er the terrible sea,
    I and thou?"

One boat-cloak did cover
The loved and the lover—
Their blood beats one measure,
They murmur proud pleasure
    Soft and low;—

While around, the lash'd Ocean,
Like mountains in motion,
Is withdrawn and uplifted,
Sunk, shatter'd, and shifted,
    To and fro.

IV.

In the court of the fortress
Beside the pale portress,
Like a bloodhound well beaten
The bridegroom stands, eaten
    By shame;

On the topmost watch-turret,
As a death-boding spirit,
Stands the grey tyrant father,—
To his voice the mad weather
    Seems tame;

    And with curses as wild
    As e'er cling to child,
  He devotes to the blast
  The best, loveliest, and last
    Of his name.
SHELLEY.

[TO A DEPARTED FRIEND.]

DOST thou look back on what hath been,
    As some divinely gifted man,
  Whose life in low estate began
And on a simple village green;

Who breaks his birth's invidious bar,
    And grasps the skirts of happy chance,
    And breasts the blows of circumstance,
And grapples with his evil star;

Who makes by force his merit known
    And lives to clutch the golden keys,
    To mould a mighty state's decrees,
And shape the whisper of the throne;

And moving up from high to higher,
    Becomes on Fortune's crowning slope
    The pillar of a people's hope,
The centre of a world's desire;

Yet feels as in a pensive dream,
    When all his active powers are still,
    A distant dearness in the hill,
A secret sweetness in the stream,

The limit of his narrow fate,
    While yet beside its vocal springs
    He play'd at counsellors and kings,
With one that was his earliest mate;

Who ploughs with pain his native lea
    And reaps the labour of his hands,
    Or in the furrow musing stands;
Does my old friend remember me?
              In Memoriam.

SONG.

[FROM "AS YOU LIKE IT."]

UNDER the greenwood tree
    Who loves to lie with me,
And tune his merry note
    Unto the sweet bird's throat,
Come hither, come hither, come hither:
      Here shall he see
      No enemy
But winter and rough weather.

Who doth ambition shun,
    And loves to live i' the sun;
Seeking the food he eats,
    And pleased with what he gets,
Come hither, come hither, come hither:
      Here shall he see
      No enemy
But winter and rough weather.
              SHAKESPEARE.

SONNET.

ON FIRST LOOKING INTO CHAPMAN'S HOMER.

MUCH have I travell'd in the realms of gold,
    And many goodly states and kingdoms seen;
Round many western islands have I been
Which bards in fealty to Apollo hold.
Oft of one wide expanse had I been told
    That deep-brow'd Homer ruled as his demesne:
    Yet did I never breathe its pure serene
Till I heard Chapman speak out loud and bold:
Then felt I like some watcher of the skies,
    When a new planet swims into his ken;
Or like stout Cortez when with eagle eyes
    He stared at the Pacific—and all his men
Look'd at each other with a wild surmise—
    Silent, upon a peak in Darien.

                      KEATS.

THE APOLOGY.

THINK me not unkind or rude,
    That I walk alone in grove and glen;
I go to the god of the wood,
    To fetch his word to men.

Tax not my sloth that I
    Fold my arms beside the brook;
Each cloud that floated in the sky
    Writes a letter in my book.

Chide me not, laborious band,
　For the idle flowers I brought;
Every aster in my hand
　Goes home loaded with a thought.

There was never mystery
　But 'tis figured in the flowers,
Was never secret history,
　But birds tell it in the bowers.

One harvest from thy field
　Homeward brought the oxen strong;
A second crop thine acres yield,
　Which I gather in a song.
　　　　　　　　EMERSON.

TIBBIE.

TUNE "INVERCAULD'S REEL."

O TIBBIE, I hae seen the day
　　Ye wadna been sae shy!
For laik o' gear ye lightly me;—
　But, trowth, I carena by!

Yestreen I met you on the moor,
　Ye spak na, but gaed by like stoure;[1]
Ye geck at me because I'm poor;
　But fient a hair care I.
Chorus.　O Tibbie, &c.

I doubtna, lass, but ye may think,
Because ye hae the name o' clink,

---

[1] *Stoure*, a whirl of dust.

That ye can please me at a wink,
　　Whene'er ye like to try:

But sorrow tak him that's sae mean,
Although his pouch o' coin were clean,
Wha follows ony saucy quean
　　That looks sae proud and high!

Although a lad were ne'er sae smart,
If that he want the yellow dirt
Ye'll cast your head anither airt
　　And answer him fu' dry:

But if he hae the name o' gear
Ye'll fasten to him like a brier,
Though hardly he, for sense or lear,
　　Be better than the kye.

But Tibbie, lass, tak my advice,—
Your daddie's gear maks you sae nice;
The deil a ane wad spier your price
　　Were ye as poor as I;

There lives a lass in yonder park,
I wadna gie her in her sark
For thee wi' a' thy thousan' mark,—
　　Ye needna look sae high!

Chorus. O Tibbie, I hae seen the day
　　Ye wadna been sae shy!
　For laik o' gear ye lightly me;—
　　But, trowth, I carena by!

　　　　　　　　　　　BURNS.

CHORAL SONG OF ILLYRIAN PEASANTS.

[FROM "ZAPOLYA."]

UP! up! ye dames, ye lasses gay!
    To the meadows trip away.
'Tis you must tend the flocks this morn,
And scare the small birds from the corn.
Not a soul at home may stay:
    For the shepherds must go
    With lance and bow
To hunt the wolf in the woods to-day.

Leave the hearth and leave the house
To the cricket and the mouse:
Find grannam out a sunny seat,
With babe and lambkin at her feet.
Not a soul at home may stay:
    For the shepherds must go
    With lance and bow
To hunt the wolf in the woods to-day.
COLERIDGE.

THE RAVEN.

ONCE upon a midnight dreary, while I
    ponder'd, weak and weary,
Over many a quaint and curious volume of for-
    gotten lore,

While I nodded, nearly napping, suddenly there
    came a tapping,
As of some one gently rapping, rapping at my
    chamber door.
" 'Tis some visitor," I mutter'd, " tapping at my
    chamber door—
        Only this, and nothing more."

Ah, distinctly I remember it was in the bleak
    December,
And each separate dying ember wrought its ghost
    upon the floor.
Eagerly I wish'd the morrow ;—vainly I had
    sought to borrow
From my books surcease of sorrow—sorrow for
    the lost Lenore—
For the rare and radiant maiden whom the angels
    name Lenore—
        Nameless here for evermore.

And the silken sad uncertain rustling of each
    purple curtain
Thrill'd me—fill'd me with fantastic terrors never
    felt before ;
So that now, to still the beating of my heart, I
    stood repeating
" 'Tis some visitor entreating entrance at my
    chamber door—
Some late visitor entreating entrance at my
    chamber door ;—
        This it is, and nothing more."

Presently my soul grew stronger ; hesitating then
    no longer,
" Sir," said I, " or Madam, truly your forgiveness
    I implore ;

But the fact is I was napping, and so gently you
    came rapping,
And so faintly you came tapping, tapping at my
    chamber door,
That I scarce was sure I heard you"—here I
    open'd wide the door;—
        Darkness there, and nothing more.

Deep into that darkness peering, long I stood
    there wondering, fearing,
Doubting, dreaming dreams no mortal ever dared
    to dream before;
But the silence was unbroken, and the darkness
    gave no token,
And the only word there spoken was the whisper'd
    word, " Lenore!"
This I whisper'd, and an echo murmur'd back the
    word, " Lenore!"
        Merely this, and nothing more.

Back into the chamber turning, all my soul within
    me burning,
Soon I heard again a tapping somewhat louder
    than before,
" Surely," said I, " surely that is something at my
    window lattice;
Let me see, then, what thereat is, and this mystery
    explore—
Let my heart be still a moment and this mystery
    explore;—
        'Tis the wind, and nothing more!"

Open here I flung a shutter, when, with many a
    flirt and flutter,
In there stepp'd a stately raven of the saintly days
    of yore;

Not the least obeisance made he; not an instant
    stopp'd or stay'd he;
But, with mien of lord or lady, perch'd above my
    chamber door—
Perch'd upon a bust of Pallas just above my
    chamber door—
        Perch'd, and sat, and nothing more.

Then this ebony bird beguiling my sad fancy into
    smiling,
By the grave and stern decorum of the countenance
    it wore,
" Though thy crest be shorn and shaven, thou," I
    said, " art sure no craven,
Ghastly, grim, and ancient raven wandering from
    the Nightly shore—
Tell me what thy lordly name is on the Night's
    Plutonian shore!"
        Quoth the raven, " Nevermore."

Much I marvell'd this ungainly fowl to hear dis-
    course so plainly,
Though its answer little meaning—little relevancy
    bore;
For we cannot help agreeing that no living human
    being
Ever yet was blest with seeing bird above his
    chamber door—
Bird or beast upon the sculptured bust above his
    chamber door,
        With such name as " Nevermore."

But the raven, sitting lonely on the placid bust,
    spoke only
That one word, as if his soul in that one word he
    did outpour.

Nothing farther then he utter'd—not a feather then
    he flutter'd—
Till I scarcely more than mutter'd " Other friends
    have flown before—
On the morrow *he* will leave me, as my hopes
    have flown before."
        Then the bird said " Nevermore."

Startled at the stillness broken by reply so aptly
    spoken,
" Doubtless," said I, " what it utters is its only
    stock and store
Caught from some unhappy master whom unmer-
    ciful Disaster
Follow'd fast, and follow'd faster, till his songs one
    burden bore—
Till the dirges of his Hope that melancholy burden
    bore
        Of ' Never—nevermore.' "

But the raven still beguiling all my sad soul into
    smiling,
Straight I wheel'd a cushion'd seat in front of bird,
    and bust, and door;
Then, upon the velvet sinking, I betook myself to
    linking
Fancy unto fancy, thinking what this ominous bird
    of yore—
What this grim, ungainly, ghastly, gaunt, and
    ominous bird of yore
        Meant in croaking " Nevermore."

This I sat engaged in guessing, but no syllable
    expressing
To the fowl whose fiery eyes now burnt into my
    bosom's core;

This and more I sat divining, with my head at
    ease reclining
On the cushion's velvet lining that the lamplight
    gloated o'er,
But whose velvet violet lining, with the lamplight
    gloating o'er,
      She shall press, ah, nevermore!

Then, methought, the air grew denser, perfumed
    from an unseen censer
Swung by angels whose faint foot-falls tinkled on
    the tufted floor.
" Wretch," I cried, " thy God hath lent thee—by
    these angels he hath sent thee
Respite—respite and nepenthe from thy memories
    of Lenore!
Quaff, oh quaff this kind nepenthe and forget this
    lost Lenore!"
      Quoth the raven, " Nevermore."

" Prophet!" said I, " thing of evil!—prophet
    still, if bird or devil!—
Whether Tempter sent, or whether tempest toss'd
    thee here ashore,
Desolate yet all undaunted, on this desert land
    enchanted—
On this home by Horror haunted—tell me truly,
    I implore—
Is there—*is* there balm in Gilead?—tell me—tell
    me, I implore!"
      Quoth the raven, " Nevermore."

" Prophet!" said I, "thing of evil—prophet still,
    if bird or devil!
By that Heaven that bends above us—by that God
    we both adore—

Tell this soul with sorrow laden if, within the
    distant Aidenn,
It shall clasp a sainted maiden whom the angels
    name Lenore—
Clasp a rare and radiant maiden whom the angels
    name Lenore."
        Quoth the raven, " Nevermore."

" Be that word our sign of parting, bird or fiend ! "
    I shriek'd, upstarting—
" Get thee back into the tempest and the Night's
    Plutonian shore !
Leave no black plume as a token of the lie thy
    soul hath spoken !
Leave my loneliness unbroken !—quit the bust
    above my door !
Take thy beak from out my heart, and take thy
    form from off my door ! "
        Quoth the raven, " Nevermore."

And the raven, never flitting, still is sitting, still
    is sitting
On the pallid bust of Pallas just above my
    chamber door ;
And his eyes have all the seeming of a demon's
    that is dreaming,
And the lamplight o'er him streaming throws his
    shadow on the floor ;
And my soul from out that shadow that lies
    floating on the floor
        Shall be lifted—nevermore !
                E. A. Poe.

FLOWERS.

I WILL not have the mad Clytie,
   Whose head is turn'd by the sun;
The Tulip is a courtly quean,
   Whom therefore I will shun;
The Cowslip is a country wench,
   The Violet is a nun;—
But I will woo the dainty Rose,
   The queen of every one.

The Pea is but a wanton witch,
   In too much haste to wed,
And clasps her rings on every hand;
   The Wolfsbane I should dread;
Nor will I dreary Rosemarye,
   That always mourns the dead;—
But I will woo the dainty Rose,
   With her cheeks of tender red.

The Lily is all in white, like a saint,
   And so is no mate for me—
And the Daisy's cheek is tipp'd with a blush,
   She is of such low degree;
Jasmin is sweet, and has many loves,
   And the Broom's betroth'd to the Bee;—
But I will plight with the dainty Rose,
   For fairest of all is she!

HOOD.

FABLE.

THE Mountain and the Squirrel
    Had a quarrel,
And the former call'd the latter " Little Prig :"
Bun replied,
" You are doubtless very big,
But all sorts of things and weather
Must be taken in together
To make up a year,
And a sphere.
And I think it no disgrace
To occupy my place.
If I'm not so large as you,
You are not so small as I,
And not half so spry:
I'll not deny you make
A very pretty squirrel-track ;
Talents differ ; all is well and wisely put ;
If I cannot carry forests on my back,
Neither can you crack a nut."
                   EMERSON.

AS I LAY A-THINKING.

AS I lay a-thinking, a-thinking, a-thinking,
    Merry sang the Bird as she sat upon the
        spray ;
  There came a noble Knight
  With his hauberk shining bright,

   And his gallant heart was light,
    Free, and gay;
And as I lay a-thinking, he rode upon his way.

As I lay a-thinking, a-thinking, a-thinking,
 Sadly sang the Bird as she sat upon the tree;
  There seem'd a crimson plain,
  Where a gallant Knight lay slain,
  And a steed with broken rein
   Ran free;
As I lay a-thinking—most pitiful to see.

As I lay a-thinking, a-thinking, a-thinking,
 Merry sang the Bird as she sat upon the bough;
  A lovely Maid came by,
  And a gentle Youth was nigh,
  And he breathed many a sigh
   And a vow;
As I lay a-thinking—her heart was gladsome now.

As I lay a-thinking, a-thinking, a-thinking,
 Sadly sang the Bird as she sat upon the thorn;
  No more a Youth was there,
  But a Maiden rent her hair,
  And cried in sad despair,
   "That I was born!"
As I lay a-thinking—she perished forlorn.

As I lay a-thinking, a-thinking, a-thinking,
 Sweetly sang the Bird as she sat upon the briar;
  There came a lovely Child,
  And his face was meek and mild,
  Yet joyously he smiled
   On his sire;
As I lay a-thinking—a cherub might admire.

But as I lay a-thinking, a-thinking, a-thinking,
  And sadly sang the Bird as it perch'd upon a bier;
    That joyous smile was gone,
    And the face was white and wan,
    As the down upon the swan
      Doth appear;
As I lay a-thinking—oh, bitter flow'd the tear!

As I lay a-thinking, the golden sun was sinking,
  O merry sang that Bird as it glitter'd on her
      breast
    With a thousand gorgeous dyes,
    While soaring to the skies
    'Mid the stars she seem'd to rise
      As to her nest;
As I lay a-thinking, her meaning was exprest:
    " Follow, follow me away!
    It boots not to delay,"—
    ('Twas so she seem'd to say)
      " Here is rest!"
        RICHARD H. BARHAM.

A MAN'S REQUIREMENTS.

LOVE me, sweet, with all thou art,
  Feeling, thinking, seeing,—
Love me in the lightest part,
  Love me in full being.

Love me with thine open youth
  In its frank surrender;
With the vowing of thy mouth,
  With its silence tender.

Love me with thine azure eyes
    Made for earnest granting;—
Taking colour from the skies,
    Can Heaven's truth be wanting?

Love me with their lids that fall
    Snow-like at first meeting:
Love me with thine heart, that all
    The neighbours then see beating.

Love me with thy hand stretch'd out
    Freely—open-minded:
Love me with thy loitering foot,—
    Hearing one behind it.

Love me with thy voice that turns
    Sudden faint above me;
Love me with thy blush that burns
    When I murmur " *Love me!* "

Love me with thy thinking soul—
    Break it to love-sighing;
Love me with thy thoughts that roll
    On through living—dying.

Love me in thy gorgeous airs,
    When the world has crown'd thee:
Love me, kneeling at thy prayers,
    With the angels round thee.

Love me pure, as musers do,
    Up the woodlands shady:
Love me gaily, fast, and true,
    As a winsome lady.

Through all hopes that keep us brave,
    Further off or nigher,

Love me for the house and grave,—
   And for something higher.

Thus, if thou wilt prove me, dear,
   Woman's love no fable,
I will love *thee*—half-a-year—
   As a man is able.

            ELIZABETH BARRETT BROWNING.

MEA CULPA.

AT me one night the angry moon
      Suspended to a rim of cloud
Glared through the courses of the wind.
Suddenly there my spirit bow'd
And shrank into a fearful swoon
That made me deaf and blind.

We sinn'd—we sin—is that a dream?
We wake—there is no voice nor stir;
Sin and repent from day to day,
As though some reeking murderer
Should dip his hand in a running stream,
And lightly go his way.

Embrace me, fiends and wicked men,
For I am of your crew. Draw back,
Pure women, children with clear eyes.
Let Scorn confess me on his rack,—
Stretch'd down by force, uplooking then
Into the solemn skies!

Singly we pass the gloomy gate;
Some robed in honour, full of peace,

Who of themselves are not aware;
Being fed with secret wickedness,
And comforted with lies: my fate
Moves fast; I shall come there.

All is so usual, hour by hour;
Men's spirits are so lightly twirl'd
By every little gust of sense;
Who lays to heart this common world?
Who lays to heart the Ruling Power,
Just, infinite, intense—?

Thou wilt not frown, O God. Yet we
Escape not thy transcendent law;
It reigns within us and without.
What earthly vision never saw
Man's naked soul may suddenly see,
Dreadful, past thought or doubt.

BREAK, break, break,
   On thy cold gray stones, O Sea!
And I would that my tongue could utter
   The thoughts that arise in me.

O well for the fisherman's boy,
   That he shouts with his sister at play!
O well for the sailor lad,
   That he sings in his boat on the bay!

And the stately ships go on
   To their haven under the hill;
But O for the touch of a vanish'd hand,
   And the sound of a voice that is still!

> Break, break, break,
>   At the foot of thy crags, O Sea,
> But the tender grace of a day that is dead
>   Will never come back to me.
>
> TENNYSON.

SONNET.

[ABSENCE.]

FROM you I have been absent in the spring,
  When proud-pied April, dress'd in all his trim,
Hath put a spirit of youth in everything,
That heavy Saturn laugh'd and leap'd with him.
Yet not the lays of birds, nor the sweet smell
Of different flowers in odour and in hue,
Could make me any summer story tell,
Or from their proud lap pluck them where they grew,
Nor did I wonder at the lilies' white,
Nor praise the deep vermillion of the rose,
They were but sweet, but figures of delight,
Drawn after you, you pattern of all those,—
Yet seem'd it winter still; and, you away,
As with your shadow I with these did play.

SHAKESPEARE.

THE TIGER.

TIGER, tiger, burning bright
  In the forest of the night!
What immortal hand or eye
Could frame thy fearful symmetry?

In what distant deeps or skies
Burnt the ardour of thine eyes?
On what wings dare he aspire—
What the hand dare seize the fire?

And what shoulder, and what art
Could twist the sinews of thy heart?
And when thy heart began to beat,
What dread hand form'd thy dread feet?

What the hammer, what the chain?
In what furnace was thy brain?
Did God smile his work to see?
Did He who made the lamb make thee?

WILLIAM BLAKE.

SONG.

(FROM THE SPANISH OF IGLESIAS.)

ALEXIS calls me cruel;
    The rifted crags that hold
The gather'd ice of winter,
    He says, are not more cold.

When even the very blossoms
    Around the fountain's brim,
And forest walks can witness
    The love I bear to him.

I would that I could utter
    My feelings without shame;
And tell him how I love him,
    Nor wrong my virgin fame.

Alas! to seize the moment
When heart inclines to heart,
And press a suit with passion,
Is not a woman's part.

If no one comes to gather
The roses where they stand,
They fade among their foliage;
They cannot seek his hand.

W. C. BRYANT.

YARROW UNVISITED.

(See the various Poems, the scene of which is laid upon the banks of the Yarrow; in particular the exquisite Ballad of Hamilton, beginning:—
"*Busk ye, busk ye, my bonny, bonny Bride,
Busk ye, busk ye, my winsome Marrow!*")

FROM Stirling castle we had seen
   The mazy Forth unravell'd;
Had trod the banks of Clyde, and Tay,
And with the Tweed had travell'd;
And when we came to Clovenford,
Then said my "*winsome Marrow*,"
"Whate'er betide, we'll turn aside,
And see the Braes of Yarrow."

"Let Yarrow folk, *frae* Selkirk town,
Who have been buying, selling,
Go back to Yarrow, 'tis their own;
Each maiden to her dwelling!
On Yarrow's banks let herons feed,
Hares couch, and rabbits burrow!

But we will downward with the Tweed.
Nor turn aside to Yarrow.

" There's Galla Water, Leader Haughs,
Both lying right before us;
And Dryborough, where with chiming Tweed
The lintwhites sing in chorus ;
There's pleasant Tiviot-dale, a land
Made blithe with plough and harrow :
Why throw away a needful day
To go in search of Yarrow ?

" What's Yarrow but a river bare,
That glides the dark hills under ?
There are a thousand such elsewhere
As worthy of your wonder."
Strange words they seem'd of slight and scorn :
My True-love sigh'd for sorrow ;
And look'd me in the face, to think
I thus could speak of Yarrow !

" Oh ! green," said I, " are Yarrow's holms,
And sweet is Yarrow flowing !
Fair hangs the apple frae the rock,[1]
But we will leave it growing.
O'er hilly path, and open Strath,
We'll wander Scotland thorough ;
But, though so near, we will not turn
Into the dale of Yarrow.

" Let beeves and home-bred kine partake
The sweets of Burn-mill meadow ;
The swan on still St. Mary's Lake
Float double, swan and shadow !

---

[1] See Hamilton's Ballad as above.

We will not see them; will not go,
To-day, nor yet to-morrow;
Enough if in our hearts we know
There's such a place as Yarrow.

" Be Yarrow stream unseen, unknown!
It must, or we shall rue it:
We have a vision of our own;
Ah! why should we undo it?
The treasured dreams of times long past,
We'll keep them, winsome Marrow!
For when we're there, although 'tis fair,
'Twill be another Yarrow!

" If Care with freezing years should come,
And wandering seem but folly,—
Should we be loath to stir from home,
And yet be melancholy;
Should life be dull, and spirits low,
'Twill soothe us in our sorrow,
That earth has something yet to show,
The bonny holms of Yarrow!"
WORDSWORTH.

ADIEU.

LET time and chance combine, combine,
    Let time and chance combine;
The fairest love from heaven above,
    That love of yours was mine,
        My dear,
    That love of yours was mine.

The past is fled and gone, and gone,
    The past is fled and gone;
If nought but pain to me remain,
    I'll fare in memory on,
        My dear,
    I'll fare in memory on.

The saddest tears must fall, must fall,
    The saddest tears must fall;
In weal or woe, in this world below,
    I love you ever and all,
        My dear,
    I love you ever and all.

A long road full of pain, of pain,
    A long road full of pain;
One soul, one heart, sworn ne'er to part,—
    We ne'er can meet again,
        My dear,
    We ne'er can meet again.

Hard fate will not allow, allow,
    Hard fate will not allow;
We blessed were as the angels are,—
    Adieu for ever now,
        My dear,
    Adieu for ever now.
            T. C<small>ARLYLE</small>.

TO A SKY-LARK.

I.

ETHEREAL minstrel! pilgrim of the sky!
    Dost thou despise the earth where cares
        abound?
Or, while the wings aspire, are heart and eye
    Both with thy nest upon the dewy ground?
Thy nest which thou canst drop into at will,
Those quivering wings composed, that music still!

II.

To the last point of vision, and beyond,
    Mount, daring warbler!—that love-prompted
        strain
('Twixt thee and thine a never-failing bond)
    Thrills not the less the bosom of the plain:
Yet might'st thou seem, proud privilege! to sing
All independent of the leafy spring.

III.

Leave to the nightingale her shady wood;
    A privacy of glorious light is thine;
Whence thou dost pour upon the world a flood
    Of harmony, with instinct more divine;
Type of the wise who soar, but never roam;
True to the kindred points of Heaven and Home!

                    WORDSWORTH.

THE TWA CORBIES.[1]

AS I was walking all alane,
    I heard twa corbies making a mane;
The tane unto the t'ither did say,
    "Whar sall we gang and dine the day?"

---

[1] *Corbies*, ravens.

"In behint you auld fail¹ dyke,
I wot there lies a new-slain knight;
And naebody kens that he lies there
But his hawk, his hound, and his lady fair.

"His hound is to the hunting gane,
His hawk to fetch the wild-fowl hame,
His lady's ta'en anither mate,
Sae we may mak' our dinner sweet.

"Ye'll sit on his white ²hause-bane,
And I'll pike out his bonny blue een;
Wi' ae lock o' his gowden hair
We'll theek³ our nest when it grows bare.

"Mony a one for him makes mane,
But nane sall ken whar he is gane.
O'er his white banes, when they are bare,
The wind sall blaw for evermair."

SCOTT's *Border Minstrelsy*.

DIRGE FOR THE YEAR.

ORPHAN hours, the Year is dead,
 Come and sigh, come and weep!
Merry hours, smile instead,
 For the Year is but asleep:
See, it smiles as it is sleeping,
Mocking your untimely weeping.

As an earthquake rocks a corse
 In its coffin in the clay,
So white Winter, that rough nurse,
 Rocks the dead-cold Year to-day.

---

¹ *Fail*, turf, sod.   ² *Hause*, neck.   ³ *Theek*, thatch.

Solemn hours, wail aloud
For your mother in her shroud!

As the wild air stirs and sways
   The tree-rock'd cradle of a child,
So the breath of these rude days
   Rocks the Year: be calm and mild,
Trembling hours, she will arise
With new love within her eyes.

January grey is here,
   Like a sexton by her grave;
February bears the bier,
   March with grief doth howl and rave,
And April weeps,—but, O ye hours!
Follow with May's fairest flowers.
SHELLEY.

SONG OF ARIEL.

[FROM "THE TEMPEST."]

COME unto these yellow sands,
   And then take hands,—
Curtsied when you have and kiss'd;
   (The wild waves whist)—
Foot it featly here and there;
And, sweet sprites, the burden bear.
    Hark, hark!
    Bough, wough. (*dispersedly*)
   The watch-dogs bark.
    Bough, wough. (*dispersedly*)
Hark, hark! I hear
The strain of strutting chanticleer
   Cry, cock-a-doodle-doo.
SHAKESPEARE.

SONNET.

ON HIS BLINDNESS.

WHEN I consider how my light is spent,
    Ere half my days in this dark world and
      wide;
And that one talent which is death to hide
Lodged with me useless, though my soul more bent
To serve therewith my Maker, and present
    My true account, lest he, returning, chide;
    " Doth God exact day-labour, light denied?"
I fondly ask: but Patience, to prevent
That murmur, soon replies, " God doth not need
    Either man's work, or his own gift; who best
    Bear his mild yoke, they serve him best; his
      state
Is kingly; thousands at his bidding speed,
    And post o'er land and ocean without rest;
    They also serve who only stand and wait."

MILTON.

SONG ON MAY MORNING.

NOW the bright Morning-Star, day's har-
    binger,
Comes dancing from the east, and leads with her
The flowery May, who from her green lap throws
The yellow cowslip and the pale primrose.

Hail! bounteous May, that dost inspire
Mirth, and youth, and warm desire:
Woods and groves are of thy dressing,
Hill and dale doth boast thy blessing.
Thus we salute thee with our early song,
And welcome thee, and wish thee long.

MILTON.

ULYSSES.

IT little profits that an idle king,
By his still hearth, among these barren crags,
Match'd with an aged wife, I mete and dole
Unequal laws unto a savage race,
That hoard, and sleep, and feed, and know not me.
I cannot rest from travel: I will drink
Life to the lees: all life I have enjoy'd
Greatly, have suffer'd greatly, both with those
That loved me, and alone; on shore, and when
Through scudding drifts the rainy Hyades
Vext the dim sea: I am become a name;
For always roaming with a hungry heart
Much have I seen and know; cities of men
And manners, climates, councils, governments,
Myself not least, but honour'd of them all;
And drunk delight of battle with my peers,
Far on the ringing plains of windy Troy.
I am a part of all that I have met;
Yet all experience is an arch wherethro'
Gleams that untravell'd world, whose margin fades
For ever and for ever when I move.
How dull it is to pause, to make an end,
To rust unburnish'd, not to shine in use!
As though to breathe were life. Life piled on life

Were all too little, and of one to me
Little remains: but every hour is saved
From that eternal silence, something more,
A bringer of new things; and vile it were
For some three suns to store and hoard myself,
And this grey spirit yearning in desire
To follow knowledge, like a sinking star,
Beyond the utmost bound of human thought.

    This is my son, mine own Telemachus,
To whom I leave the sceptre and the isle—
Well-loved of me, discerning to fulfil
This labour, by slow prudence to make mild
A rugged people, and through soft degrees
Subdue them to the useful and the good.
Most blameless is he, centered in the sphere
Of common duties, decent not to fail
In offices of tenderness, and pay
Meet adoration to my household gods
When I am gone. He works his work, I mine.

    There lies the port: the vessel puffs her sail:
There gloom the dark broad seas. My mariners,
Souls that have toil'd, and wrought, and thought
        with me—
That ever with a frolic welcome took
The thunder and the sunshine, and opposed
Free hearts, free foreheads—you and I are old;
Old age hath yet his honour and his toil;
Death closes all: but something ere the end,
Some work of noble note, may yet be done,
Not unbecoming men that strove with Gods.
The lights begin to twinkle from the rocks:
The long day wanes: the slow moon climbs: the
    deep
Moans round with many voices. Come, my friends,
'Tis not too late to seek a newer world.
Push off, and sitting well in order smite

The sounding furrows; for my purpose holds
To sail beyond the sunset, and the baths
Of all the western stars, until I die.
It may be that the gulfs will wash us down:
It may be we shall touch the Happy Isles,
And see the great Achilles whom we knew.
Though much is taken, much abides; and tho'
We are not now that strength which in old days
Moved earth and heaven; that which we are, we are;
One equal temper of heroic hearts
Made weak by time and fate, but strong in will
To strive, to seek, to find, and not to yield.

TENNYSON.

SONG OF ARIEL.

[FROM "THE TEMPEST."]

FULL fathom five thy father lies;
   Of his bones are coral made;
Those are pearls that were his eyes:
   Nothing of him that doth fade
But doth suffer a sea-change
Into something rich and strange.
Sea-nymphs hourly ring his knell.
Hark! now I hear them,—ding-dong bell!

SHAKESPEARE.

TO AUTUMN.

SEASON of mists and mellow fruitfulness!
   Close bosom-friend of the maturing sun;
Conspiring with him how to load and bless

With fruit the vines that round the thatch-eaves
    run;
To bend with apples the moss'd cottage-trees,
    And fill all fruit with ripeness to the core;
    To swell the gourd, and plump the hazel shells
With a sweet kernel; to set budding more,
    And still more, later flowers for the bees,
Until they think warm days will never cease,
    For Summer has o'er-brimm'd their clammy cells.

Who hath not seen thee oft amid thy store?
    Sometimes whoever seeks abroad may find
Thee sitting careless on a granary floor,
    Thy hair soft-lifted by the winnowing wind;
Or on a half-reap'd furrow sound asleep,
    Drowsed with the fume of poppies, while thy hook
    Spares the next swath and all its twined flowers;
And sometime like a gleaner thou dost keep
    Steady thy laden head across a brook;
Or by a cider-press, with patient look,
    Thou watchest the last oozings, hours by hours.

Where are the songs of Spring! Aye, where are
    they?
Think not of them, thou hast thy music too,
While barred clouds bloom the soft-dying day,
    And touch the stubble-plains with rosy hue.
Then in a wailful choir the small gnats mourn
    Among the river sallows, borne aloft
    Or sinking as the light wind lives or dies;
And full-grown lambs loud bleat from hilly bourn;
    Hedge-crickets sing; and now with treble soft
The redbreast whistles from a garden-croft,
    And gathering swallows twitter in the skies.

                        KEATS.

I DO confesse thou'rt smooth and faire;
    And I might have gone near to love thee,
Had I not found the slightest prayer
    That lips could speak, had power to move thee:
But I can let thee now alone
As worthy to be loved by none.

I do confesse thou'rt sweet; yet find
    Thee such an unthrift of thy sweets,
Thy favours are but like the wind
    That kisseth everything it meets,
And since thou canst with more than one,
Thou'rt worthy to be kiss'd by none.

The morning rose that untouch'd stands
    Arm'd with her briars, how sweetly smells!
But pluck'd and strain'd through ruder hands
    Her sweets no longer with her dwells,
But scent and beautie both are gone,
And leaves fall from her, one by one.

Such fate, ere long, will thee betide,
    When thou hast handled been awhile;
Like sere flowers to be throwne aside;—
    And I shall sigh, while some will smile,
To see thy love to everyone
Hath brought thee to be loved by none.

NED BOLTON.

A JOLLY comrade in the port, a fearless
  mate at sea,—
When I forget thee, to my hand false may the
  cutlass be!
And may my gallant battle-flag be beaten down
  in shame,
If, when the social can goes round, I fail to pledge
  thy name!
Up, up, my lads!—his memory!—we'll give it
  with a cheer,—
Ned Bolton, the commander of the Black Snake
  privateer!

Poor Ned! he had a heart of steel, with neither
  flaw nor speck;
Firm as a rock, in strife or storm, he stood the
  quarter-deck;
He was, I trow, a welcome man to many an Indian
  dame,
And Spanish planters cross'd themselves at whisper
  of his name;
But now, Jamaica girls may weep, rich Dons
  securely smile,—
His bark will take no prize again, nor e'er touch
  Indian isle.

'Sblood! 'twas a sorry fate he met on his own
  mother-wave!
The foe far off, the storm asleep, and yet to find a
  grave!
With store of the Peruvian gold, and spirit of the
  cane,—

No need would he have had to cruise in tropic
    climes again :
But some are born to sink at sea, and some to
    hang on shore,
And Fortune cried God speed! at last, and wel-
    comed Ned no more.

'Twas off the coast of Mexico—the tale is bitter
    brief—
The Black Snake, under press of sail, stuck fast
    upon a reef;
Upon a cutting coral reef, scarce a good league
    from land—
But hundreds both of horse and foot were ranged
    upon the strand.
His boats were lost before Cape Horn; and, with
    an old canoe,
Even had he number'd ten for one, what could
    Ned Bolton do?

Six days and nights the vessel lay upon the coral
    reef;
Nor favouring gale, nor friendly flag, brought
    prospect of relief:
For a land-breeze the wild one pray'd, who never
    pray'd before,
And when it came not at his call, he bit his lip
    and swore.
The Spaniards shouted from the beach, but did
    not venture near;
Too well they knew the mettle of the daring
    privateer!

A calm!—a calm!—a hopeless calm!—the red
    sun, burning high,
Glared blisteringly and wearily in a transparent
    sky;

The grog went round the gallant crew, and loudly
    rose the song,
The only pastime at an hour when rest seem'd far
    too long.
So boisterously they took their rouse upon the
    crowded deck,
They look'd like men who had escaped, not men
    who fear'd a wreck.

Up sprung the breeze the seventh day. Away!
    away to sea
Drifted the bark, with riven planks, over the
    waters free;
Their battle-flag these rovers bold then hoisted
    top-mast high,
And to the swarthy foe sent back a fierce defying
    cry.
" One last broadside!" Ned Bolton cried; deep
    boom'd the cannon roar,
And echo's hollow growl return'd an answer from
    the shore.

The thundering gun, the broken song, the mad
    tumultuous cheer,
Ceased not, so long as ocean spared the shatter'd
    privateer.
I saw her,—I,—she shot by me like lightning, in
    the gale;
We strove to save, we tack'd, and fast we shorten'd
    all our sail:
I knew the wave of Ned's right hand,—farewell!
    —you strive in vain!
And he, or one of his ship's crew, ne'er enter'd
    port again.

WILLIAM KENNEDY.

GOODBYE.

GOODBYE, proud world, I'm going home,
Thou'rt not my friend, and I'm not thine;
Long through thy weary crowds I roam;
A river-ark on the ocean brine,
Long I've toss'd like the driven foam;
But now, proud world, I'm going home.

Goodbye to Flattery's fawning face,
To Grandeur, with his wise grimace,
To upstart Wealth's averted eye,
To supple Office low and high,
To crowded halls, to court, and street,
To frozen hearts, and hustling feet,
To those who go, and those who come;
Goodbye, proud world, I'm going home.

I'm going to my own hearth-stone
Bosom'd in yon green hills, alone,
A secret nook in a pleasant land,
Whose groves the frolic fairies plann'd;
Where arches green the livelong day
Echo the blackbird's roundelay,
And vulgar feet have never trod
A spot that is sacred to thought and God.

O when I am safe in my sylvan home,
I tread on the pride of Greece and Rome,
And when I am stretch'd beneath the pines
Where the evening star so holy shines,

I laugh at the lore and the pride of man,
At the sophist schools, and the learned clan;
For what are they all in their high conceit,
When man in the bush with God may meet.

EMERSON.

THE CAIQUE.

YONDER to the kiosk, beside the creek,
   Paddle the swift caique,
Thou brawny oarsman with the sun-burnt cheek,
Quick! for it soothes my heart to hear the Bulbul
   speak!

Ferry me quickly to the Asian shores,
Swift bending to your oars.
Beneath the melancholy sycamores
Hark! what a ravishing note the love-lorn Bulbul
   pours.

Behold, the boughs seem quivering with delight,
The stars themselves more bright,
As 'mid the waving branches out of sight
The Lover of the Rose sits singing through the
   night.

Under the boughs I sat and listen'd still,
I could not have my fill.
"How comes," I said, "such music to his bill?
Tell me for whom he sings so beautiful a trill."

"Once I was dumb," then did the Bird disclose,
But look'd upon the Rose;

And in the garden where the loved-one grows
I straightway did begin sweet music to compose."

" O bird of song, there's one in this caique
The Rose would also seek,
So he might learn like you to love and speak."
Then answer'd me the bird of dusky beak,
" The Rose, the Rose of Love blushes on Leilah's
    cheek."
W. M. THACKERAY.

TO ——

MUSIC, when soft voices die,
    Vibrates in the memory;
Odours, when sweet violets sicken,
Live within the sense they quicken.

Rose-leaves, when the rose is dead,
Are heaped for the beloved's bed;
And so thy thoughts, when thou art gone,
Love itself shall slumber on.
SHELLEY.

THERANIA.

O UNKNOWN Belov'd One! to the mellow
    season
    Branches in the lawn make drooping bow'rs;
Vase and plot burn scarlet, gold, and azure;

Honeysuckles wind the tall grey turret,
    And pale passion-flow'rs.
Come thou, come thou to my lonely thought,
    O Unknown Belov'd One.

Now at evening twilight, dusky dew down-wavers,
    Soft stars crown the grove-encircled hill;
Breathe the new-mown meadows, broad and
    misty;
Through the heavy grass the rail is talking;
    All beside is still.
Trace with me the wandering avenue,
    O Unknown Belov'd One.

In the mystic realm, and in the time of visions,
    I thy lover have no need to woo;
There I hold thy hand in mine, thou dearest,
And thy soul in mine, and feel its throbbing,
    Tender, deep, and true:
Then my tears are love, and thine are love,
    O Unknown Belov'd One.

Is thy voice a wavelet on the listening darkness?
    Are thine eyes unfolding from their veil?
Wilt thou come before the signs of winter—
Days that shred the bough with trembling fingers,
    Nights that weep and wail?
Art thou Love indeed, or art thou Death,
    O Unknown Belov'd One?

                WILLIAM ALLINGHAM.

THE BLOSSOM.

MERRY, merry Sparrow!
    Under leaves so green
A happy Blossom

Sees you, swift as arrow,
Seek your cradle narrow,
   Near my bosom.

Pretty, pretty Robin!
  Under leaves so green
   A happy Blossom
Hears you sobbing, sobbing,
Pretty, pretty Robin,
   Near my bosom.
WILLIAM BLAKE.

SONNET.

[LOVE'S SLAVE.]

BEING your slave, what should I do but tend
  Upon the hours and times of your desire?
I have no precious time at all to spend,
Nor services to do, till you require.
Nor dare I chide the world-without-end hour,
Whilst I, my Sovereign, watch the clock for you,
Nor think the bitterness of absence sour,
When you have bid your servant once adieu;
Nor dare I question with my jealous thought
Where you may be, or your affairs suppose,
But, like a sad slave, stay and think of nought,
Save, where you are how happy you make those:
So true a fool is love, that in your will
(Though you do anything) he thinks no ill.
SHAKESPEARE.

SONG.

GO, lovely rose!
  Tell her, that wastes her time and me,
    That now she knows,
When I resemble her to thee,
How sweet and fair she seems to be.

  Tell her, that's young
And shuns to have her graces spy'd,
    That hadst thou sprung
In deserts where no men abide,
Thou must have uncommended dy'd.

  Small is the worth
Of beauty from the light retired:
    Bid her come forth,
Suffer herself to be desired,
And not blush so to be admired.

  Then die! that she
The common fate of all things rare
    May read in thee:
How small a part of time they share
That are so wondrous sweet and fair.

                    EDMUND WALLER.

TAM GLEN.

MY heart is a-breaking, dear Tittie!
 Some counsel unto me come len';
To anger them a' is a pity,
 But what will I do wi' Tam Glen?

I'm thinking, wi' sic a braw fallow,
 In poortith I might mak a fen';
What care I in riches to wallow,
 If I may not marry Tam Glen?

There's Laurie the laird o' Drumeller,
 " Guid day to you,"—brute! he comes ben:
He brags and he blaws o' his siller,
 But when will he dance like Tam Glen?

My minnie does constantly deave me,
 And bids me beware o' young men;
They flatter, she says, to deceive me,—
 But wha can think sae o' Tam Glen?

My daddie says, gin I'll forsak' him
 He'll gie me guid hunder marks ten,—
But if its ordain'd I maun tak' him,
 O wha will I get but Tam Glen?

Yestreen at the Valentine's dealing
 My heart to my mou' gied a sten;
For thrice I drew ane without failing,
 And thrice it was written—Tam Glen.

The last Halloween I lay waukin
 My droukit sark-sleeve, as ye ken,

His likeness cam up the house staulkin,
  And the vera grey breeks o' Tam Glen!

Come counsel, dear Tittie,—don't tarry!
  I'll gie you my bonnie black hen
Gif ye will advise me to marry
  The lad I loe dearly, Tam Glen.

                                BURNS.

ODE TO EVENING.

IF aught of oaten stop or pastoral song
  May hope, chaste Eve, to soothe thy modest ear
    (Like thy own solemn springs,
    Thy springs, and dying gales);
O Nymph reserved,—while now the bright-hair'd sun
Sits in yon western tent, whose cloudy skirts,
    With brede ethereal wove,
    O'erhang his wavy bed,
And air is hush'd, save where the weak-eyed bat
With short shrill shriek flits by on leathern wing,
    Or where the beetle winds
    His small but sullen horn,
As oft he rises 'midst the twilight path,
Against the pilgrim borne in heedless hum,—
    Now teach me, Maid composed,
    To breathe some soften'd strain,
Whose numbers, stealing through thy darkening vale,
May not unseemly with its stillness suit,
    As, musing slow, I hail
    Thy genial, loved return!

For when thy folding-star arising shows
His paly circlet, at his warning lamp
    The fragrant Hours, and Elves
    Who slept in buds the day,
And many a Nymph who wreathes her brow with
    sedge
And sheds the freshening dew, and, lovelier still,
    The pensive Pleasures sweet,
    Prepare thy shadowy car.

Then let me rove some wild and heathy scene;
Or find some ruin 'midst its dreary dells,
    Whose walls more awful nod
    By thy religious gleams.
Or if chill blustering winds or driving rain
Prevent my willing feet, be mine the hut
    That from the mountain-side
    Views wilds, and swelling floods,
And hamlets brown, and dim-discover'd spires,
And hears their simple bell, and marks o'er all
    Thy dewy fingers draw
    The gradual dusky veil.

While Spring shall pour his showers, as oft he wont,
And bathe thy breathing tresses, meekest Eve!
    While Summer loves to sport
    Beneath thy lingering light:
While sallow Autumn fills thy lap with leaves,
Or Winter, yelling through the troublous air,
    Affrights thy shrinking train,
    And rudely rends thy robes,
[Till thou hast refuged where the cheerful glow
Bids welcome, and the wind-unshaken lamp,
    To household mirth and song,
    And dear domestic joy :]
So long, regardful of thy quiet rule,

Shall Fancy, Friendship, Science, smiling Peace,
   Thy gentlest influence own,
   And love thy favourite name!
                 WILLIAM COLLINS.

[LOSS.]

YOU thought my heart too far diseased;
   You wonder when my fancies play
   To find me gay among the gay,
Like one with any trifle pleased.

The shade by which my life was crost,
   Which makes a desert in the mind,
   Has made me kindly with my kind,
And like to him whose sight is lost;

Whose feet are guided through the land,
   Whose jest among his friends is free,
   Who takes the children on his knee,
And winds their curls about his hand:

He plays with threads, he beats his chair
   For pastime, dreaming of the sky;
   His inner day can never die,
His night of loss is always there.
                 In Memoriam.

THE LADY'S YES.

"YES!" I answer'd you last night;
   "No!" this morning, Sir, I say.
Colours, seen by candle-light,
   Will not look the same by day.

When the tabors play'd their best,
   Lamps above, and laughs below—
Love me sounded like a jest,
   Fit for *Yes* or fit for *No!*

Call me false, or call me free—
   Vow, whatever light may shine,
No man on thy face shall see
   Any grief for change on mine.

Yet the sin is on us both—
   Time to dance is not to woo—
Wooer light makes fickle troth—
   Scorn of *me* recoils on *you!*

Learn to win a lady's faith
   Nobly, as the thing is high;
Bravely, as for life and death—
   With a loyal gravity.

Lead her from the festive boards,
   Point her to the starry skies,
Guard her, by your faithful words,
   Pure from courtship's flatteries.

By your truth she shall be true—
Ever true, as wives of yore—
And her *Yes*, once said to you,
Shall be Yes for evermore.

ELIZABETH BARRETT BROWNING.

A LAMENT.

SWIFTER far than summer's flight,
Swifter far than youth's delight,
Swifter far than happy night,
    Art thou come, art thou gone:
As the earth when leaves are dead,
As the night when sleep is sped,
As the heart when joy is fled,
    I am left lone, alone.

The swallow Summer comes again,
The owlet Night resumes her reign,
But the wild swan Youth is fain
    To fly with thee, false as thou.
My heart each day desires the morrow,
Sleep itself is turn'd to sorrow,
Vainly would my winter borrow
    Sunny leaves from any bough.

Lilies for a bridal bed,
Roses for a matron's head,
Violets for a maiden dead,—
    Pansies let my flowers be:
On the living grave I bear
Scatter them without a tear;
Let no friend, however dear,
    Waste one hope, one fear for me.

SHELLEY.

THE FORGING OF THE ANCHOR.

COME, see the Dolphin's anchor forged—'tis
    at a white heat now:
The bellows ceased, the flames decreased—though
    on the forge's brow
The little flames still fitfully play through the
    sable mound,
And fitfully you still may see the grim smiths
    ranking round,
All clad in leathern panoply, their broad hands
    only bare—
Some rest upon their sledges here, some work the
    windlass there.

The windlass strains the tackle chains, the black
    mound heaves below,
And red and deep a hundred veins burst out at
    every throe:
It rises, roars, rends all outright—O, Vulcan, what
    a glow!
'Tis blinding white, 'tis blasting bright—the high
    sun shines not so!
The high sun sees not, on the earth, such fiery
    fearful show;
The roof-ribs swarth, the candent hearth, the ruddy
    lurid row
Of smiths that stand, an ardent band, like men
    before the foe.
As, quivering through his fleece of flame, the sail-
    ing monster, slow
Sinks on the anvil—all about the faces fiery grow.

"Hurrah!" they shout, "leap out—leap out;"
    bang, bang the sledges go :
Hurrah! the jetted lightnings are hissing high
    and low—
A hailing fount of fire is struck at every squashing
    blow,
The leathern mail rebounds the hail, the rattling
    cinders strow
The ground around : at every bound the swelter-
    ing fountains flow,
And thick and loud the swinking crowd at every
    stroke pant " ho !"

Leap out, leap out, my masters; leap out and lay
    on load !
Let's forge a goodly anchor—a bower thick and
    broad ;
For a heart of oak is hanging on every blow, I
    bode,
And I see the good ship riding, all in a perilous
    road—
The low reef roaring on her lee—the roll of ocean
    pour'd
From stem to stern, sea after sea ; the mainmast
    by the board ;
The bulwarks down, the rudder gone, the boats
    stove at the chains !
But courage still, brave mariners—the bower yet
    remains,
And not an inch to flinch he deigns, save when ye
    pitch sky high ;
Then moves his head, as though he said, " Fear
    nothing—here am I."

Swing in your strokes in order, let foot and hand
    keep time ;
Your blows make music sweeter far than any
    steeple's chime.

But, while you sling your sledges, sing— and let
    the burthen be,
The anchor is the anvil king, and royal craftsmen
    we!
Strike in, strike in—the sparks begin to dull their
    rustling red;
Our hammers ring with sharper din, our work will
    soon be sped.
Our anchor soon must change his bed of fiery rich
    array
For a hammock at the roaring bows, or an oozy
    couch of clay;
Our anchor soon must change the lay of merry
    craftsmen here,
For the yeo-heave-o', and the heave-away, and the
    sighing seaman's cheer;
When, weighing slow, at eve they go—far, far
    from love and home;
And sobbing sweethearts, in a row, wail o'er the
    ocean foam.

In livid and obdurate gloom he darkens down at
    last;
A shapely one he is, and strong, as e'er from cat
    was cast.
O trusted and trustworthy guard, if thou hadst
    life like me,
What pleasures would thy toils reward beneath
    the deep green sea!
O deep Sea-diver, who might then behold such
    sights as thou?
The hoary-monster's palaces! methinks what joy
    'twere now
To go plumb plunging down amid the assembly of
    the whales,
And feel the churn'd sea round me boil beneath
    their scourging tails!

Then deep in tangle-woods to fight the fierce sea
    unicorn,
And send him foil'd and bellowing back, for all
    his ivory horn;
To leave the subtle sworder-fish of bony blade
    forlorn;
And for the ghastly-grinning shark to laugh his
    jaws to scorn;
To leap down on the kraken's back, where 'mid
    Norwegian isles
He lies, a lubber anchorage for sudden shallow'd
    miles;
'Till snorting, like an under-sea volcano, off he
    rolls;
Meanwhile to swing, a-buffeting the far astonish'd
    shoals
Of his back-browsing ocean-calves; or, haply in
    a cove,
Shell-strown, and consecrate of old to some Un-
    diné's love,
To find the long-hair'd mermaidens; or, hard by
    icy lands,
To wrestle with the Sea-serpent, upon cerulean
    sands.

O broad-arm'd Fisher of the deep, whose sports
    can equal thine?
The Dolphin weighs a thousand tons, that tugs
    thy cable line;
And night by night, 'tis thy delight, thy glory day
    by day,
Through sable sea and breaker white, the giant
    game to play—
But shamer of our little sports! forgive the name
    I gave—
A fisher's joy is to destroy—thine office is to save.

O lodger in the sea-kings' halls, couldst thou but
    understand
Whose be the white bones by thy side, or who
    that dripping band,
Slow swaying in the heaving wave, that round
    about thee bend,
With sounds like breakers in a dream blessing
    their ancient friend—
Oh, couldst thou know what heroes glide with
    larger steps round thee,
Thine iron side would swell with pride; thou'dst
    leap within the sea.

Give honour to their memories who left the plea-
    sant strand,
To shed their blood so freely for the love of Fa-
    therland,
Who left their chance of quiet age and grassy
    churchyard grave,
So freely, for a restless bed amid the tossing wave—
Oh, though our anchor may not be all I have
    fondly sung,
Honour him for their memory, whose bones he
    goes among!

    Samuel Ferguson.

TO DAFFODILS.

FAIR daffodils, we weep to see
 You haste away so soon;
As yet the early rising sun
 Has not attain'd his noon:
  Stay, stay,

K

    Until the hastening day
      Has run
    But to the even-song;
And, having pray'd together, we
    Will go with you along.

We have short time to stay, as you;
    We have as short a spring;
As quick a growth to meet decay
    As you, or any thing:
      We die,
As your hours do; and dry
    Away
Like to the summer's rain,
Or as the pearls of morning dew,
    Ne'er to be found again.
              HERRICK.

AN ANGEL IN THE HOUSE.

HOW sweet it were, if without feeble fright,
    Or dying of the dreadful beauteous sight,
An angel came to us, and we could bear
To see him issue from the silent air
At evening in our room, and bend on ours
His divine eyes, and bring us from his bowers
News of dear friends and children who have never
Been dead indeed,—as we shall know for ever.
Alas! we think not what we daily see
About our hearths,—angels, that *are* to be,
Or may be if they will, and we prepare
Their souls and ours to meet in happy air,—
A child, a friend, a wife whose soft heart sings
In unison with ours, breeding its future wings.
              LEIGH HUNT.

BONNIE GEORGE CAMPBELL.

HIE upon Hielands,
    And low upon Tay,
Bonnie George Campbell
    Rode out on a day;
Saddled and bridled,
    And gallant to see:
Hame cam' his gude horse,
    But hame cam' na he.

Out ran his auld mither,
    Greeting fu' sair;
Out ran his bonnie bride,
    Reaving her hair.
He rade saddled and bridled,
    Wi' boots to the knee:
Hame cam' his gude horse,
    But never cam' he.

" My meadow lies green,
    And my corn is unshorn,
My barn is to bigg,[1]
    And my babie's unborn."
He rade saddled and bridled,
    Careless and free:
Toom[2] hame cam' the saddle,
    And never cam' he.

---

[1] *Bigg*, build.   [2] *Toom*, empty.

THE HUMBLE-BEE.

BURLY dozing humble-bee!
Where thou art is clime for me.
Let them sail for Porto Rique,
Far off heats through seas to seek,
I will follow thee alone,
Thou animated torrid-zone!
Zig-zag steerer, desert-cheerer,
Let me chase thy waving lines,
Keep me nearer, me thy hearer,
Singing over shrubs and vines.

Insect-lover of the sun,
Joy of thy dominion!
Sailor of the atmosphere,
Swimmer through the waves of air,
Voyager of light and noon,
Epicurean of June,
Wait, I prithee, till I come
Within ear-shot of thy hum;
All without is martyrdom.

When the south wind, in May days,
With a net of shining haze
Silvers the horizon wall,
And, with softness touching all,
Tints the human countenance
With a colour of romance,
And infusing subtle heats,
Turns the sod to violets,
Thou in sunny solitudes,
Rover of the underwoods,
The green silence dost displace,
With thy mellow breezy bass.

Hot midsummer's petted crone,
Sweet to me thy drowsy tone,
Telling of countless sunny hours,
Long days, and solid banks of flowers,
Or gulfs of sweetness without bound
In Indian wildernesses found,
Of Syrian peace, immortal leisure,
Firmest cheer and bird-like pleasure.

Aught unsavoury or unclean,
Hath my insect never seen,
But violets and bilberry bells,
Maple sap and daffodels,
Grass with green flag half-mast high,
Succory to match the sky,
Columbine with horn of honey,
Scented fern, and agrimony,
Clover, catch-fly, adder's-tongue,
And briar-roses dwelt among;
All beside was unknown waste,
All was picture as he pass'd.

Wiser far than human seer,
Yellow-breech'd philosopher!
Seeing only what is fair,
Sipping only what is sweet,
Thou dost mock at fate and care,
Leave the chaff and take the wheat.
When the fierce north-western blast
Cools sea and land so far and fast,
Thou already slumberest deep,—
Wo and want thou canst outsleep,—
Want and wo which torture us,
Thy sleep makes ridiculous.

EMERSON.

DISDAIN RETURNED.

HE that loves a rosie cheeke,
    Or a corall lip admires,
Or from star-like eyes doth seeke
    Fuel to maintain his fires;
As old Time makes these decay,
So his flames must waste away.

But a smooth and stedfast minde,
    Gentle thoughts and calm desires,
Hearts with equal love combined,
    Kindle never-dying fires.
Where these are not, I despise
Lovely cheekes, or lips, or eyes.

No tears, Celia, now shall win
    My resolved hearte to return;
I have search'd thy soul within,
    And find nought but pride and scorn;
I have learn'd thy arts, and now
Can disdain as much as thou.
THOMAS CAREW.

AULD ROBIN GRAY.

WHEN the sheep are in the fauld and the kye at hame,
And a' the weary warld to sleep are gane,
The waes o' my heart fa' in showers frae my e'e,
While my gudeman lies sound by me.

Young Jamie lo'ed me weel, and sought me for
 his bride;
But saving a crown he had naething else beside.
To mak' the crown a pound, my Jamie gaed to sea;
And the crown and the pound were baith for me.

He hadna been gane a year and a day,
When my father brake his arm, and our cow was
 stown away;
My mither she fell sick, and Jamie at the sea;
And Auld Robin Gray cam' a-courting me.

My father couldna' work, and my mither doughtna
 spin,
I toil'd day and night, but their bread I couldna
 win;
Auld Rab maintain'd them baith, and wi' tears in
 his e'e,
Said, " Jenny, for their sakes, O marry me!"

My heart it said na; I look'd for Jamie back;
But the wind it blew high, and the ship it was a
 wrack;
His ship it was a wrack,—why didna Jenny dee?
O why do I live, to cry, Wae's me!

My father urgit sair, my mither didna speak,
But she lookit in my face till my heart was like to
 break.
They gied him my hand, though my heart was at
 the sea;
Sae Auld Robin Gray he is gudeman to me.

I hadna been a wife a week but only four,
When sitting sae mournfully ae night at the door,
I saw my Jamie's wraith, for I couldna think it he,
Till he said, " I'm come back, love, to marry thee."

O sair did we greet, and muckle did we say;
We took but ae kiss, and we tore ourselves away.
I wish that I were dead, but I'm no like to dee.
O why do I live, to say, Wae's me!

I gang like a ghaist, and I carena to spin.
I darena think on Jamie, for that wad be a sin.
But I'll do my best a gude wife to be;
For Auld Robin Gray is kind to me.

LADY ANNE LINDSAY.

SONG.

[FROM "ZAPOLYA."]

A SUNNY shaft did I behold,
    From sky to earth it slanted,
And poised therein a bird so bold,—
    Sweet bird, thou wert enchanted!
He sank, he rose, he twinkled, he troll'd
    Within that shaft of sunny mist;
His eyes of fire, his beak of gold,
    All else of amethyst.
And thus he sang, "Adieu! adieu!
Love's dreams prove seldom true.
The blossoms they make no delay,
The sparkling dewdrops will not stay.
    Sweet month of May,
    We must away,
    Far, far away!
    To-day! to-day!"

COLERIDGE.

SONNET.

MARY QUEEN OF SCOTS.

(LANDING AT THE MOUTH OF THE DERWENT, WORKINGTON.)

DEAR to the Loves and to the Graces vow'd,
    The Queen drew back the wimple that she wore;
And to the throng, that on the Cumbrian shore
Her landing hail'd, how touchingly she bow'd!
And like a Star (that, from a heavy cloud
Of pine-tree foliage poised in air, forth darts,
When a soft summer gale at evening parts
The gloom that did its loveliness enshroud)
She smiled; but Time, the old Saturnian Seer,
Sigh'd on the wing as her foot press'd the strand,
With step prelusive to a long array
Of woes and degradations hand in hand—
Weeping captivity, and shuddering fear
Still'd by the ensanguined block of Fotheringay.

WORDSWORTH.

LINES COMPOSED IN A CONCERT ROOM.

*   *   *   *   *

O GIVE me, from this heartless scene released,
    To hear our old musician, blind and gray,
(Whom stretching from my nurse's arms I kiss'd)

His Scottish tunes and warlike marches play,
By moonshine, on the balmy summer-night,
  The while I dance amid the tedded hay
With merry maids, whose ringlets toss in light.

Or lies the purple evening on the bay
Of the calm glossy lake, O let me hide
  Unheard, unseen, behind the alder-trees,
For round their roots the fisher's boat is tied,
  On whose trim seat doth Edmund stretch at ease,
And while the lazy boat sways to and fro,
  Breathes in his flute sad airs, so wild and slow,
  That his own cheek is wet with quiet tears.

But O, dear Anne! when midnight wind careers,
And the gust pelting on the out-house shed
  Makes the cock shrilly on the rain-storm crow,
To hear thee sing some ballad full of woe,
Ballad of ship-wreck'd sailor floating dead
  Whom his own true-love buried in the sands!
Thee, gentle woman, for thy voice re-measures
Whatever tones and melancholy pleasures
  The things of Nature utter; birds or trees
Or moan of ocean-gale in weedy caves,
Or, when the stiff grass 'mid the heath-plant waves,
  Murmur and music thin of sudden breeze.

COLERIDGE.

[FROM "A MIDSUMMER NIGHT'S DREAM."]

Fairy. OVER hill, over dale,
    Thorough bush, thorough briar,
Over park, over pale,
    Thorough flood, thorough fire,

I do wander everywhere,
Swifter than the moone's sphere;
And I serve the Fairy Queen
To dew her orbs upon the green:
The cowslips tall her pensioners be,
In their gold coats spots you see,
These be rubies, fairy favours,
In those freckles live their savours:
I must go seek some dewdrops here,
And hang a pearl in every cowslip's ear.

SHAKESPEARE.

CIRCUMSTANCE.

TWO children in two neighbour villages
    Playing mad pranks along the heathy leas;
Two strangers meeting at a festival;
Two lovers whispering by an orchard wall;
Two lives bound fast in one with golden ease;
Two graves grass-green beside a gray church-tower,
Wash'd with still rains and daisy-blossomèd;
Two children in one hamlet born and bred;
So runs the round of life from hour to hour.

TENNYSON.

THE SANDS O' DEE.

I.

"O MARY, go and call the cattle home,
    And call the cattle home,
  And call the cattle home,
Across the sands o' Dee:"

The western wind was wild and dank wi' foam,
    And all alone went she.

II.

The creeping tide came up along the sand,
    And o'er and o'er the sand,
    And round and round the sand,
  As far as eye could see;
The blinding mist came down and hid the land—
    And never home came she.

III.

Oh, is it weed, or fish, or floating hair?—
    A tress o' golden hair,
    O' drowned maiden's hair,
  Above the nets at sea.
Was never salmon yet that shone so fair,
    Among the stakes on Dee.

IV.

They row'd her in across the rolling foam,
    The cruel crawling foam,
    The cruel hungry foam,
  To her grave beside the sea:
But still the boatmen hear her call the cattle home,
    Across the sands o' Dee.

          CHARLES KINGSLEY.

ODE TO A NIGHTINGALE.

I.

MY heart aches, and a drowsy numbness pains
    My sense, as though of hemlock I had drunk,
Or emptied some dull opiate to the drains

One minute past, and Lethe-wards had sunk :
'Tis not through envy of thy happy lot,
  But being too happy in thy happiness,—
    Where thou, light-wingèd Dryad of the trees,
      In some melodious plot
  Of beechen green, and shadows numberless,
    Singest of summer in full-throated ease.

II.

O for a draught of vintage, that hath been
  Cool'd a long age in the deep-delvèd earth,
Tasting of Flora and the country-green,
  Dance, and Provençal song and sun-burnt mirth !
O for a beaker full of the warm South,
  Full of the true, the blushful Hippocrene,
    With beaded bubbles winking at the brim,
      And purple-stainèd mouth ;
  That I might drink, and leave the world unseen,
    And with thee fade away into the forest dim :

III.

Fade far away, dissolve, and quite forget
  What thou among the leaves hast never known,
The weariness, the fever, and the fret
  Here, where men sit and hear each other groan ;
Where palsy shakes a few, sad, last grey hairs,
  Where youth grows pale and spectre-thin, and dies ;
    Where but to think is to be full of sorrow
      And leaden-eyed despairs ;
  Where Beauty cannot keep her lustrous eyes,
    Or new Love pine at them beyond to-morrow.

IV.

Away ! away ! for I will fly to thee,
  Not charioted by Bacchus and his pards,

But on the viewless wings of Poesy,
  Though the dull brain perplexes and retards:
Already with thee! tender is the night,
    And haply the Queen-Moon is on her throne,
      Cluster'd around by all her starry Fays;
        But here there is no light,
  Save what from heaven is with the breezes blown
    Through verdurous glooms and winding mossy
      ways.

V.

I cannot see what flowers are at my feet,
  Nor what soft incense hangs upon the boughs,
But in embalmèd darkness, guess each sweet
    Wherewith the seasonable month endows
The grass, the thicket, and the fruit-tree wild;
    White hawthorn, and the pastoral eglantine;
      Fast-fading violets cover'd up in leaves;
        And mid-May's eldest child,
  The coming musk-rose, full of dewy wine,
    The murmurous haunt of flies on summer eves.

VI.

Darkling I listen; and for many a time
  I have been half in love with easeful Death,
Call'd him soft names in many a musèd rhyme,
    To take into the air my quiet breath;
Now more than ever seems it rich to die,
    To cease upon the midnight with no pain,
      While thou art pouring forth thy soul abroad
        In such an ecstacy!
  Still wouldst thou sing, and I have ears in vain—
    To thy high requiem become a sod.

VII.

Thou wast not born for death, immortal Bird!
  No hungry generations tread thee down;

The voice I hear this passing night was heard
  In ancient days by emperor and clown :
Perhaps the self-same song that found a path
    Through the sad heart of Ruth when, sick for
      home,
      She stood in tears amid the alien corn ;
        The same that ofttimes hath
Charm'd magic casements opening on the foam
  Of perilous seas, in faery lands forlorn.

VIII.

Forlorn! the very word is like a bell
  To toll me back from thee to my sole self!
Adieu! the fancy cannot cheat so well
  As she is famed to do, deceiving elf.
Adieu! adieu! thy plaintive anthem fades
    Past the near meadows, over the still stream,
      Up the hill-side; and now 'tis buried deep
        In the next valley-glades :
  Was it a vision, or a waking dream?
    Fled is that music :—do I wake or sleep?
               KEATS.

THE LABORATORY.

(ANCIEN REGIME.)

I.

NOW that I, tying thy glass mask tightly,
  May gaze through these faint smokes curl-
    ing whitely,
As thou pliest thy trade in this devil's smithy—
Which is the poison to poison her, prithee?

II.

He is with her; and they know that I know
Where they are; what they do: they believe my
    tears flow
While they laugh, laugh at me, at me fled to the
    drear
Empty church to pray God in for them!—I am here.

III.

Grind away, moisten and mash up thy paste,
Pound at thy powder,—am I in haste?
Better sit thus, and observe thy strange things,
Than go where men wait me and dance at the
    King's.

IV.

That in the mortar—you call it a gum?
Ah, the brave tree whence such gold oozings
    come!
And yonder soft phial, the exquisite blue,
Sure to taste sweetly,—is that poison too?

V.

Had I but all of them, thee and thy treasures,
What a wild crowd of invisible pleasures!
To carry pure death in an earring, a casket,
A signet, a fan-mount, a fillagree-basket!

VI.

Soon, at the King's, but a lozenge to give
And Pauline should have just thirty minutes to
    live!
To light a pastille, and Elise, with her head,
And her breast, and her arms, and her hands,
    should drop dead!

VII.

Quick—is it finish'd? The colour's too grim!
Why not like the phial's, enticing and dim?
Let it brighten her drink, let her turn it and stir,
And try it and taste, ere she fix and prefer!

VIII.

What a drop! She's not little, no minion like me—
That's why she ensnared him: this never will free
The soul from those masculine eyes,—say, "no!"
To that pulse's magnificent come-and-go.

IX.

For only last night, as they whisper'd, I brought
My own eyes to bear on her so, that I thought
Could I keep them one half minute fix'd, she
    would fall,
Shrivell'd; she fell not; yet this does it all!

X.

Not that I bid you spare her the pain!
Let death be felt and the proof remain;
Brand, burn up, bite into its grace—
He is sure to remember her dying face!

XI.

Is it done? take my mask off! Nay, be not morose.
It kills her, and this prevents seeing it close—
The delicate droplet, my whole fortune's fee—
If it hurts her, beside, can it ever hurt me?

XII.

Now, take all my jewels, gorge gold to your fill,
You may kiss me, old man, on my mouth if you
    will!
But brush this dust off me, lest horror it brings
Ere I know it—next moment I dance at the King's.

                    ROBERT BROWNING.

INSCRIPTION FOR A FOUNTAIN.

(MORE GRÆCO.)

REST! this little Fountain runs
    Thus for aye:—It never stays
For the look of summer suns,
    Nor the cold of winter days.
Whosoe'er shall wander near,
    When the Syrian heat is worst,
Let him hither come, nor fear
    Lest he may not slake his thirst:
He will find this little river
Running still, as bright as ever.
Let him drink, and onwards hie,
Bearing but in thought, that I,
EROTAS, bade the Naiad fall,
And thank the great god Pan for all!

BARRY CORNWALL.

THE RUOSE THAT DECK'D HER BREAST.

[DORSET DIALECT.]

POOR Jenny were her Roberd's bride
    Two happy years, an' then 'e died;
And zoo[1] the wold vo'ke[2] maide her come
Varsiaken,[3] to her maiden huome,
But Jenny's merry tongue were dum';

---

[1] *Zoo*, so.   [2] *Wold vo'ke*, old folk.   [3] *Varsiaken*, forsaken.

An' roun' her comely neck she wore
A moornèn¹ kerchief, wher avore
    The ruose did deck her breast.

She wā'k'd² aluone wi' eyeballs wet
To zee the flow'rs that she'd a-zet;
The lilies, white's her mâiden frocks,
The spik,³ to put 'ithin her box,
Wi' columbines an' hollyhocks;
The jilliflow'r an' noddèn pink,
An' ruose that touch'd her soul to ðink⁴
    O' ðik that deck'd her breast.

Var⁵ at her weddèn, jist avore
Her mâiden han' had yert⁶ a-wore
A wife's goold ring, wi' hangèn head
She wā'k'd along ðik flower-bed,
Wher bloodywâ'iors,⁷ stain'd wi' red,
An' miarygoolds did skirt the wā'k,
An' gather'd vrom the ruose's stā'k
    A bud to deck her breast.

An' then her cheäk wi' youthvul blood
Were bloomen as the ruose's bud;
But now, as she wi' grief da pine,
'Tis piale's the milk-white jassamine.
But Roberd 'ave a-left behine
A little biaby wi' his fiace,
To smile an' nessle in the pliace
    Wher the ruose did deck her breast.

                    WILLIAM BARNES.

---

¹ *Moornèn*, mourning.   ² *Wā'k'd*, walked.   ³ *Spik*, lavender.   ⁴ *Ðink*, think. ("Ð" is an Anglo-Saxon letter, used by Mr. Barnes, and *nearly* equivalent to "th.")   ⁵ *Var*, for.   ⁶ *Yert*, yet.   ⁷ *Bloodywâ'iors*, (warriors,) name given to the garden wall-flower.

FITZ-EUSTACE'S SONG.

[FROM " MARMION."]

WHERE shall the lover rest,
    Whom the fates sever
From his true maiden's breast,
    Parted for ever?
Where through groves deep and high
    Sounds the loud billow;
Where early violets die,
    Under the willow;
Chorus. Eleu loro, &c.
    Soft shall be his pillow.

There, through the summer day,
    Cool streams are laving;
There, whilst the tempests sway,
    Scarce are boughs waving;
There thy rest shalt thou take,
    Parted for ever;
Never again to wake,
    Never, O never.
Chorus. Eleu loro, &c.
    Never, O never.

Where shall the traitor rest,
    He, the deceiver,
Who could win maiden's breast,
    Ruin and leave her?
In the lost battle,
    Borne down by the flying,

Where mingles war's rattle
  With the groans of the dying.
Chorus. Eleu loro, &c.
  There shall he be lying.

Her wing shall the eagle flap
  O'er the false-hearted;
His warm blood the wolf shall lap
  Ere life be parted.
Shame and dishonour sit
  By his grave ever:
Blessing shall hallow it,—
  Never! O never!
Chorus. Eleu loro, &c.
  Never! O never!
             SCOTT.

THE EXILE.

THE swallow with summer
  Will wing o'er the seas,
The wind that I sigh to
  Will visit thy trees,
The ship that it hastens
  Thy ports shall contain,
But me—I must never
  See England again.

There's many that weep there;
  But one weeps alone
For the tears that are falling
  So far from her own;—
So far from thy own, love,
  We know not our pain;
If death is between us,
  Or only the main.

When the white cloud reclines
  On the verge of the sea,
I fancy the white cliffs
  And dream upon thee.
But the cloud spreads its wings
  To the blue heav'n, and flies.
We never shall meet, love,
  Except in the skies.
HOOD.

SONNET.

[LOVE'S CONSOLATION.]

WHEN, in disgrace with fortune and men's eyes,
I all alone beweep my outcast state,
And trouble deaf Heaven with my bootless cries,
And look upon myself, and curse my fate,
Wishing me like to one more rich in hope,
Featured like him, like him with friends possess'd,
Desiring this man's art, and that man's scope,
With what I most enjoy contented least,
Yet in these thoughts myself almost despising;
Haply I think on thee,—and then my state
(Like to the lark at break of day arising
From sullen earth) sings hymns at heaven's gate;
For thy sweet love remember'd such wealth brings,
That then I scorn to change my state with kings.
SHAKESPEARE.

O'BRIEN OF ARRA.[1]

(AIR "THE PIPER OF BLESSINGTON.")

TALL are the towers of O'Kennedy,
    Broad are the lands of MacCarha,
Desmond feeds five hundred men a-day;
    Yet, here's to O'Brien of Arra!
      Up from the Castle of Drumineer,
        Down from the top of Camalta,
      Clansman and kinsman are coming here,
        To give him the *Cead Millia Falta!*[2]

See you the mountains look huge at eve—
    So is our chieftain in battle!
Welcome he has for the fugitive,
    Usquebaugh, fighting, and cattle.
      Up from the Castle of Drumineer,
        Down from the top of Camalta,
      Gossip and ally are coming here,
        To give him the *Cead Millia Falta.*

Horses the valleys are tramping on,
    Sleek from the Sassenach manger;
Cre-aghts the hills are encamping on—
    Empty the bawns of the stranger!
      Up from the Castle of Drumineer,
        Down from the top of Camalta,
      Kern and bonaght are coming here,
        To give him the *Cead Millia Falta.*

---

[1] An Irish Chieftain, fighting against the English of "The Pale."

[2] Irish words, meaning, "A hundred thousand welcomes!" and pronounced like *Kade Meel-ya Fault-ya.*

He has black silver from Killaloe,
    Ryan and Carroll are neighbours,
Nenagh submits with a pillalcu,
    Butler is meat for our sabres!
        Up from the Castle of Drumineer,
            Down from the top of Camalta,
        Ryan and Carroll are coming here,
            To give him the *Cead Millia Falta.*

Scarce 'tis a week since through Ossory
    Chased he the Baron of Durrow,
Forced him five rivers to cross, or he
    Had died by the sword of Red Murrough!
        Up from the Castle of Drumineer,
            Down from the top of Camalta,
        All the O'Briens are coming here,
            To give him the *Cead Millia Falta.*

Tall are the towers of O'Kennedy,
    Broad are the lands of MacCarha,
Desmond feeds five hundred men a-day;
    Yet, here's to O'Brien of Arra!
        Up from the Castle of Drumineer,
            Down from the top of Camalta,
        Clansman and kinsman are coming here,
            To give him the *Cead Millia Falta!*

                    THOMAS DAVIS.

LORD AMIENS' SONG, IN THE FOREST OF ARDEN.

[FROM "AS YOU LIKE IT."]

1.

BLOW, blow, thou winter wind!
    Thou art not so unkind
As man's ingratitude;

Thy tooth is not so keen,
Because thou art not seen,
   Although thy breath be rude.
Heigh-ho! sing heigh-ho unto the green holly!
Most friendship is feigning, most loving mere folly.
   Then heigh-ho the holly!
   This life is most jolly.

II.

Freeze, freeze, thou bitter sky!
That dost not bite so nigh
   As benefits forgot:
Though thou the waters warp
Thy sting is not so sharp
   As friend remember'd not.
Heigh-ho! sing heigh-ho unto the green holly!
Most friendship is feigning, most loving mere folly.
   Then heigh-ho the holly!
   This life is most jolly.

SHAKESPEARE.

SONNET.

SEPTEMBER.

THE dark green Summer with its massive hues
Fades into Autumn's tincture manifold;
A gorgeous garniture of fire and gold
The high slope of the ferny hill indues;
The mists of morn in slumbering layers diffuse
O'er glimmering rock, smooth lake, and spiked array
Of hedgerow thorns, a unity of grey;
All things appear their tangible form to lose
In ghostly vastness. But anon the gloom

Melts, as the Sun puts off his muddy veil;
And now the birds their twittering songs resume,
All Summer silent in the leafy dale.
In Spring they piped of love on every tree,
But now they sing the song of memory.

Hartley Coleridge.

THE TWO APRIL MORNINGS.

WE walk'd along, while bright and red
    Uprose the morning sun;
And Matthew stopp'd, he look'd and said,
    "The will of God be done!"

A village schoolmaster was he,
    With hair of glittering grey;
As blithe a man as you could see
    On a Spring holiday.

And on that morning, through the grass,
    And by the steaming rills,
We travell'd merrily, to pass
    A day among the hills.

"Our work," said I, "was well begun;
    Then, from thy breast what thought,
Beneath so beautiful a sun,
    So sad a sigh has brought?"

A second time did Matthew stop;
    And fixing still his eye
Upon the eastern mountain-top,
    To me he made reply:

" Yon cloud with that long purple cleft
   Brings fresh into my mind
A day like this which I have left
   Full thirty years behind.

" And just above yon slope of corn
   Such colours, and no other,
Were in the sky, that April morn,
   Of this the very brother.

" With rod and line I sued the sport
   Which that sweet season gave,
And, to the churchyard come, stopp'd short
   Beside my daughter's grave.

" Nine summers had she scarcely seen,
   The pride of all the vale;
And then she sang;—she would have been
   A very nightingale.

" Six feet in earth my Emma lay;
   And yet I loved her more,
For so it seem'd, than till that day
   I e'er had loved before.

" And, turning from her grave, I met,
   Beside the churchyard yew,
A blooming Girl whose hair was wet
   With points of morning dew.

" A basket on her head she bare;
   Her brow was smooth and white:
To see a child so very fair,
   It was a pure delight!

" No fountain from its rocky cave
   Ere tripp'd with foot so free;

She seem'd as happy as a wave
　　　　That dances on the sea.

" There came from me a sigh of pain
　　Which I could ill confine;
I look'd at her, and look'd again:
　　And did not wish her mine!"

Matthew is in his grave, yet now,
　　Methinks, I see him stand,
As at that moment, with a bough
　　Of wilding in his hand.
　　　　　　　　WORDSWORTH.

LORD ULLIN'S DAUGHTER.

A CHIEFTAIN, to the Highlands bound,
　　Cries, " Boatman, do not tarry!
And I'll give thee a silver pound
　　To row us o'er the ferry."

"Now who be ye, would cross Lochgyle,
　　This dark and stormy water?"
" O, I'm the chief of Ulva's isle,
　　And this, Lord Ullin's daughter.

" And fast before her father's men
　　Three days we've fled together,
For should he find us in the glen
　　My blood would stain the heather.

" His horsemen hard behind us ride;
　　Should they our steps discover,
Then who will cheer my bonny bride
　　When they have slain her lover?"

Out spoke the hardy Highland wight,
    " I'll go, my chief—I'm ready :
It is not for your silver bright,
    But for your winsome lady.

" And by my word, the bonny bird
    In danger shall not tarry !
So though the waves are raging white,
    I'll row you o'er the ferry."

By this the storm grew loud apace,
    The water-wraith was shrieking ;
And in the scowl of heaven each face
    Grew dark as they were speaking.

But still as wilder blew the wind,
    And as the night grew drearer,
Adown the glen rode armed men,
    Their trampling sounded nearer.

" O haste thee, haste !" the lady cries,
    " Though tempests round us gather ;
I'll meet the raging of the skies,
    But not an angry father."

The boat has left a stormy land,
    A stormy sea before her ;
When, oh ! too strong for human hand,
    The tempest gather'd o'er her.

And still they row'd amidst the roar
    Of waters fast prevailing :
Lord Ullin reach'd that fatal shore,
    His wrath was changed to wailing.

For sore dismay'd, through storm and shade,
    His child he did discover :
One lovely hand she stretch'd for aid,
    And one was round her lover.

"Come back! come back!" he cried in grief,
  "Across this stormy water;
And I'll forgive your Highland chief,
  My daughter! Oh my daughter!"

'Twas vain:—the loud waves lash'd the shore,
  Return or aid preventing.
The waters wild went o'er his child,
  And he was left lamenting.

CAMPBELL.

THE ARROW AND THE SONG.

I SHOT an arrow into the air,
  It fell to earth, I knew not where;
For, so swiftly it flew, the sight
Could not follow it in its flight.

I breathed a song into the air,
It fell to earth, I knew not where;
For who has sight so keen and strong
That it can follow the flight of song?

Long, long afterward, in an oak
I found the arrow still unbroke;
And the song, from beginning to end,
I found again in the heart of a friend.

H. W. LONGFELLOW.

O WHISTLE, AND I'LL COME TO YOU, MY LAD.

O WHISTLE, and I'll come to you, my lad,
  O whistle, and I'll come to you, my lad;
Tho' father and mither and a' should gae mad,
O whistle, and I'll come to you, my lad!

But warily tent, when you come to court me,
And come na unless the back-yett be a-jee;
Syne up the back-stile and let naebody see,
And come as ye were na comin' to me.

At kirk, or at market, whene'er ye meet me,
Gang by me as tho' that ye cared na a flie;
But steal me a blink o' your bonnie black e'e;
Yet look as ye were na lookin' at me.

Aye vow and protest that ye care na for me,
And whyles ye may lightly my beauty a wee;
But court na anither, tho' jokin' ye be,
For fear that she wyle your fancy frae me.

O whistle, and I'll come to you, my lad,
O whistle, and I'll come to you, my lad;
Tho' father and mither and a' should gae mad,
O whistle, and I'll come to you, my lad!

BURNS.

SONNET.

[ABSENCE AND PRESENCE.]

SO am I as the rich, whose blessed key
  Can bring him to his sweet up-lockèd treasure,
The which he will not every hour survey,
For blunting the fine point of seldom pleasure.
Therefore are feasts so solemn and so rare,
Since seldom coming, in the long year set,
Like stones of worth they thinly placed are,
Or captain-jewels in the carcanet.
So is the time that keeps you, as my chest,

Or as the wardrobe which the robe doth hide,
To make some special instant special-blest
By new unfolding his imprison'd pride.
    Blessed are you, whose worthiness gives scope,
    Being had, to triumph, or being lack'd, to hope.
                                SHAKESPEARE.

KUBLA KHAN; OR, A VISION IN A DREAM.

A FRAGMENT.

[*One day in the summer of* 1797, *Coleridge tells us, being at a farm-house on Exmoor, he fell asleep in his chair after reading in* " *Purchas's Pilgrimage*" *these or some such words,* " *Here the Khan Kubla commanded a palace to be built, and a stately garden thereunto: and thus ten miles of fertile ground were enclosed with a wall,*" *and waking after three hours, was aware that a long chain of verse had linked itself in his mind. He instantly wrote down the following words; but being then called away on business and detained above an hour, he found on his return that, save some scattered lines and images, the remainder of the beautiful dream-symphony was fled: nor could he ever after recover it.*]

IN Xanadu did Kubla Khan
    A stately pleasure-dome decree:
Where Alpha, the sacred river, ran
Through caverns measureless to man,
    Down to a sunless sea.
So twice five miles of fertile ground
With walls and towers were girdled round:

And there were gardens bright with sinuous rills,
Where blossom'd many an incense-bearing tree;
And here were forests ancient as the hills,
Enfolding sunny spots of greenery.

But oh! that deep romantic chasm which slanted
Down the green hill athwart a cedarn cover!
A savage place! as holy and enchanted
As e'er beneath a waning moon was haunted
By woman wailing for her demon-lover!
And from this chasm with ceaseless turmoil seething,
As if this earth in fast thick pants were breathing,
A mighty fountain momently was forced:
Amid whose swift half-intermitted burst
Huge fragments vaulted like rebounding hail,
Or chaffy grain beneath the thresher's flail:
And 'mid these dancing rocks at once and ever
It flung up momently the sacred river.
Five miles meandering with a mazy motion
Through wood and dale the sacred river ran,
Then reach'd the caverns measureless to man,
And sank in tumult to a lifeless ocean:
And 'mid this tumult Kubla heard from far
Ancestral voices prophesying war!

The shadow of the dome of pleasure
Floated midway on the waves;
Where was heard the mingled measure
From the fountain and the caves.
It was a miracle of rare device,
A sunny pleasure-dome with caves of ice!

 A damsel with a dulcimer
 In a vision once I saw:
 It was an Abyssinian maid,
 And on her dulcimer she play'd,
 Singing of Mount Abora.

          Could I revive within me
          Her symphony and song,
          To such a deep delight 'twould win me
      That with music loud and long
      I would build that dome in air,
      That sunny dome! those caves of ice!
      And all who heard should see them there,
      And all should cry, Beware! Beware!
      His flashing eyes, his floating hair!
      Weave a circle round him thrice,
      And close your eyes with holy dread,
      For he on honey-dew hath fed,
      And drunk the milk of Paradise.
                              COLERIDGE.

SHE dwelt among the untrodden ways
 Beside the springs of Dove,
A Maid whom there were none to praise
 And very few to love:

A violet by a mossy stone
 Half-hidden from the eye!
Fair as a star, when only one
 Is shining in the sky.

She lived unknown, and few could know
 When Lucy ceased to be;
But she is in her grave,—and, oh,
 The difference to me!
                              WORDSWORTH.

UP AT A VILLA—DOWN IN THE CITY.

(AS DISTINGUISHED BY AN ITALIAN PERSON OF QUALITY.)

I.

HAD I but plenty of money, money enough and to spare,
The house for me, no doubt, were a house in the city-square.
Ah such a life, such a life, as one leads at the window there!

II.

Something to see, by Bacchus, something to hear, at least!
There, the whole day long, one's life is a perfect feast;
While up at a villa one lives, I maintain it, no more than a beast.

III.

Well now, look at our villa! stuck like the horn of a bull
Just on a mountain's edge as bare as the creature's skull,
Save a mere shag of a bush with hardly a leaf to pull!
I scratch my own, sometimes, to see if the hair's turn'd wool.

IV.

But the city, oh the city—the square with the houses! Why

They are stone-faced, white as a curd, there's some-
  thing to take the eye!
Houses in four straight lines, not a single front
  awry!
You watch who crosses and gossips, who saunters,
  who hurries by:
Green blinds, as a matter of course, to draw when
  the sun gets high;
And the shops with fanciful signs which are painted
  properly.

V.

What of a villa? Though winter be over in March
  by rights,
'Tis May perhaps ere the snow shall have wither'd
  well off the heights:
You've the brown plough'd land before, where the
  oxen steam and wheeze,
And the hills over-smoked behind by the faint
  grey olive trees.

VI.

Is it better in May, I ask you? you've summer
  all at once;
In a day he leaps complete with a few strong April
  suns!
'Mid the sharp short emerald wheat, scarce risen
  three fingers well,
The wild tulip, at end of its tube, blows out its
  great red bell
Like a thin clear bubble of blood, for the children
  to pick and sell.

VII.

Is it ever hot in the square? There's a fountain
  to spout and splash!

In the shade it sings and springs ; in the shine
    such foam-bows flash
On the horses with curling fish-tails, that prance
    and paddle and pash
Round the lady atop in the conch—fifty gazers do
    not abash,
Though all that she wears is some weeds round
    her waist in a sort of sash !

VIII.

All the year long at the villa, nothing's to see
    though you linger,
Except yon cypress that points like Death's lean
    lifted forefinger.
Some think fireflies pretty, when they mix in the
    corn and mingle,
Or thrid the stinking hemp till the stalks of it seem
    a-tingle.
Late August or early September, the stunning
    cicada is shrill,
And the bees keep their tiresome whine round the
    resinous firs on the hill.
Enough of the seasons,—I spare you the months
    of the fever and chill.

IX.

Ere opening your eyes in the city, the blessed
    church-bells begin :
No sooner the bells leave off, than the diligence
    rattles in :
You get the pick of the news, and it costs you
    never a pin.
By and by there's the travelling doctor gives pills,
    lets blood, draws teeth ;
Or the Punchinello-trumpet breaks up the market
    beneath.

At the post-office such a scene-picture—the new
    play, piping hot!
And a notice how, only this morning, three liberal
    thieves were shot.
Above it behold the archbishop's most fatherly of
    rebukes,
And beneath, with his crown and his lion, some
    little new law of the Duke's!
Or a sonnet with flowery marge to the Reverend
    Don So-and-so,
Who is Dante, Boccaccio, Petrarca, Saint Jerome,
    and Cicero,
" And moreover," (the sonnet goes rhyming,) "the
    skirts of Saint Paul has reach'd,
Having preach'd us those six Lent-lectures more
    unctuous than ever he preach'd."
Noon strikes,—here sweeps the procession! our
    Lady borne smiling and smart
With a pink gauze gown all spangles, and seven
    swords stuck in her heart!
Bang, whang, whang, goes the drum, *tootle-te-
    tootle* the fife;
No keeping one's haunches still: it's the greatest
    pleasure in life.

X.

But bless you, it's dear—it's dear! fowls, wine, at
    double the rate.
They have clapp'd a new tax upon salt, and what
    oil pays passing the gate
It's a horror to think of. And so, the villa for
    me, not the city!
Beggars can scarcely be choosers—but still—ah,
    the pity, the pity!
Look, two and two go the priests, then the monks
    with cowls and sandals,

And the penitents dress'd in white skirts, a-holding
  the yellow candles.
One, he carries a flag up straight, and another a
  cross with handles,
And the Duke's guard brings up the rear, for the
  better prevention of scandals.
Bang, whang, whang, goes the drum, *tootle-te-
  tootle* the fife.
Oh, a day in the city-square, there is no such
  pleasure in life!

ROBERT BROWNING.

FORBEARANCE.

HAST thou named all the birds without a gun;
  Loved the wood-rose, and left it on its stalk;
At rich men's tables eaten bread and pulse;
Unarm'd faced danger with a heart of trust;
And loved so well a high behaviour
In man or maid that thou from speech refrain'd,
Nobility more nobly to repay?—
O be my friend, and teach me to be thine!

EMERSON.

THE BROOK.

I COME from haunts of coot and hern,
    I make a sudden sally
And sparkle out among the fern,
    To bicker down a valley.

By thirty hills I hurry down,
  Or slip between the ridges,
By twenty thorps, a little town,
  And half a hundred bridges.

Till last by Philip's farm I flow
  To join the brimming river,
For men may come and men may go,
  But I go on for ever.

I chatter over stony ways,
  In little sharps and trebles,
I bubble into eddying bays,
  I babble on the pebbles.

With many a curve my banks I fret
  By many a field and fallow,
And many a fairy foreland set
  With willow-weed and mallow.

I chatter, chatter, as I flow
  To join the brimming river,
For men may come and men may go,
  But I go on for ever.

I wind about, and in and out,
  With here a blossom sailing,
And here and there a lusty trout,
  And here and there a grayling,

And here and there a foamy flake
  Upon me, as I travel
With many a silvery waterbreak
  Above the golden gravel,

And draw them all along, and flow
  To join the brimming river,

For men may come and men may go,
   But I go on for ever.

I steal by lawns and grassy plots,
   I slide by hazel covers;
I move the sweet forget-me-nots
   That grow for happy lovers.

I slip, I slide, I gloom, I glance,
   Among my skimming swallows;
I make the netted sunbeam dance
   Against my sandy shallows.

I murmur under moon and stars
   In brambly wildernesses;
I linger by my shingly bars;
   I loiter round my cresses;

And out again I curve and flow
   To join the brimming river,
For men may come and men may go,
   But I go on for ever.
                TENNYSON.

LA BELLE DAME SANS MERCY.

AH, what can ail thee, wretched wight,
   Alone and palely loitering?
The sedge is wither'd from the lake,
   And no birds sing.

Ah, what can ail thee, wretched wight,
   So haggard and so woe-begone?

The squirrel's granary is full,
　　　　And the harvest's done.

I see a lily on thy brow,
　　With anguish moist and fever-dew;
And on thy cheek a fading rose
　　Fast withereth too.

I met a Lady in the meads,
　　Full beautiful, a fairy's child;
Her hair was long, her foot was light,
　　And her eyes were wild.

I set her on my pacing steed,
　　And nothing else saw all day long;
For sideways would she lean, and sing
　　A fairy's song.

I made a garland for her head,
　　And bracelets too, and fragrant zone:
She look'd at me as she did love,
　　And made sweet moan.

She found me roots of relish sweet,
　　And honey wild, and manna dew;
And sure in language strange she said,
　　I love thee true.

She took me to her elfin grot,
　　And there she gazed and sigh'd deep,
And there I shut her wild sad eyes—
　　So kiss'd to sleep.

And there we slumber'd on the moss,
　　And there I dream'd, ah woe betide,
The latest dream I ever dream'd
　　On the cold hill-side.

I saw pale kings, and princes too,
   Pale warriors, death-pale were they all;
Who cried " La belle Dame sans mercy
      Hath thee in thrall!"

I saw their starved lips in the gloom
   With horrid warning gapèd wide,
And I awoke and found me here,
      On the cold hill-side.

And this is why I sojourn here
   Alone and palely loitering,
Though the sedge is wither'd from the lake,
      And no birds sing.
KEATS.

SONNET.

[THE SENSE OF LOSS.]

SURPRISED by joy—impatient as the Wind
   I turn'd to share the transport—oh! with whom
But Thee, deep buried in the silent tomb,
That spot which no vicissitude can find?
Love, faithful love, recall'd thee to my mind—
But how could I forget thee? Through what power,
Even for the least division of an hour,
Have I been so beguiled as to be blind
To my most grievous loss?—That thought's return
Was the worst pang that sorrow ever bore,
Save one, one only, when I stood forlorn,
Knowing my heart's best treasure was no more;
That neither present time, nor years unborn
Could to my sight that heavenly face restore.
WORDSWORTH.

THE HOUR OF PRAYER.

CHILD, amidst the flowers at play,
While the red light fades away;
Mother, with thine earnest eye
Ever following silently;
Father, by the breeze of eve
Call'd thy harvest work to leave;
Pray! ere yet the dark hours be,
Lift the heart and bend the knee!

Traveller, in the stranger's land,
Far from thine own household band;
Mourner, haunted by the tone
Of a voice from this world gone;
Captive, in whose narrow cell
Sunshine hath not leave to dwell;
Sailor, on the darkening sea;
Lift the heart and bend the knee!

Warrior, that from battle won
Breathest now at set of sun;
Woman, o'er the lowly slain
Weeping on the burial plain;
Ye that triumph, ye that sigh,
Kindred by one holy tie,
Heaven's first star alike ye see,—
Lift the heart and bend the knee!

FELICIA HEMANS.

SONNET.

[LOVE'S SILENCE.]

BECAUSE I breathe not love to everie one,
    Nor do not use set colours for to weare,
Nor nourish special locks of vowèd haire,
Nor give each speech a full point of a groan;
The courtlie nymphs, acquainted with the moan
Of them who in their lips Love's standard beare,
"What, he?" say they of me, "now I dare sweare
He cannot love! No, no, let him alone."
And think so still! if Stella know my minde.
Profess indeed I do not Cupid's art;
But you, fair maids, at length this true shall finde,
That his right badge is but worne in the heart:
Dumb swans, not chattering pies, do lovers prove:
They love indeed, who quake to say they love.

                  SIR PHILIP SIDNEY.

SONG.

[FROM "THE PRINCESS."]

TEARS, idle tears, I know not what they mean,
    Tears from the depth of some divine despair
Rise in the heart, and gather to the eyes,
In looking on the happy Autumn fields,
And thinking of the days that are no more.

Fresh as the first beam glittering on a sail,
That brings our friends up from the under world,
Sad as the last which reddens over one

That sinks with all we love below the verge,
So sad, so fresh, the days that are no more.

Ah, sad and strange as in dark summer dawns
The earliest pipe of half awaken'd birds
To dying ears, when unto dying eyes
The casement slowly grows a glimmering square;
So sad, so strange, the days that are no more.

Dear as remember'd kisses after death,
And sweet as those by hopeless fancy feign'd
On lips that are for others; deep as love,
Deep as first love, and wild with all regret;
O Death in Life, the days that are no more.

TENNYSON.

TO MY SISTER.

WRITTEN AT A SMALL DISTANCE FROM MY HOUSE, AND SENT BY MY LITTLE BOY.

IT is the first mild day of March:
    Each minute sweeter than before
The redbreast sings from the tall larch
    That stands beside our door.

There is a blessing in the air,
    Which seems a sense of joy to yield
To the bare trees, and mountains bare,
    And grass in the green field.

My Sister! ('tis a wish of mine)
    Now that our morning meal is done,
Make haste, your morning task resign;
    Come forth and feel the sun.

Edward will come with you;—and, pray,
　　Put on with speed your woodland dress;
And bring no book: for this one day
　　We'll give to idleness.

No joyless forms shall regulate
　　Our living calendar:
We from to-day, my Friend, will date
　　The opening of the year.

Love, now a universal birth,
　　From heart to heart is stealing,
From earth to man, from man to earth:
　　It is the hour of feeling.

One moment now may give us more
　　Than years of toiling reason:
Our minds shall drink at every pore
　　The spirit of the season.

Some silent laws our hearts will make,
　　Which they shall long obey:
We for the year to come may take
　　Our temper from to-day.

And from the blessed power that rolls
　　About, below, above,
We'll frame the measure of our souls:
　　They shall be turn'd to love.

Then come, my Sister! come, I pray,
　　With speed put on your woodland dress;
And bring no book: for this one day
　　We'll give to idleness.

　　　　　　　　　　WORDSWORTH.

YE MARINERS OF ENGLAND.

(A NAVAL ODE.)

YE mariners of England,
    That guard our native seas;
Whose flag has braved, a thousand years,
    The battle and the breeze!
Your glorious standard launch again
    To match another foe!
And sweep through the deep,
    While the stormy tempests blow;
While the battle rages loud and long,
    And the stormy tempests blow.

The spirits of your fathers
    Shall start from every wave!
For the deck it was their field of fame,
    And Ocean was their grave:
Where Blake and mighty Nelson fell
    Your manly hearts shall glow,
As ye sweep through the deep,
    While the stormy tempests blow;
While the battle rages loud and long,
    And the stormy tempests blow.

Britannia needs no bulwark,
    No towers along the steep;
Her march is o'er the mountain waves
    Her home is on the deep.
With thunders from her native oak
    She quells the floods below—

As they roar on the shore
  When the stormy tempests blow;
When the battle rages loud and long,
  And the stormy tempests blow.

The meteor flag of England
  Shall yet terrific burn;
Till danger's troubled night depart,
  And the star of peace return.
Then, then, ye ocean warriors!
  Our song and feast shall flow
To the fame of your name,
  When the storm has ceased to blow;
When the fiery fight is heard no more,
  And the storm has ceased to blow.

CAMPBELL.

SONNET.

TO CYRIACK SKINNER.

CYRIACK, this three years' day these eyes, though clear,
  To outward view, of blemish or of spot,
  Bereft of light, their seeing have forgot;
Nor to their idle orbs doth sight appear
Of sun, or moon, or star, throughout the year,
  Or man, or woman. Yet I argue not
  Against Heaven's hand or will, nor bate a jot
Of heart or hope; but still bear up and steer
Right onward. What supports me, dost thou ask?
  The conscience, friend, to have lost them over-
    plied

In liberty's defence, my noble task,
  Of which all Europe rings from side to side.
This thought might lead me through the world's
      vain masque,
  Content though blind, had I no better guide.
MILTON.

[FAIRY SONG.]

COME, follow, follow me,
  You fairy elves that be,
Which circle on the greene;
  Come, follow Mab your queene.
Hand in hand let's dance around,
For this place is fairy ground.

  When mortals are at rest,
  And snoring in their nest;
  Unheard and unespy'd,
    Through key-holes we do glide;
Over tables, stools, and shelves,
We trip it with our fairy elves.

  And, if the house be foul,
  Or platter, dish, or bowl,
  Up stairs we nimbly creep,
  And find the sluts asleep:
There we pinch their arms and thighs;
None escapes, nor none espies.

  But if the house be swept,
  And from uncleanness kept,
  We praise the household maid,
  And duely she is paid:

For we use before we goe
To drop a tester in her shoe.

 Upon a mushroome's head
 Our table-cloth we spread;
 A grain of rye or wheat
 Is manchet which we eat;
Pearly drops of dew we drink
In acorn cups fill'd to the brink.

 The grasshopper, gnat, and fly
 Serve for our minstrelsie;
 Grace said, we dance awhile,
 And so the time beguile:
And if the moon doth hide her head,
The glow-worm lights us home to bed.

 On tops of dewie grasse
 So nimbly do we passe,
 The young and tender stalk
 Ne'er bends when we do walk:
Yet in the morning may be seen
Where we the night before have been.

SONNET.

[A PARTING.]

SINCE there's no help, come let us kiss and parte:
Nay, I have done: you get no more of me:
And I am glad, yea, glad with all my heart,
That thus so cleanly I myself can free;
Shake hands for ever, cancel all our vows,
And when we meet at any time againe,

Be it not seen in either of our brows
That we one jot of former love retaine.

. . Now at the last gasp of Love's latest breath,
When, his pulse failing, Passion speechless lies,
When Faith is kneeling by his bed of death,
And Innocence is closing up his eyes,
Now, if thou wouldst, when all have given him over,
From death to life thou might'st him yet recover!
MICHAEL DRAYTON.

[NOSE VERSUS EYES.]

REPORT OF AN ADJUDGED CASE NOT TO BE FOUND
IN ANY OF THE BOOKS.

BETWEEN Nose and Eyes a strange contest arose,
   The spectacles set them unhappily wrong;
The point in dispute was, as well the world knows,
   To which the said spectacles ought to belong.

So Tongue was the lawyer, and argued the cause
   With a great deal of skill, and a wig full of learning:
While chief baron Ear sat to balance the laws,
   So famed for his talent in nicely discerning.

In behalf of the Nose it will quickly appear,
   And your lordship, he said, will undoubtedly find,
That the Nose has had spectacles always in wear,
   Which amounts to possession time out of mind.

Then holding the spectacles up to the court—
   Your lordship observes they are made with a straddle

As wide as the ridge of the Nose is ; in short,
  Design'd to sit close to it, just like a saddle.

Again, would your lordship a moment suppose
  ('Tis a case that has happen'd, and may be again,)
That the visage or countenance had not a nose,
  Pray who would, or who could, wear spectacles then ?

On the whole it appears, and my argument shows,
  With a reasoning the court will never condemn,
That the spectacles plainly were made for the Nose,
  And the Nose was as plainly intended for them.

Then shifting his side (as a lawyer knows how),
  He pleaded again in behalf of the Eyes ;
But what were his arguments few people know,
  For the court did not think they were equally wise.

So his lordship decreed, with a grave solemn tone,
  Decisive and clear, without one if or but,
That whenever the Nose put his spectacles on,
  By daylight, or candlelight,—Eyes should be shut.

COWPER.

CUPID'S CURSE.

[SUNG BY ŒNONE AND PARIS.

FROM " THE ARRAIGNMENT OF PARIS:" A DRAMATIC PASTORAL—1584.]

Œn. **F**AIRE, and faire, and twice so faire,
    As faire as anie may be,
  The fairest shepherd on our greene,
    A Love for any Lady.

Paris. Faire, and faire, and twice so faire,
    As faire as any may be,
  Thy Love is fair for thee alone,
    And for no other Lady.

Œn. My Love is faire, my Love is gay,
  And fresh as bin the flowers in May,
  And of my Love my roundelay,
  My merry, merry, merry roundelay,
    Concludes with Cupid's Curse:
  They that do change old love for newe,
    Pray Gods they change for worse!

Œn. Faire, and faire, and twice so faire,
    As faire as any may be,
  The fairest shepherd on our greene,
    A Love for any Lady.

Paris. Faire, and faire, and twice so faire,
    As faire as anie may be,
  Thy Love is faire for thee alone,
    And for no other Lady.

Œn. My Love can pipe, my Love can sing,
  My Love can manie a pretty thing,
  And of his lovely praises ring
  My merry, merry, merry roundelays.
    Amen to Cupid's Curse:
  They that do change old love for newe,
    Pray Gods they change for worse!

                        GEORGE PEELE.

SONG.

[FROM " THE LADY OF THE LAKE."]

SOLDIER, rest! thy warfare o'er,
   Sleep the sleep that knows not breaking;
Dream of battle-fields no more,
   Days of danger, nights of waking.
In our isle's enchanted hall
   Hands unseen thy couch are strewing,
Fairy strains of music fall,
   Every sense with slumber dewing.
Soldier, rest! thy warfare o'er,
Dream of fighting fields no more;
Sleep the sleep that knows no breaking,
Morn of toil, nor night of waking.

No rude sound shall reach thine ear,
   Armour's clang, or war-steed's champing,
Trump nor pibroch summon here
   Mustering clan, or squadron tramping.
Yet the lark's shrill fife may come
   At the day-break from the fallow,
And the bittern sound his drum,
   Booming from the sedgy shallow.
Ruder sounds shall none be near,
Guards nor warders challenge here.
Here's no war-steed's neigh and champing,
Shouting clans or squadron's tramping.
SCOTT.

THE LADY'S GRAVE.

THEY laid my lady in her grave,
    My lady with the deep blue eye;
      'Twas not in sainted ground
      Where crosses stand around,
But by the river's side, where the green sedges wave.

They had not seen that lady's smile
Ere her unhappy days were come;
      Or the last bed of rest,
      Hallow'd by prayer and priest,
Would not have been withheld, as if from something vile.

They would have loved that deep blue eye,
Because it told a tale of heav'n;
      And in her candid look
      Read, as in holy book,
Immortal things and pure, belonging to the sky.

But by the river's sedgy brink,
Where her cold corse was floating found,
      They hid my lady fair
      Unbless'd by priest or pray'r,
Where yellow iris and pale reeds the water drink.

The river lily's humid flow'r,
And cresses with their cold green leaf,
      In place of tomb, denied
      By harsh and impious pride,
Grow there; and sounds from heav'n sweep by at evening hour.

                MARY BODDINGTON.

TO THE CUCKOO.

O BLITHE New-comer! I have heard,
   I hear thee and rejoice.
O Cuckoo! shall I call thee Bird,
   Or but a wandering Voice?

While I am lying on the grass
   Thy twofold shout I hear,
That seems to fill the whole air's space,
   As loud far off as near.

Though babbling only to the Vale,
   Of sunshine and of flowers,
Thou bringest unto me a tale
   Of visionary hours.

Thrice welcome, darling of the Spring!
   Even yet thou art to me
No bird, but an invisible thing,
   A voice, a mystery;

The same whom in my school-boy days
   I listen'd to; that Cry
Which made me look a thousand ways
   In bush, and tree, and sky.

To seek thee did I often rove
   Through woods and on the green;
And thou wert still a hope, a love;
   Still long'd for, never seen.

And I can listen to thee yet;
   Can lie upon the plain
And listen, till I do beget
   That golden time again.

O blessed Bird! the earth we pace
   Again appears to be
An unsubstantial, faery place;
   That is fit home for Thee!
WORDSWORTH.

IN THE STILLNESS O' THE NIGHT.

[DORSET DIALECT.]

OV all the housen[1] o' the pliace,
   There's oone[2] wher I da[3] like to call
By dae ar night the best ov all,
To zee my Fanny's smilèn fiace;
   An' dere[4] the stiately tress da grow,
   A-rockèn as the win' da blow,
   While she da sweetly sleep below,
   In the stillness o' the night.

An' dere at evemen,[5] I da goo,
   A-hoppèn auver[6] ghiates[7] an' bars,
By twinklen light o' winter stars,
When snow da clumper[8] to my shoe;
   An' zometimes we da slyly catch
   A chat an hour upon the stratch,[9]
   An' piart wi' whispers at the hatch[10]
   In the stillness o' the night.

---

[1] *Housen*, houses.   [2] *Oone*, one.   [3] *Da*, do.   [4] *Dere*, there.   [5] *Evemen*, evening.   [6] *Auver*, over.   [7] *Ghiates*, gates.   [8] *Clumper*, gather in a lump, (an excellent word.)   [9] *Stratch*, stretch.   [10] *Hatch*, wicket-gate.

An' zometimes she da goo¹ to zome
   Young nâighbours' housen down the plaice,
   An' I da² get a clue to triace
Her out, an' goo to zee her huome;³
   An' I da wish a vield⁴ a mile,
   As she da sweetly chat an' smile,
   Along the drove,⁵ or at the stile,
     In the stillness o' the night.
WILLIAM BARNES.

SONG.

A SPIRIT haunts the year's last hours,
   Dwelling amid these yellowing bowers:
   To himself he talks;
For at eventide, listening earnestly,
At his work you may hear him sob and sigh
   In the walks;
   Earthward he boweth the heavy stalks
Of the mouldering flowers:
     Heavily hangs the broad sunflower
       Over its grave i' the earth so chilly;
     Heavily hangs the hollyhock,
     Heavily hangs the tiger-lily.

The air is damp, and hush'd, and close,
As a sick man's room when he taketh repose
   An hour before death:
My very heart faints and my whole soul grieves
At the moist rich smell of the rotting leaves,
   And the breath

---

¹ *Goo*, go. ² *Da*, doth. ³ *Huome*, home. ⁴ *Vield*, field. ⁵ *Drove*, a cow-path between hedges.

Of the fading edges of box beneath,
And the year's last rose.
>> Heavily hangs the broad sunflower
>> Over its grave i' the earth so chilly;
>> Heavily hangs the hollyhock,
>> Heavily hangs the tiger-lily.

TENNYSON.

HERRICK'S LITANY.

IN the hour of my distress,
When temptations me oppress,
And when I my sins confess,
  Sweet Spirit, comfort me!

When I lie within my bed,
Sick in heart and sick in head,
And with doubts discomforted,
  Sweet Spirit, comfort me!

When the house doth sigh and weep,
And the world is drown'd in sleep,
Yet mine eyes the watch do keep,
  Sweet Spirit, comfort me!

When the priest his last hath pray'd,
And I nod to what is said,
'Cause my speech is now decay'd,
  Sweet Spirit, comfort me!

When the judgment is reveal'd,
And that open'd which was seal'd,
When to thee I have appeal'd,
  Sweet Spirit, comfort me!

HERRICK.

SONNET.

FROM THE ITALIAN OF MICHAEL ANGELO.

THE might of one fair face sublimes my love,
    For it hath wean'd my heart from low desires,
Nor death I need, nor purgatorial fires;
Thy beauty, antepart of joys above,
Instructs me in the bliss that saints approve;
For oh! how good, how beautiful must be
The God that made so good a thing as thee,
So fair an image of the heavenly Dove.
Forgive me if I cannot turn away
From those sweet eyes that are my earthly heaven,
For they are guiding stars benignly given
To tempt my footsteps to the upward way;
And if I dwell too fondly in thy sight,
I live and love in God's peculiar light.
HARTLEY COLERIDGE.

[SPRING AND SORROW.]

NOW fades the last long streak of snow,
    Now burgeons every maze of quick
About the flowering squares, and thick,
By ashen roots the violets blow.

Now rings the woodland loud and long,
    The distance takes a lovelier hue,
    And drown'd in yonder living blue
The lark becomes a sightless song.

Now dance the lights on lawn and lea,
  The flocks are whiter down the vale,
  And milkier every milky sail
On winding stream or distant sea;

Where now the seamew pipes, or dives
  In yonder greening gleam, and fly
  The happy birds that change their sky
To build and brood; that live their lives

From land to land; and in my breast
  Spring wakens too; and my regret
  Becomes an April violet,
And buds and blossoms like the rest.
In Memoriam.

CHORUS OF THE FLOWERS.

WE are the sweet Flowers,
    Born of sunny showers,
Think, whene'er you see us, what our beauty saith:
    Utterance mute and bright
    Of some unknown delight,
We fill the air with pleasure, by our simple breath:
    All who see us, love us;
    We befit all places;
Unto sorrow we give smiles; and unto graces,
    graces.

    Mark our ways, how noiseless
    All, and sweetly voiceless,
Though the March winds pipe to make our passage
    clear;

Not a whisper tells
Where our small seed dwells,
Nor is known the moment green, when our tips
    appear.
We thread the earth in silence,
In silence build our bowers,
And leaf by leaf in silence show, till we laugh atop,
    sweet Flowers!

The dear lumpish baby,
Humming with the May-bee,
Hails us with his bright stare, stumbling through
    the grass;
The honey-dropping moon,
On a night in June,
Kisses our pale pathway leaves, that felt the bride-
    groom pass;
Age, the wither'd clinger,
On us mutely gazes,
And wraps the thought of his last bed in his
    childhood's daisies.

See, and scorn all duller
Taste, how heav'n loves colour,
How great Nature, clearly, joys in red and green;
What sweet thoughts she thinks
Of violets and pinks,
And a thousand flushing hues, made solely to be
    seen;
See her whitest lilies
Chill the silver showers,
And what a red mouth has her rose, the woman of
    the flowers!

Uselessness divinest
Of a use the finest

Painteth us, the teachers of the end of use;
　　Travellers weary-eyed
　　Bless us far and wide;
Unto sick and prison'd thoughts we give sudden
　　　truce;
　　Not a poor town-window
　　Loves its sickliest planting,
But its wall speaks loftier truth than Babylon's
　　　whole vaunting.

　　Sage are yet the uses
　　Mix'd with our sweet juices,
Whether man or may-fly profit of the balm;
　　As fair fingers heal'd
　　Knights from the olden field,
We hold cups of mightiest force to give the wildest
　　　calm.
　　E'en the terror Poison
　　Hath its plea for blooming;
Life it gives to reverent lips, though death to the
　　　presuming.

　　And oh! our sweet soul-taker,
　　That thief the honey-maker,
What a house hath he, by the thymy glen!
　　In his talking rooms
　　How the feasting fumes,
Till his gold cups overflow to the mouths of men!
　　The butterflies come aping
　　Those fine thieves of ours,
And flutter round our rifled tops, like tickled
　　　flowers with flowers.

　　See those tops, how beauteous!
　　What fair service duteous

Round some idol waits, as on their lord the Nine?
    Elfin court 'twould seem;
    And taught perchance that dream
Which the old Greek mountain dreamt upon nights divine.
    To expound such wonder
    Human speech avails not;
Yet there dies no poorest weed, that such a glory exhales not.

    Think of all these treasures,
    Matchless works and pleasures,
Every one a marvel, more than thought can say;
    Then think in what bright showers
    We thicken fields and bowers,
And with what heaps of sweetness half stifle wanton May:
    Think of the mossy forests
    By the bee-birds haunted,
And all those Amazonian plains, lone lying as enchanted!

    Trees themselves are ours;
    Fruits are born of flowers;
Peach and roughest nut were blossoms in the spring;
    The lusty bee knows well
    The news, and comes pell-mell,
And dances in the bloomy thicks with darksome antheming.
    Beneath the very burthen
    Of planet-pressing ocean
We wash our smiling cheeks in peace, a thought for meek devotion.

    Tears of Phœbus,—missings
    Of Cytherea's kissings,

  Have in us been found, and wise men find them
      still;
    Drooping grace unfurls
    Still Hyacinthus' curls,
And Narcissus loves himself in the selfish rill;
    Thy red lip, Adonis,
    Still is wet with morning;
And the step that bled for thee, the rosy briar
      adorning.

    Who shall say that flowers
    Dress not heav'n's own bowers?
Who its love, without them, can fancy,—or sweet
      floor?
    Who shall even dare
    To say we sprang not there,
And came not down that Love might bring one
      piece of heav'n the more?
    Oh pray believe that angels
    From those blue dominions
Brought us in their white laps down, 'twixt their
      golden pinions.
         LEIGH HUNT.

AN END.

LOVE, strong as death, is dead.
 Come, let us make his bed
  Among the dying flowers;
A green turf at his head,
And a stone at his feet,
Whereon we may sit
  In the quiet evening hours.

He was born in the spring,
And died before the harvesting;
   On the last warm summer day
He left us;—he would not stay
For autumn twilights, cold and grey;
Sit we by his grave and sing.
   " He is gone away."

To few chords, and sad, and low,
   Sing we so.
Be our eyes fix'd on the grass,
Shadow-veil'd, as the years pass,
While we think of all that was
   In the long ago.
           CHRISTINA ROSSETTI.

TO A WATER-FOWL.

WHITHER, 'midst falling dew,
   While glow the heavens with the last steps
      of day,
Far through their rosy depths, dost thou pursue
   Thy solitary way!

   Vainly the fowler's eye
Might mark thy distant flight to do thee wrong,
As, darkly painted on the crimson sky,
   Thy figure floats along.

   Seek'st thou the plashy brink
Of weedy lake, or marge of river wide,
Or where the rocking billows rise and sink
   On the chafed ocean side?

   There is a Power whose care
'Teaches thy way along that pathless coast,—
The desert and illimitable air,—
   Lone wandering, but not lost.

   All day thy wings have fann'd,
At that far height, the cold thin atmosphere,
Yet stoop not, weary, to the welcome land,
   Though the dark night is near.

   And soon that toil shall end;
Soon shalt thou find a summer home, and rest,
And scream among thy fellows; reeds shall bend,
   Soon, o'er thy shelter'd nest.

   Thou'rt gone, the abyss of heaven
Hath swallow'd up thy form; yet, on my heart
Deeply hath sunk the lesson thou hast given,
   And shall not soon depart.

   He, who from zone to zone
Guides through the boundless sky thy certain
    flight,
In the long way that I must tread alone,
   Will lead my steps aright.
        W. C. BRYANT.

VENUS OF THE NEEDLE.

O MARYANNE, you pretty girl,
  Intent on silky labour,
Of sempstresses the pink and pearl,
  Excuse a peeping neighbour!

Those eyes for ever drooping, give
  The long brown lashes rarely;
But violets in the shadows live,—
  For once unveil them fairly.

Hast thou not lent that flounce enough
  Of looks so long and earnest?
Lo, here's more " penetrable stuff "
  To which thou never turnest.

Ye graceful fingers, deftly sped!
  How slender, and how nimble!
O might I wind their skeins of thread,
  Or but pick up their thimble!

How blest the youth whom love shall bring,
  And happy stars embolden,
To change the dome into a ring,
  The silver into golden!

Who'll steal some morning to her side
  To take her finger's measure,
While Maryanne pretends to chide,
  And blushes deep with pleasure.

Who'll watch her sew her wedding-gown,
  Well conscious that it *is* hers;
Who'll glean a tress, without a frown,
  With those so ready scissors.

Who'll taste those ripenings of the south,
  The fragrant and delicious—
Don't put the pins into your mouth,
  O Maryanne, my precious!

I almost wish it were my trust
  To teach how shocking that is;

I wish I had not, as I must,
  To quit this tempting lattice.

Sure aim takes Cupid, fluttering foe,
  Across a street so narrow;
A thread of silk to string his bow,
  A needle for his arrow!

WILLIAM ALLINGHAM.

SONG OF ARIEL.

[FROM " THE TEMPEST."]

WHERE the bee sucks, there suck I;
  In a cowslip's bell I lie;
There I couch when owls do cry;
On the bat's back I do fly
After summer, merrily.
Merrily, merrily, shall I live now,
Under the blossom that hangs on the bough!

SHAKESPEARE.

TO A COLD BEAUTY.

I.

LADY, wouldst thou heiress be
  To Winter's cold and cruel part?
When he sets the rivers free,
  Thou dost still lock up thy heart;
Thou that shouldst outlast the snow
But in the whiteness of thy brow.

II.

Scorn and cold neglect are made
   For winter gloom and winter wind,
But thou wilt wrong the summer air,
   Breathing it to words unkind,—
Breath which only should belong
To love, to sunlight, and to song.

III.

When the little buds unclose,
   Red, and white, and pied, and blue,
And that virgin flower, the rose,
   Opes her heart to hold the dew,
Wilt thou lock thy bosom up,
With no jewel in its cup?

IV.

Let not cold December sit
   Thus in Love's peculiar throne:
Brooklets are not prison'd now,
   But crystal frosts are all agone;
And that which hangs upon the spray,
It is no snow, but flower of May.

                        HOOD.

I CANNOT see the features right,
   When on the gloom I strive to paint
The face I know; the hues are faint
And mix with hollow masks of night:

Cloud-towers by ghostly masons wrought,
  A gulf that ever shuts and gapes,
  A hand that points, and palled shapes
In shadowy thoroughfares of thought;

And crowds that stream from yawning doors,
  And shoals of pucker'd faces drive;
  Dark bulks that tumble half alive,
And lazy lengths on boundless shores:

Till all at once beyond the will
  I hear a wizard music roll,
  And through a lattice on the soul
Looks thy fair face and makes it still.
                    In Memoriam.

ULALUME.

THE skies they were ashen and sober;
    The leaves they were crispèd and sere—
    The leaves they were withering and sere;
It was night in the lonesome October
    Of my most immemorial year;
It was hard by the dim lake of Auber,
    In the misty mid-region of Weir—
It was down by the dank tarn of Auber,
    In the ghoul-haunted woodland of Weir.

Here once, through an alley titanic,
    Of cypress, I roam'd with my Soul—
    Of cypress, with Psyche, my Soul.
These were days when my heart was volcanic
    As the scoriac rivers that roll—
    As the lavas that restlessly roll

Their sulphurous currents down Yaanek
    In the ultimate climes of the pole—
That groan as they roll down Mount Yaanek
    In the realms of the boreal pole.

Our talk had been serious and sober,
    But our thoughts they were palsied and sere—
    Our memories were treacherous and sere—
For we knew not the month was October,
    And we mark'd not the night of the year—
    (Ah, night of all nights in the year!)
We noted not the dim lake of Auber—
(Though once we had journey'd down here)—
Remember'd not the dank tarn of Auber,
    Nor the ghoul-haunted woodland of Weir.

And now as the night was senescent
    And star-dials pointed to morn—
    As the star-dials hinted of morn—
At the end of our path a liquescent
    And nebulous lustre was born,
Out of which a miraculous crescent
    Arose with a duplicate horn—
Astarte's bediamonded crescent
    Distinct with its duplicate horn.

And I said—" She is warmer than Dian:
    She rolls through an ether of sighs—
    She revels in a region of sighs:
She has seen that the tears are not dry on
    These cheeks, where the worm never dies,
And has come past the stars of the Lion
    To point us the path to the skies—
    To the Lethean peace of the skies—
Come up, in despite of the Lion,
    To shine on us with her bright eyes—

Come up through the lair of the Lion,
   With love in her luminous eyes."

But Psyche, uplifting her finger,
   Said—" Sadly this star I mistrust—
   Her pallor I strangely mistrust :—
Oh, hasten !—oh, let us not linger !
   Oh, fly !—let us fly !—for we must."
In terror she spoke, letting sink her
   Plumes till they trail'd in the dust—
   Till they sorrowfully trail'd in the dust.

I replied—" This is nothing but dreaming :
   Let us on by this tremulous light !
   Let us bathe in this crystalline light !
Its Sibylic splendour is beaming
   With Hope and in Beauty to-night :—
   See !—it flickers up the sky through the night !
Ah, we safely may trust to its gleaming,
   And be sure it will lead us aright—
We safely may trust to a gleaming
   That cannot but guide us aright,
   As it flickers up to Heaven through the night."

Thus I pacified Psyche and kiss'd her,
   And tempted her out of her gloom—
   And conquer'd her scruples and gloom ;
And we pass'd from the shade, as I kiss'd her,
   But were stopp'd by the door of a tomb—
   By the door of a legended tomb ;
And I said—" What is written, sweet sister,
   On the door of this legended tomb ?"
   She replied—" Ulalume—Ulalume—
   'Tis the vault of thy lost Ulalume !"

Then my heart it grew ashen and sober
   As the leaves that were crispèd and sere—

As the leaves that were withering and sere,
And I cried—" It was surely October,
　Was this very night of last year,
　That I journey'd—I journey'd down here—
　That I brought a dread burthen down here—
　On this night of all nights in the year,
　Ah, what demon has tempted me here?
Well I know now this dim lake of Auber—
　This misty mid-region of Weir—
Well I know now the dank tarn of Auber,
　This ghoul-haunted woodland of Weir."

EDGAR A. POE.

LINES

WRITTEN IN EARLY SPRING. 1798.

I HEARD a thousand blended notes,
　While in a grove I sate reclined,
In that sweet mood when pleasant thoughts
Bring sad thoughts to the mind.

To her fair works did Nature link
The human soul that through me ran;
And much it grieved my heart to think
What man has made of man.

Through primrose tufts, in that green bower.
The periwinkle trailed its wreaths;
And 'tis my faith that every flower
Enjoys the air it breathes.

The birds around me hopp'd and play'd,
Their thoughts I cannot measure:—
But the least motion which they made,
It seem'd a thrill of pleasure.

The budding twigs spread out their fan,
  To catch the breezy air;
And I must think, do all I can,
  That there was pleasure there.

If this belief from heaven be sent,
If such be Nature's holy plan,
Have I not reason to lament
What man has made of man?

              WORDSWORTH.

THE MAID'S LAMENT.

I LOVED him not; and yet now he is gone
  I feel I am alone.
I check'd him while he spoke; yet could he speak,
  Alas! I would not check.
For reasons not to love him once I sought,
  And wearied all my thought
To vex myself and him: I now would give
  My love could he but live
Who lately lived for me, and when he found
  'Twas vain, in holy ground
He hid his face amid the shades of death.
  I waste for him my breath
Who wasted his for me: but mine returns,
  And this lorn bosom burns
With stifling heat, heaving it up in sleep,
  And making me to weep
Tears that had melted his soft heart: for years
  Wept he as bitter tears.
Merciful God! such was his latest prayer,
  These may she never share!
Quieter is his breath, his breast more cold
  Than daisies in the mould,

Where children spell, athwart the churchyard gate,
    His name and life's brief date.
Pray for him, gentle souls, whoe'er you be,
    And oh! pray too for me!

W. S. LANDOR.

FAIRY SONG.

[FROM "THE MAID'S METAMORPHOSIS."]

BY the moon we sport and play,
    With the night begins our day;
As we dance the dew doth fall;
Trip it, little urchins all!
Lightly as the wingèd bee,
Two by two, and three by three,
And about go we, and about go we!

JOHN LYLY.

[EVENING.]

LOW-FLOWING breezes are roaming the
    broad valley dimm'd in the gloaming:
  Thorough the black-stemm'd pines only the far
    river shines.
Creeping through blossomy rushes and bowers of
    rose-blowing bushes,
  Down by the poplars tall rivulets babble and
    fall.
Barketh the shepherd-dog cheerly; the grass-
    hopper carolleth clearly;
  Deeply the turtle coos; shrilly the owlet halloos:

Winds creep; dews fall chilly; in her first sleep
    earth breathes stilly:
  Over the pools in the burn watergnats murmur
    and mourn.
Sadly the far kine loweth: the glimmering water
    out-floweth:
  Twin peaks shadow'd with pine slope to the
    dark hyaline.
Low-throned Hesper is stayèd between the two
    peaks; but the Naiad,
  Throbbing in mild unrest, holds him beneath in
    her breast.
The ancient poetess singeth that Hesperus all things
    bringeth,
  Soothing the wearied mind. Bring me my love,
    Rosalind!
Thou comest morning and even; she cometh not
    morning or even.
  False-eyed Hesper, unkind, where is my sweet
    Rosalind?

TENNYSON.

EDOM O' GORDON.

[OLD BALLAD.]

IT fell about the Martinmas,
    When the wind blew shrill and cauld,
Said Edom o' Gordon to his men,
    "We maun draw to a hauld.

"And whatna hauld sall we draw to,
    My merry men and me?
We will gae to the house of the Rodes,
    To see that fair ladye."

The ladye stood on her castle wa',
   Beheld baith dale and down;
There she was avare of a host of men
   Came riding towards the toun.[1]

"O see ye not, my merry men a'?
   O see ye not what I see?
Methinks I see a host of men;
   I marvel who they be."

She ween'd it had been her luvely lord,
   As he cam' riding hame;
It was the traitor, Edom o' Gordon,
   Wha reck'd nor sin nor shame.

She had nae sooner buskit hersell
   And putten on her goun,
Till Edom o' Gordon an' his men
   Were round about the toun.

They had nae sooner supper set,
   Nae sooner said the grace,
But Edom o' Gordon an' his men
   Were lighted about the place.

The ladye ran up to her tower-head,
   As fast as she could hie,
To see if by her fair speeches
   She could wi' him agree.

"Come doun to me, ye ladye gay,
   Come doun, come doun to me;
This night sall ye lig within mine armes,
   To-morrow my bride sall be."

"I winna come down, ye fause Gordon,
   I winna come down to thee;

---

[1] *Toun* (town), an enclosed place.

I winna forsake my ain dear lord,—
    And he is na far frae me."

" Gie owre your house, ye lady fair,
    Gie owre your house to me;
Or I sall burn yoursell therein,
    But and your babies three."

" I winna gie owre, ye fause Gordon,
    To nae sic traitor as thee.
And if ye burn my ain dear babes,
    My lord sall mak' ye dree.

" Now reach my pistoll, Glaud, my man,
    And charge ye weel my gun;
For, but an I pierce that bluidy butcher,
    My babes, we been undone!"

She stude upon her castle wa'
    And let twa bullets flee:
She miss'd that bluidy butcher's heart,
    And only razed his knee.

" Set fire to the house!" quo' fause Gordon,
    Wud[1] wi' dule and ire:
" Fause ladye, ye sall rue that shot,
    As ye burn in the fire!"

" Wae worth, wae worth ye, Jock, my man!
    I paid ye weel your fee;
Why pu' ye out the grund-wa' stane.
    Lets in the reek to me?

" And e'en wae worth ye, Jock, my man!
    I paid ye weel your hire;
Why pu' ye out the grund-wa' stane,
    To me lets in the fire?"

---

[1] *Wud*, mad.

"Ye paid me weel my hire, ladye,
   Ye paid me weel my fee:
But now I'm Edom o' Gordon's man,—
   Maun either do or dee."

O then bespake her little son,
   Sat on the nurse's knee:
Says, "Mither dear, gie owre this house,
   For the reek it smothers me."

"I wad gie a' my gowd, my bairn,
   Sae wad I a' my fee,
For ae blast o' the western wind,
   To blaw the reek frae thee."

O then bespake her daughter dear,—
   She was baith jimp and sma':
"O row' me in a pair o' sheets,
   And tow me owre the wa'!"

They row'd her in a pair o' sheets,
   And tow'd her owre the wa';
But on the point o' Gordon's spear
   She gat a deadly fa'.

O bonnie, bonnie was her mouth,
   And cherry were her cheeks,
And clear, clear was her yellow hair,
   Whereon the red blood dreeps.

Then wi' his spear he turn'd her owre;
   O gin her face was wan!
He said, "Ye are the first that e'er
   I wish'd alive again."

He turn'd her owre and owre again ;
  O gin her skin was white !
" I might hae spared that bonnie face
  To hae been some man's delight."

" Busk and boun, my merry men a',
  For ill dooms I do guess ;—
I cannot look on that bonnie face
  As it lies on the grass."

" Wha looks to freits,[1] my master dear,
  Its freits will follow them ;
Let it ne'er be said that Edom o' Gordon
  Was daunted by a dame."

But when the ladye saw the fire
  Come flaming o'er her head,
She wept, and kiss'd her children twain,
  Says, " Bairns, we been but dead."

The Gordon then his bugle blew,
  And said, " Awa', awa' !
This House o' the Rodes is a' in a flame,
  I hauld it time to ga'."

And this way lookit her ain dear lord,
  As he came owre the lea ;
He saw his castle a' in a lowe,
  Sae far as he could see.

" Put on, put on, my wighty men,
  As fast as ye can dri'e !
For he that's hindmost o' the thrang
  Sall ne'er get good o' me."

---

[1] *Freits*, (frights?), ill-omens, ill-luck.

Then some they rade, and some they ran,
   Out-owre the grass and bent;
But ere the foremost could win up,
   Baith lady and babes were brent.

And after the Gordon he is gane,
   Sae fast as he might dri'e;
And soon i' the Gordon's foul heart's blude
   He's wroken his fair ladye.

PHILLIDA AND CORYDON.

IN the merry month of May,
   In a morn, by break of day,
Forth I walk'd by the wood-side,
Whenas May was in his pride:
There I spièd, all alone,
Phillida and Corydon.
Much ado there was, God wot;
He would love, and she would not.
She said, never man was true;
He said, none was false to you.
He said, he had loved her long;
She said, love should have no wrong.
Corydon would kiss her then;
She said, maids must kiss no men,
Till they do for good and all:
Then she made the shepherd call
All the heavens to witness truth,
Never loved a truer youth.
Then with many a pretty oath,
Yea and nay, and faith and troth,
Such as silly shepherds use,
When they will not love abuse,

Love, which had been long deluded,
Was with kisses sweet concluded;
And Phillida with garlands gay
Was made the Lady of the May.

Nicholas Breton.

LORD RANDAL.

"O WHERE hae ye been, Lord Randal, my
    son?
O where hae ye been, my handsome young man?"
" I hae been to the wood; mother, make my bed
    soon,
For I'm weary wi' hunting, and fain would lie
    down."

" Where gat ye your dinner, Lord Randal, my son?
Where gat ye your dinner, my handsome young
    man?"
" I dined wi' my love; mother, make my bed soon,
For I'm weary wi' hunting, and fain would lie
    down."

" What gat ye to dinner, Lord Randal, my son?
What gat ye to dinner, my handsome young man?"
" I gat eels boil'd in broo'; mother, make my bed
    soon,
For I'm weary wi' hunting, and fain would lie
    down."

" And where are your bloodhounds, Lord Randal,
    my son?
And where are your bloodhounds, my handsome
    young man?"

" O they swell'd and they died; mother, make my
       bed soon,
For I'm weary wi' hunting, and fain would lie
       down."

" O I fear ye are poison'd, Lord Randal, my son!
O I fear ye are poison'd, my handsome young man!"
" O yes, I am poison'd! mother, make my bed
       soon,
For I'm sick at the heart, and I fain would lie down."
     Scott's *Border Minstrelsy*.

[EVENING.]

SWEET after showers, ambrosial air,
 That rollest from the gorgeous gloom
 Of evening over brake and bloom
And meadow, slowly breathing bare

The round of space, and rapt below
 Through all the dewy-tassell'd wood,
 And shadowing down the horned flood
In ripples, fan my brows and blow

The fever from my cheek, and sigh
 The full new life that feeds thy breath
 Throughout my frame till Doubt and Death,
Ill brethren, let the fancy fly

From belt to belt of crimson seas
 On leagues of odour streaming far,
 To where in yonder orient star
A hundred spirits whisper " Peace."
     In Memoriam.

THE BRIDGE OF SIGHS.

"Drown'd! drown'd!"—HAMLET.

ONE more Unfortunate,
Weary of breath,
Rashly importunate,
Gone to her death!

Take her up tenderly,
Lift her with care;
Fashion'd so slenderly,
Young, and so fair!

Look at her garments
Clinging like cerements;
Whilst the wave constantly
Drips from her clothing;
Take her up instantly,
Loving, not loathing.—

Touch her not scornfully;
Think of her mournfully,
Gently and humanly;
Not of the stains of her,
All that remains of her
Now is pure womanly.

Make no deep scrutiny
Into her mutiny
Rash and undutiful:
Past all dishonour,
Death has left on her
Only the beautiful.

Still, for all slips of hers,
One of Eve's family—
Wipe those poor lips of hers
Oozing so clammily.

Loop up her tresses
Escaped from the comb,
Her fair auburn tresses;
Whilst wonderment guesses
Where was her home?

Who was her father?
Who was her mother?
Had she a sister?
Had she a brother?
Or was there a dearer one
Still, and a nearer one
Yet, than all other?

Alas! for the rarity
Of Christian charity
Under the sun!
Oh! it was pitiful!
Near a whole city full,
Home she had none.

Sisterly, brotherly,
Fatherly, motherly
Feelings had changed:
Love, by harsh evidence,
Thrown from its eminence;
Even God's providence
Seeming estranged.

Where the lamps quiver
So far in the river,

With many a light
From window and casement,
From garret to basement,
She stood, with amazement,
Houseless by night.

The bleak wind of March
Made her tremble and shiver:
But not the dark arch,
Or the black flowing river:
Mad from life's history
Glad to death's mystery
Swift to be hurl'd—
Any where, any where
Out of the world!

In she plunged boldly,
No matter how coldly
The rough river ran,—
Over the brink of it;—
Picture it—think of it,
Dissolute man!

Take her up tenderly,
Lift her with care;
Fashion'd so slenderly,
Young, and so fair!

Ere her limbs frigidly
Stiffen too rigidly,
Decently,—kindly,—
Smoothe, and compose them;
And her eyes, close them,
Staring so blindly!
Dreadfully staring
Through muddy impurity,

As when with the daring
Last look of despairing
Fix'd on futurity.

Perishing gloomily,
Spurr'd by contumely,
Cold inhumanity,
Burning insanity,
Into her rest.—
Cross her hands humbly
As if praying dumbly,
Over her breast!

Owning her weakness,
Her evil behaviour,
And leaving, with meekness,
Her sins to her Saviour!

     HOOD.

SONG.

[AT A LADY'S WINDOW.]

FROM " CYMBELINE."

HARK! hark! the lark at heaven's gate sings,
 And Phœbus 'gins arise,
His steeds to water at those springs
 On chaliced flowers that lies;
And winking marybuds begin
 To ope their golden eyes;
With every thing that pretty bin:
 My lady sweet, arise.
  Arise, arise!
    SHAKESPEARE.

SONG.

FALSE friend, wilt thou smile or weep
   When my life is laid asleep?
Little cares for a smile or a tear
The clay-cold corpse upon the bier;
   Farewell! Heigh-ho!
   What is this whispers low?
There is a snake in thy smile, my dear,
And bitter poison within thy tear.

Sweet sleep, were death like to thee,
Or if thou couldst mortal be,
I would close these eyes of pain,—
When to wake? Never again.
   O world, farewell!
   Listen to the passing-bell!
It says thou and I must part,
With a light and a heavy heart.
                                SHELLEY.

THE WIFE OF USHER'S WELL.

[OLD BALLAD.]

THERE lived a wife at Usher's Well,
   And a wealthy wife was she,
She had three stout and stalwart sons,
   And sent them o'er the sea.

They hadna been a week from her,
    A week but barely ane,
When word cam' to the carline wife,
    That her three sons were gane.

They hadna been a week from her,
    A week but barely three,
When word cam' to the carline wife,
    That her sons she'd never see.

" I wish the wind may never cease,
    Nor fish be in the flood,
Till my three sons come hame to me,
    In earthly flesh and blood!"

It fell about the Martinmas,
    When nights are lang and mirk,
The carline wife's three sons cam' hame,
    And their hats were o' the birk.

It neither grew in syke nor ditch,
    Nor yet in ony sheugh;
But at the gates o' Paradise
    That birk grew fair eneugh.

" Blow up the fire, my maidens!
    Bring water from the well!
For a' my house shall feast this night,
    Since my three sons are well."

And she has made to them a bed,
    She's made it large and wide;
And she's ta'en her mantle round about,
    Sat down at the bed-side.

Up then crew the red, red cock,
    And up and crew the gray;

The eldest to the youngest said
  " 'Tis time we were away.

" The cock doth craw, the day doth daw,
  The channerin' worm doth chide ;
Gin we be miss'd out o' our place,
  A sair pain we maun bide."

" Lie still, lie still but a little wee while,
  Lie still but if we may ;
Gin my mother should miss us when she wakes,
  She'll go mad ere it be day.

" Our mother has nae mair but us ;
  See where she leans asleep ;
The mantle that was on herself,
  She has happ'd it round our feet."

O it's they have ta'en up their mother's mantle,
  And they've hung it on a pin :
" O lang may ye hing, my mother's mantle,
  Ere ye hap us again !

" Fare-ye-weel, my mother dear !
  Fareweel to barn and byre !
And fare-ye-weel, the bonny lass,
  That kindles my mother's fire."

THE KNIGHT'S TOMB.

WHERE is the grave of Sir Arthur O'Kellyn?
  Where may the grave of that good man be ?
By the side of a spring on the breast of Helvellyn,
  Under the twigs of a young birch tree.

The oak that in summer was sweet to hear
And rustled its leaves in the fall of the year,
And whistled and roar'd in the winter alone,
Is gone, and the birch in its stead has grown.
The Knight's bones are dust,
And his good sword rust;
His soul is with the saints, I trust.

COLERIDGE.

THE SHADOW OF NIGHT.

I.

HOW strange it is to wake
   And watch while others sleep,
Till sight and hearing ache
   For objects that may keep
The awful inner sense
   Unroused, lest it should mark
The life that haunts the emptiness
   And horror of the dark.

II.

How strange the distant bay
   Of dogs; how wild the note
Of cocks that scream for day,
   In homesteads far remote;
How strange and wild to hear
   The old and crumbling tower,
Amidst the darkness, suddenly
   Take life and speak the hour!

III.

If dreams or panic dread
   Reveal the gloom of gloom,

Kiss thou the pillow'd head
  By thine, and soft resume
The confident embrace,
  And so each other keep
In the sure league of amity,
  And the safe lap of sleep.

IV.

Albeit the love-sick brain
  Affects the dreary moon,
Ill things alone refrain
  From life's nocturnal swoon:
Men melancholy mad,
  Beasts ravenous and sly,
The robber and the murderer,
  Remorse, with lidless eye.

V.

The nightingale is gay,
  For she can vanquish night;
Dreaming, she sings of day,
  Notes that make darkness bright:
But when the refluent gloom
  Saddens the gaps of song,
We charge on her the dolefulness,
  And call her crazed with wrong.

VI.

'Tis well that men should lie
  All senseless, while the sun,
Coursing the nether sky,
  Leaves half the world o'er-run
With baleful shapes unseen;
  And foul it is when we
By loud carousal desecrate
  Night's evil sanctity.

VII.

'Twere good that all should pray,
    And so lie down to rest,
While yet the wholesome day
    Is lingering in the West.
His prayer shall turn to peace,
    Who still regards with awe
The midnight's noxious mystery,
    And nature's genial law.

            COVENTRY PATMORE.

THE FAIRY THORN.

AN ULSTER BALLAD.

"GET up, our Anna dear, from the weary
    spinning wheel;
For your father's on the hill, and your mother
    is asleep:
Come up above the crags, and we'll dance a high-
    land reel
Around the fairy thorn on the steep."

At Anna Grace's door 'twas thus the maidens cried,
    Three merry maidens fair in kirtles of the green;
And Anna laid the rock and the weary wheel aside,
    The fairest of the four, I ween.

They're glancing through the glimmer of the quiet
    eve,
    Away in milky wavings of neck and ankle bare;
The heavy-sliding stream in its sleepy song they
    leave,
    And the crags in the ghostly air:

And linking hand and hand, and singing as they go,
   The maids along the hill-side have ta'en their fearless way,
Till they come to where the rowan trees in lonely beauty grow
   Beside the Fairy Hawthorn grey.

The hawthorn stands between the ashes tall and slim,
   Like matron with her twin grand-daughters at her knee;
The rowan berries cluster o'er her low head grey and dim
   In ruddy kisses sweet to see.

The merry maidens four have ranged them in a row,
   Between each lovely couple a stately rowan stem,
And away in mazes wavy, like skimming birds they go,
   Oh, never caroll'd bird like them!

But solemn is the silence of the silvery haze
   That drinks away their voices in echoless repose,
And dreamily the evening has still'd the haunted braes,
   And dreamier the gloaming grows.

And sinking one by one, like lark-notes from the sky
   When the falcon's shadow saileth across the open shaw,
Are hush'd the maiden's voices, as cowering down they lie
   In the flutter of their sudden awe.

For, from the air above, and the grassy ground beneath,

And from the mountain-ashes and the old
    Whitethorn between,
A power of faint enchantment doth through their
    beings breathe,
And they sink down together on the green.

They sink together silent, and stealing side to side,
    They fling their lovely arms o'er their drooping
    necks so fair,
Then vainly strive again their naked arms to hide,
    For their shrinking necks again are bare.

Thus clasp'd and prostrate all, with their heads
    together bow'd,
    Soft o'er their bosom's beating—the only human
    sound—
They hear the silky footsteps of the silent fairy
    crowd,
    Like a river in the air, gliding round.

Nor scream can any raise, nor prayer can any say,
    But wild, wild, the terror of the speechless
    three—
For they feel fair Anna Grace drawn silently away,
    By whom they dare not look to see.

They feel their tresses twine with her parting
    locks of gold,
    And the curls elastic falling, as her head with-
    draws;
They feel her sliding arms from their tranced arms
    unfold,
    But they dare not look to see the cause:

For heavy on their senses the faint enchantment
    lies
    Through all that night of anguish and perilous
    amaze;

And neither fear nor wonder can ope their quiver-
   ing eyes
  Or their limbs from the cold ground raise.

Till out of Night the Earth has roll'd her dewy side,
  With every haunted mountain and streamy vale
   below ;
When, as the mist dissolves in the yellow morning-
   tide,
  The maidens' trance dissolveth so.

Then fly the ghastly three as swiftly as they may,
  And tell their tale of sorrow to anxious friends
   in vain—
They pined away and died within the year and day,
  And ne'er was Anna Grace seen again.
                    SAMUEL FERGUSON.

THE HOUSE.

THERE is no architect can build
   As the Muse can ;
She is skilful to select
   Materials for her plan ;

Rafters warily to choose
   Of immortal pine,
Or cedar incorruptible,
   Worthy her design.

She threads dark Alpine forests,
   Or valleys by the sea,
In many lands, with painful steps,
   Ere she can find a tree.

She ransacks mines and ledges,
  And quarries every rock,
To hew the famous adamant
  For each eternal block.

She lays her beams in music,
  In music every one,
To the cadence of the whirling world
  Which dances round the sun.

That so they shall not be displaced
  By lapses or by wars,
But for the love of happy souls
  Outlive the newest stars.

EMERSON.

HIS WISH TO PRIVACY.

GIVE me a cell
  To dwell,
Where no foot hath
  A path;
There will I spend,
  And end,
My wearied years
  In tears.

HERRICK.

LOVE.

ALL thoughts, all passions, all delights,
  Whatever stirs this mortal frame,
All are but ministers of Love,
  And feed his sacred flame.

Oft in my waking dreams do I
Live o'er again that happy hour,
When midway on the mount I lay,
    Beside the ruin'd tower.

The moonshine, stealing o'er the scene
Had blended with the light of eve;
And she was there, my hope, my joy,
    My own dear Genevieve!

She lean'd against the armèd man,
The statue of the armèd knight;
She stood and listen'd to my lay,
    Amid the lingering light.

Few sorrows hath she of her own,
My hope! my joy! my Genevieve!
She loves me best whene'er I sing
    The songs that make her grieve.

I play'd a soft and doleful air,
I sang an old and moving story—
An old rude song, that suited well
    That ruin wild and hoary.

She listen'd with a flitting blush,
With downcast eyes and modest grace;
For well she knew I could not choose
    But gaze upon her face.

I told her of the Knight that wore
Upon his shield a burning brand;
And that for ten long years he woo'd
    The Lady of the Land.

I told her how he pined: and ah!
The deep, the low, the pleading tone

With which I sang another's love,
    Interpreted my own.

She listen'd with a flitting blush,
With downcast eyes, and modest grace;
And she forgave me, that I gazed
    Too fondly on her face!

But when I told the cruel scorn
That crazed that bold and lovely Knight,
And that he cross'd the mountain-woods,
    Nor rested day nor night;

That sometimes from the savage den,
And sometimes from the darksome shade,
And sometimes starting up at once
    In green and sunny glade,—

There came and look'd him in the face
An angel beautiful and bright;
And that he knew it was a Fiend,
    This miserable Knight!

And that unknowing what he did,
He leap'd among a murderous band,
And saved from outrage worse than death
    The Lady of the Land;—

And how she wept, and clasp'd his knees;
And how she tended him in vain—
And ever strove to expiate
    The scorn that crazed his brain;—

And that she nursed him in a cave;
And how his madness went away,
When on the yellow forest-leaves
    A dying man he lay;—

His dying words—but when I reach'd
That tenderest strain of all the ditty,
My faltering voice and pausing harp
    Disturbed her soul with pity!

All impulses of soul and sense
Had thrill'd my guileless Genevieve;
The music and the doleful tale,
    The rich and balmy eve;

And hopes, and fears that kindle hope,
An undistinguishable throng,
And gentle wishes long subdued,
    Subdued and cherish'd long!

She wept with pity and delight,
She blush'd with love, and virgin shame;
And like the murmur of a dream,
    I heard her breathe my name.

Her bosom heaved—she stepp'd aside,
As conscious of my look she stept—
Then suddenly, with timorous eye
    She fled to me and wept.

She half inclosed me with her arms,
She press'd me with a meek embrace;
And bending back her head look'd up,
    And gazed upon my face.

'Twas partly love, and partly fear,
And partly 'twas a bashful art,
That I might rather feel, than see
    The swelling of her heart.

I calm'd her fears, and she was calm,
And told her love with virgin pride;
And so I won my Genevieve,
   My bright and beauteous Bride.

COLERIDGE.

SONG FOR AUGUST.

BENEATH this starry arch
  Nought resteth or is still;
But all things hold their march
  As if by one great will.
    Moves one, move all,—
    Hark to the footfall,—
      On, on, for ever.

Yon sheaves were once but seed;
Will ripens into deed:
As cave-drops swell the streams
Day thoughts feed nightly dreams;
And sorrow tracketh wrong
As echo follows song,—
    On, on, for ever.

By night, like stars on high,
  The hours reveal their train;
They whisper and pass by;
  I never watch in vain.
    Moves one, move all,—
    Hark to the footfall,—
      On, on, for ever.

They pass the cradle head,
And there a promise shed;

They pass the moist new grave,
And bid rank verdure wave;
They bear through every clime
The harvest of all time,—
   On, on, for ever.
       HARRIET MARTINEAU.

[LULLABY FOR TITANIA.]

FROM " A MIDSUMMER NIGHT'S DREAM."

First Fairy.
YOU spotted snakes with double tongue,
  Thorny hedgehogs, be not seen;
Newts, and blind worms, do no wrong;
  Come not near our fairy queen.

Chorus.
Philomel with melody
Sing in our sweet lullaby:
Lulla, lulla, lullaby: lulla, lulla, lullaby:
Never harm, nor spell nor charm,
  Come our lovely lady nigh!
So good-night, with lullaby.

Second Fairy.
Weaving spiders, come not here;
  Hence, you long-legg'd spinners, hence;
Beetles black, approach not near;
  Worm, nor snail, do no offence.

Chorus.
Philomel with melody
Sing in our sweet lullaby:

Lulla, lulla, lullaby: lulla, lulla, lullaby:
  Never harm, nor spell nor charm,
    Come our lovely lady nigh!
    So good-night, with lullaby.
SHAKESPEARE.

UPON THE IMAGE OF DEATH.

BEFORE my face the picture hangs
    That dailie should put me in minde
Of those cold qualms and bitter pangs
    That shortly I am like to finde :
      But yet, alas! full little I
      Do think hereon, that I must die.

I often look upon a face
    Most uglie, grislie, bare, and thin ;
I often view the hollow place
    Where eyes and nose have sometime been ;
      I see the bones across that lie ;
      Yet little think, that I must die.

I read the label underneathe,
    That telleth me whereto I must :
I see the sentence eke that saithe
    " Remember, man, that thou art duste ;"
      But yet, alas, but seldom I
      Do think indeed, that I must die!

Continually at my bed's head
    An hearse doth hang, which doth me tell
That I, ere morning, may be dead,
    Though now I feel myself full well :
      But yet, alas, for all this, I
      Have little minde that I must die !

The gowne which I do use to weare,
  The knife, wherewith I cut my meate,
And eke that old and ancient chair
  Which is my only usual seate,
    All these do tell me I must die;
    And yet my life amende not I!

My ancestors are turn'd to clay,
  And many of my mates are gone;
My youngers daily drop away;—
  And can I think to 'scape alone?
    No, no, I know that I must die;
    And yet my life amende not I!

Not Solomon, for all his wit,
  Nor Samson, though he were so strong,
No king, nor ever person yet,
  Could 'scape, but Death laid him along!
    Wherefore I know that I must die;
    And yet my life amende not I!

Though all the east did quake to hear
  Of Alexander's dreadful name,
And all the west did likewise fear
  The sound of Julius Cæsar's fame,
    Yet both by death in duste now lie;
    Who then can 'scape, but he must die?

If none can 'scape Death's dreadful darte,
  If rich and poor his beck obey,
If strong, if wise, if all do smarte,
  Then I to 'scape shall have no way.
    O grant me grace, O God, that I
    My life may mende, sith I must die!

ROBERT SOUTHWELL.

THE ANGEL.

I DREAM'D a dream, what can it mean?
    And that I was a maiden queen,
Guarded by an Angel mild:
Witless woe, was ne'er beguiled!

And I wept both night and day,
And he wiped my tears away;
And I wept both day and night,
And hid from him my heart's delight.

So he took his wings and fled;
Then the morn blush'd rosy red;
I dried my tears, and arm'd my fears
With ten thousand shields and spears.

Soon my Angel came again;
I was arm'd, he came in vain;
For the time of youth was fled,
And grey hairs were on my head.
                    WILLIAM BLAKE.

LOVELY MARY DONNELLY.

AN IRISH BALLAD.

OH, lovely Mary Donnelly, it's you I love the
        best!
If fifty girls were round you I'd hardly see the rest.

Be what it may the time of day, the place be where
　　it will,
Sweet looks of Mary Donnelly, they bloom before
　　me still.

Her eyes like mountain water that's flowing on a
　　rock,
How clear they are, how dark they are! and they
　　give me many a shock.
Red rowans warm in sunshine and wetted with a
　　show'r,
Could ne'er express the charming lip that has me
　　in its pow'r.

Her nose is straight and handsome, her eyebrows
　　lifted up,
Her chin is very neat and pert, and smooth like a
　　china cup,
Her hair's the brag of Ireland, so weighty and so
　　fine;
It's rolling down upon her neck, and gather'd in a
　　twine.

The dance o' last Whit-Monday night exceeded
　　all before,
No pretty girl for miles about was missing from
　　the floor;
But Mary kept the belt of love, and O but she
　　was gay!
She danced a jig, she sung a song, that took my
　　heart away.

When she stood up for dancing, her steps were so
　　complete,
The music nearly kill'd itself to listen to her feet;

The fiddler moan'd his blindness, he heard her so
    much praised,
But bless'd himself he wasn't deaf when once her
    voice she raised.

And evermore I'm whistling or lilting what you
    sung,
Your smile is always in my heart, your name be-
    side my tongue;
But you've as many sweethearts as you'd count on
    both your hands,
And for myself there's not a thumb or little finger
    stands.

Oh, you're the flower o' womankind in country or
    in town;
The higher I exalt you, the lower I'm cast down.
If some great lord should come this way, and see
    your beauty bright,
And you to be his lady, I'd own it was but right.

O might we live together in a lofty palace hall,
Where joyful music rises, and where scarlet cur-
    tains fall!
O might we live together in a cottage mean and
    small;
With sods of grass the only roof, and mud the only
    wall!

O lovely Mary Donnelly, your beauty's my distress.
It's far too beauteous to be mine, but I'll never
    wish it less.
The proudest place would fit your face, and I am
    poor and low;
But blessings be about you, dear, wherever you
    may go!   WILLIAM ALLINGHAM.

WALY, WALY.

[OLD BALLAD.]

O WALY, waly, up the bank,
   O waly, waly, doun the brae,
And waly, waly, yon burn-side,
   Where I and my love were wont to gae!
I lean'd my back unto an aik,
   I thocht it was a trustie tree,
But first it bow'd and syne it brak',—
   Sae my true love did lichtlie me.

O waly, waly, but love be bonnie
   A little time while it is new;
But when it's auld it waxeth cauld,
   And fadeth awa' like the morning dew.
O wherefore should I busk my heid,
   Or wherefore should I kame my hair?
For my true love has me forsook,
   And says he'll never lo'e me mair.

Noo Arthur's Seat sall be my bed,
   The sheets sall ne'er be press'd by me:
Saint Anton's well sall be my drink:
   Since my true love's forsaken me.
Martinmas wind, when wilt thou blaw,
   And shake the green leaves off the tree?
O gentle death when wilt thou come?
   For of my life I am wearie.

'Tis not the frost that freezes fell,
   Nor blawing snaw's inclemencie,

'Tis not sic cauld that makes me cry;
    But my love's heart grown cauld to me.
When we cam' in by Glasgow toun,
    We were a comely sicht to see;
My love was clad in the black velvet,
    An' I mysel' in cramasie.[1]

But had I wist before I kiss'd
    That love had been so ill to win,
I'd lock'd my heart in a case o' gowd,
    And pinn'd it wi' a siller pin.
Oh, oh! if my young babe were born,
    And set upon the nurse's knee;
And I mysel' were dead and gane,
    And the green grass growing over me!

[HYMN TO DIANA.]

QUEEN and huntress, chaste and fair,
    Now the sun is laid to sleep,
Seated in thy silver chair
    State in wonted manner keep:
Hesperus entreats thy light,
Goddess excellently bright!

Earth, let not thy envious shade
    Dare itself to interpose;
Cynthia's shining orb was made
    Heav'n to clear, when day did close:
Bless us then with wishèd sight,
Goddess excellently bright!

---

[1] *Cramasie*, cramoisie, crimson.

Lay thy bow of pearl apart,
   And thy crystal shining quiver;
Give unto the flying hart
   Space to breathe, how short soever:
Thou that mak'st a day of night,
Goddess excellently bright!

BEN JONSON.

SONNET.

EAGLES.

(COMPOSED AT DUNOLLIE CASTLE IN THE BAY OF OBAN.)

DISHONOUR'D Rock and Ruin! that, by law
Tyrannic, keep the Bird of Jove embarr'd
Like a lone criminal whose life is spared.
Vex'd is he, and screams loud. The last I saw
Was on the wing; stooping, he struck with awe
Man, bird, and beast, then, with a consort pair'd,
From a bold headland, their loved aery's guard,
Flew high above Atlantic waves, to draw
Light from the fountain of the setting sun.
Such was this Prisoner once; and, when his plumes
The sea-blast ruffles as the storm comes on,
In spirit for a moment he resumes
His rank 'mong free-born creatures that live free,
His power, his beauty, and his majesty.

WORDSWORTH.

THE REVERIE OF POOR SUSAN.

AT the corner of Wood Street, when daylight appears,
Hangs a thrush that sings loud, it has sung for three years:
Poor Susan has pass'd by the spot, and has heard
In the silence of morning the song of the Bird.

'Tis a note of enchantment; what ails her? She sees
A mountain ascending, a vision of trees;
Bright volumes of vapour through Lothbury glide,
And a river flows on through the vale of Cheapside.

Green pastures she views in the midst of the dale,
Down which she so often has tripp'd with her pail;
And a single small cottage, a nest like a dove's,
The one only dwelling on earth that she loves.

She looks, and her heart is in heaven: but they fade,
The mist and the river, the hill and the shade:
The stream will not flow, and the hill will not rise,
And the colours have all pass'd away from her eyes!
WORDSWORTH.

THE PAINS OF SLEEP.

ERE on my bed my limbs I lay,
It hath not been my use to pray
With moving lips or bended knees;
But silently by slow degrees,
My spirit I to Love compose,
In humble trust mine eye-lids close,
With reverential resignation,
No wish conceived, no thought exprest,
Only a sense of supplication;
A sense o'er all my soul imprest—
That I am weak, yet not unblest,
Since in me, round me, everywhere
Eternal strength and wisdom are.

But yester-night I pray'd aloud
In anguish and in agony,
Up-starting from the fiendish crowd
Of shapes and thoughts that tortured me:
A lurid light, a trampling throng,
Sense of intolerable wrong,
And whom I scorn'd, those only strong!
Thirst of revenge, the powerless will
Still baffled, and yet burning still!
Desire with loathing strangely mix'd
On wild or hateful objects fix'd:
Fantastic passions! maddening brawl!
And shame and terror over all!
Deeds to be hid which were not hid,
Which all confused I could not know,
Whether I suffer'd, or I did:

For all seem'd guilt, remorse or woe,
My own or others', still the same
Life-stifling fear, soul-stifling shame.

So two nights pass'd: the night's dismay
Sadden'd and stunn'd the coming day.
Sleep, the wide blessing, seem'd to me
Distemper's worst calamity.
The third night, when my own loud scream
Had waked me from the fiendish dream,
O'ercome with sufferings strange and wild,
I wept as I had been a child;
And having thus by tears subdued
My anguish to a milder mood,
Such punishments, I said, were due
To natures deepliest stain'd with sin,—
For aye entempesting anew
The unfathomable hell within,
The horror of their deeds to view,
To know and loathe, yet wish and do!
Such griefs with some men well agree,
But wherefore, wherefore fall on me?
To be beloved is all I need,
And whom I love, I love indeed.
                                COLERIDGE.

THE SKYLARK.

BIRD of the wilderness,
    Blithesome and cumberless,
Sweet be thy matin o'er moorland and lea!
    Emblem of happiness,
    Blest is thy dwelling-place—
O to abide in the desert with thee!

Wild is thy lay and loud,
Far in the downy cloud,
Love gives it energy, love gave it birth.
Where, on thy dewy wing,
Where art thou journeying?
Thy lay is in heaven, thy love is on earth.

O'er fell and fountain sheen,
O'er moor and mountain green,
O'er the red streamer that heralds the day,
Over the cloudlet dim,
Over the rainbow's rim,
Musical cherub, soar singing away!

Then, when the gloaming comes,
Low in the heather-blooms
Sweet will thy welcome and bed of love be!
Emblem of happiness,
Blest is thy dwelling-place—
O to abide in the desert with thee!

JAMES HOGG.

EDWARD, EDWARD.

[OLD BALLAD.]

"WHY does your brand sae drap wi' blude,
   Edward, Edward?
Why does your brand sae drap wi' blude,
 And why sae sad gang ye, O?"
"O, I hae kill'd my hawk sae gude,
   Mither, mither:
O, I hae kill'd my hawk sae gude:
 And I hae nae mair but he, O."

" Your hawk's blude was never sae red,
    Edward, Edward:
Your hawk's blude was never sae red,
  My dear son, I tell thee, O."
" O, I hae kill'd my red-roan steed,
    Mither, mither:
O, I hae kill'd my red-roan steed,
  That carried me fair and free, O."

" 'Gin your steed be gane, ye hae plenty mair,
    Edward, Edward,
'Gin your steed be gane, ye hae plenty mair;
  Some ither dule ye dree, O."
" O, I hae kill'd my father dear,
    Mither, mither:
O, I hae kill'd my father dear,
  Alas! and wae is me, O."

" And whatten penance will ye dree for that,
    Edward, Edward?
And whatten penance will ye dree for that?
  My dear son, now tell me, O."
" I'll set my feet in yonder boat,
    Mither, mither:
I'll set my feet in yonder boat,
  And I'll fare over the sea, O."

" And what will ye do wi' your towers and your ha',
    Edward, Edward?
And what will ye do wi' your towers and your ha',
  That were sae fair to see, O?"
" I'll let them stand till they doun fa',
    Mither, mither:
I'll let them stand till they doun fa';
  For here never mair maun I be, O."

"And what will ye leave to your bairns and your
            wife,
                Edward, Edward?
And what will ye leave to your bairns and your wife,
    When you gang over the sea, O?"
"The warld's room: let them beg through life,
            Mither, mither:
The warld's room: let them beg through life;
    For them never mair will I see, O."

"And what will ye leave to your ain mither dear,
            Edward, Edward?
And what will ye leave to your ain mither dear?
    My dear son, now tell me, O."
"The curse of hell frae me shall ye bear,
            Mither, mither!
The curse of hell frae me shall ye bear,
    Sic counsels ye gave to me, O!"

PERCY's *Reliques*.

ODE ON MELANCHOLY.

NO, no! go not to Lethe, neither twist
    Wolf's-bane, tight-rooted, for its poisonous
            wine;
Nor suffer thy pale forehead to be kiss'd
    By night-shade, ruby grape of Proserpine;
Make not your rosary of yew-berries,
    Nor let the beetle, nor the death-moth be
Your mournful Psyche, nor the downy owl
A partner in your sorrow's mysteries;
    For shade to shade will come too drowsily,
And drown the wakeful anguish of the soul.

But when the melancholy fit shall fall
    Sudden from heaven like a weeping cloud,
That fosters the droop-headed flowers all,
    And hides the green hill in an April shroud;
Then glut thy sorrow on a morning rose,
Or on the rainbow of the salt sand-wave,
    Or on the wealth of globed peonies;
Or if thy mistress some rich anger shows,
Emprison her soft hand, and let her rave,
    And feed deep, deep upon her peerless eyes.

She dwells with Beauty—Beauty that must die;
    And Joy, whose hand is ever at his lips
Bidding adieu; and aching Pleasure nigh,
    Turning to poison while the bee-mouth sips:
Ay, in the very temple of Delight
Veil'd Melancholy has her sovran shrine,
    Though seen of none save him whose strenuous tongue
Can burst Joy's grape against his palate fine;
His soul shall taste the sadness of her might,
    And be among her cloudy trophies hung.

KEATS.

SONNET.

THE TROSACHS.

THERE'S not a nook within this solemn Pass
    But were an apt confessional for One
Taught by his summer spent, his autumn gone,
That Life is but a tale of morning grass
Wither'd at eve. From scenes of art which chase
That thought away, turn, and with watchful eyes

Feed it 'mid Nature's old felicities,
Rocks, rivers, and smooth lakes more clear than
    glass
Untouch'd, unbreathed upon. Thrice happy quest,
If from a golden perch of aspen spray
(October's workmanship to rival May)
The pensive warbler of the ruddy breast
That moral sweeten by a heaven-taught lay,
Lulling the year, with all its cares, to rest!

WORDSWORTH.

BALLAD.

SHE'S up and gone, the graceless girl!
    And robb'd my failing years;
My blood before was thin and cold,
    But now 'tis turn'd to tears;
My shadow falls upon my grave,
    So near the brink I stand;
She might have stay'd a little yet,
    And led me by the hand.

Aye, call her on the barren moor,
    And call her on the hill;
'Tis nothing but the heron's cry,
    And plover's answer shrill.
My child is flown on wilder wings
    Than they have ever spread;
And I may even walk a waste
    That widen'd when she fled.

Full many a thankless child has been,
    But never one like mine;
Her meat was served on plates of gold,
    Her drink was rosy wine.

But now she'll share the robin's food,
   And sup the common rill,
Before her feet will turn again
   To meet her father's will.
                HOOD.

INCANTATION.

[FROM THE TRAGEDY OF " REMORSE."]

HEAR, sweet spirit, hear the spell,
   Lest a blacker charm compel!
So shall the midnight breezes swell
With thy deep long-lingering knell.

And at evening evermore,
In a chapel on the shore,
Shall the chaunter, sad and saintly,
Yellow tapers burning faintly,
Doleful masses chaunt for thee,
Miserere Domine!

Hark! the cadence dies away
   On the quiet moonlight sea:
The boatmen rest their oars and say,
   Miserere Domine!
           COLERIDGE.

SONG.

[FROM " ROKEBY."]

A WEARY lot is thine, fair maid,
   A weary lot is thine;
To pull the thorn thy brow to braid,
   And press the rue for wine.

A lightsome eye, a soldier's mien,
  A feather of the blue,
A doublet of the Lincoln green,—
  No more of me you knew,
        My love,
  No more of me you knew!

This morn is merry June, I trow;
  The rose is budding fain;—
But she shall bloom in winter snow
  Ere we two meet again.
He turn'd his charger as he spake,
  Upon the river shore;
He gave his bridle-reins a shake,
  Said, "Adieu for evermore,
        My love!
  And adieu for evermore!"

SCOTT.

[FROM "A MIDSUMMER NIGHT'S DREAM."]

Puck.

NOW the hungry lion roars,
  And the wolf behowls the moon,
Whilst the heavy ploughman snores,
  All with weary task foredone.
Now the wasted brands do glow;
  And the scritch-owl, scritching loud,
Puts the wretch that lies in woe
  In remembrance of a shroud.
Now it is the time of night
  That the graves, all gaping wide,
Every one lets forth his sprite,

In the church-way paths to glide.
And we fairies, that do run
  By the triple Hecat's team,
From the presence of the sun
  Following darkness like a dream,
Now are frolic : not a mouse
Shall disturb this hallow'd house.
I am sent with broom before
To sweep the dust behind the door.

SHAKESPEARE.

WHAT PLEASURE HAVE GREAT PRINCES.

[FROM BYRD'S " SONGS AND SONNETS OF SADNESS AND PIETIE." 1588.]

WHAT pleasure have great princes,
  Completer to their choice,
Than they whose humble chances
  In quiet life rejoice,
And fearing not, nor scorning,
Sing sweet in summer morning?

Their dealings plain and rightful
  Are void of all deceit;
They never know how spiteful
  It is to kneel and wait
On favourite presumptuous
Whose pride is vain and sumptuous.

All day their work each tendeth,
  At night they take their rest,
More calm than he who sendeth
  His ship into the east,—

Where gold and pearl are plenty,
   But getting very dainty.

For lawyers and their pleading,
   They 'steem it not a straw;
They think that honest meaning
   Is of itself a law,
Where conscience judgeth plainly,—
So spend no money vainly.

O happy who thus liveth,
   Not caring much for gold;
With clothing which sufficeth
   To keep him from the cold;
Though poor and plain his diet,
Yet merry is he, and quiet.

FAIR HELEN OF KIRKCONNELL.

[OLD BALLAD.]

[*Adam Fleming, says tradition, loved Helen Irving, or Bell, (for this surname is uncertain, as well as the date of the occurrence) daughter of the Laird of Kirkconnell, in Dumfriesshire. The lovers being together one day by the river Kirtle, a rival suitor suddenly appeared on the opposite bank and pointed his gun; Helen threw herself before her sweetheart, received the bullet, and died in his arms. Then Adam Fleming fought with his guilty rival and slew him.*]

I WISH I were where Helen lies!
   Night and day on me she cries;
O that I were where Helen lies,
   On fair Kirkconnell lea!

Curst be the heart that thought the thought,
And curst the hand that fired the shot,
When in my arms burd Helen dropt,
    And died to succour me!

O think na ye my heart was sair
When my love dropt, and spak' nae mair!
There did she swoon wi' meikle care,
    On fair Kirkconnell lea.

And I went down the water side,
None but my foe to be my guide,
None but my foe to be my guide,
    On fair Kirkconnell lea.

I cross'd the stream, my sword did draw,
I hack'd him into pieces sma',
I hack'd him into pieces sma',
    For her sake that died for me.

O Helen fair, beyond compare!
I'll mak' a garland o' your hair,
Shall bind my heart for evermair,
    Until the day I dee!

O that I were where Helen lies!
Night and day on me she cries;
Out of my bed she bids me rise,
    Says, " Haste, and come to me!"

O Helen fair! O Helen chaste!
Were I with thee I would be blest,
Where thou liest low and tak'st thy rest,
    On fair Kirkconnell lea.

I wish my grave were growing green,
A winding-sheet drawn o'er my e'en,

And I in Helen's arms lying,
　　　　On fair Kirkconnell lea.

　　　I wish I were where Helen lies!
　　　Night and day on me she cries;
　　　And I am weary of the skies,
　　　　For her sake that died for me.
　　　　　　　Scott's "*Border Minstrelsy.*"

DOWN ON THE SHORE.

DOWN on the shore, on the sunny shore!
　　　Where the salt smell cheers the land;
Where the tide moves bright under boundless light,
　　And the surge on the glittering strand;
Where the children wade in the shallow pools,
　　Or run from the froth in play;
Where the swift little boats with milk-white wings
　　Are crossing the sapphire bay,
And the ship in full sail, with a fortunate gale,
　　Holds proudly on her way.
Where the nets are spread on the grass to dry,
And asleep, hard by, the fishermen lie,
Under the tent of the warm blue sky,
With the hushing wave on its golden floor
　　　To sing their lullaby.

Down on the shore, on the stormy shore!
　　Beset by a growling sea,
Whose mad waves leap on the rocky steep
　　Like wolves up a traveller's tree.
Where the foam flies wide, and an angry blast
　　Blows the curlew off, with a screech;

Where the brown sea-wrack, torn up by the roots,
   Is flung out of fishes' reach ;
Where the tall ship rolls on the hidden shoals,
   And scatters her planks on the beach.
Where slate and straw through the village spin,
And a cottage fronts the fiercest din
With a sailor's wife sitting sad within,
Hearkening the wind and water's roar,
     Till at last her tears begin.

              WILLIAM ALLINGHAM.

THE JOVIAL BEGGAR.

[PLAYFORD'S " CHOICE AIRES."   1660.]

THERE was a jovial Beggar,
   He had a wooden leg,
Lame from his cradle,
   And forced for to beg.
And a-begging we will go,
     Will go, will go,
And a-begging we will go.

A bag for his oatmeal,
   Another for his salt,
And a long pair of crutches,
   To show that he can halt.

A bag for his wheat,
   Another for his rye,
And a little bottle by his side
   To drink when he's a-dry.

Seven years I begg'd
   For my old master Wilde,

He taught me how to beg
    When I was but a child.

I begg'd for my master,
    And got him store of pelf,
But Heaven now be praisèd,
    I'm begging for myself.

In a hollow tree
    I live, and pay no rent,
Providence provides for me,
    And I am well content.

Of all the occupations
    A beggar's is the best,
For whenever he's a-weary
    He can lay him down to rest.

I fear no plots against me,
    I live in open cell;
Then who would be a king, lads,
    When the Beggar lives so well?
And a-begging we will go,
    Will go, will go,
And a-begging we will go.

[LOVE FOR NO LESS THAN LOVE]

SHALL I, wasting in despair,
    Die because a woman's *fair?*
Or make pale my cheeks with care
'Cause another's rosy are?
Be she fairer than the day
Or the flowery meads in May,
    If she be not so to me
    What care I how fair she be?

Shall my foolish heart be pined
'Cause I see a woman *kind?*
Or a well-disposèd nature
Joinèd with a lovely feature?
Be she meeker, kinder than
Turtle-dove or pelican,
  If she be not so to me
  What care I how kind she be?

Shall a woman's *virtues* move
Me to perish for her love?
Or her well-deserving known
Make me quite forget my own?
Be she with that goodness blest
Which may gain her name of Best,
  If she be not such to me
  What care I how good she be?

'Cause her *fortune* seems too high
Shall I play the fool and die?
Those that bear a noble mind,
Where they want of riches find,
Think what, with them, they would do
That without them dare to woo;
  And unless that mind I see
  What care I how great she be.

Great, or good, or kind, or fair,
I will ne'er the more despair:
If she love me, this believe—
I will die ere she shall grieve;
If she slight me when I woo,
I can scorn and let her go;
  For if she be not for me
  What care I for whom she be?

GEORGE WITHER.

THE SOLDIER'S DREAM.

OUR bugles sang truce, for the night-cloud had lower'd,
    And the sentinel stars set their watch in the sky;
And thousands had sunk on the ground overpower'd,
    The weary to sleep and the wounded to die.

When reposing that night on my pallet of straw,
    By the wolf-scaring faggot that guarded the slain,
At the dead of the night a sweet vision I saw,
    And thrice ere the morning I dream'd it again.

Methought from the battle-field's dreadful array
    Far, far I had roam'd on a desolate track:
'Twas Autumn,—and sunshine arose on the way
    To the home of my fathers, that welcomed me back.

I flew to the pleasant fields traversed so oft
    In life's morning march, when my bosom was young;
I heard my own mountain goats bleating aloft,
    And knew the sweet strain that the corn-reapers sung.

Then pledged we the wine-cup, and fondly I swore
    From my home and my weeping friends never to part;
My little ones kiss'd me a thousand times o'er,
    And my wife sobb'd aloud in her fulness of heart.

Stay, stay with us,—rest; thou art weary and worn!
  And fain was their war-broken soldier to stay;—
But sorrow return'd with the dawning of morn,
  And the voice in my dreaming ear melted away.

CAMPBELL.

A LYKE-WAKE DIRGE.[1]

[OLD.]

THIS ae nighte, this ae nighte,
  Everie nighte and alle,
Fire, and selte, and candle-lighte,
  And Christe receive thy saule.

When thou from hence away art past,
  Everie nighte and alle,
To Whinny-muir thou comest at last,
  And Christe receive thy saule.

If ever thou gavest hosen and shoon,
  Everie nighte and alle,
Sit thee down and put them on,
  And Christe receive thy saule.

If hosen and shoon thou gavest nane,
  Everie nighte and alle,
The whinnes shall pricke thee to the bare bane,
  And Christe receive thy saule.

From Whinny-muir when thou mayst passe,
  Everie nighte and alle,
To Brigg o' Dread thou comest at last,
  And Christe receive thy saule.

---

[1] See Note.

* * * * *

From Brigg o' Dread when thou mayst passe,
   Everie nighte and alle,
To Purgatory Fire thou comest at last,
   And Christe receive thy saule.

If ever thou gavest meate or drinke,
   Everie nighte and alle,
The fire shall never make thee shrinke,
   And Christe receive thy saule.

If meate or drinke thou gavest nane,
   Everie nighte and alle,
The fire will burne thee to the bare bane,
   And Christe receive thy saule.

This ae nighte, this ae nighte,
   Everie nighte and alle,
Fire, and selte, and candle-lighte,
   And Christe receive thy saule.

WHERE HE WOULD HAVE HIS VERSES READ.

IN sober mornings, do not thou rehearse
   The holy incantation of a verse;—
But when that men have both well drunk and fed
Let my enchantments then be sung or read.
When laurel spirts i' the fire, and when the hearth
Smiles to itself and gilds the roof with mirth;
When up the Thyrse is raised, and when the sound
Of sacred orgies flies around around;
When the rose reigns, and locks with ointment
   shine,
Let rigid Cato read these lines of mine.

                        HERRICK.

YOUNG LOCHINVAR.

[FROM " MARMION."]

O, YOUNG Lochinvar is come out of the west!
   Through all the wide border his steed is
      the best;
And save his good broadsword he weapon had none;
He rode all unarm'd, and he rode all alone.
So faithful in love, and so dauntless in war,
There never was knight like the young Lochinvar!

He stay'd not for brake and he stopt not for stone;
He swam the Eske river where ford there was
      none;
But ere he alighted at Netherby gate,
The bride had consented, the gallant came late;
For a laggard in love and a dastard in war,
Was to wed the fair Ellen of brave Lochinvar.

So bravely he enter'd the Netherby Hall,
Among bridesmen and kinsmen and brothers and
      all;—
Then spoke the bride's father, his hand on his
      sword,
For the poor craven bridegroom said never a word,
" O come ye in peace here, or come ye in war,
Or to dance at our bridal, young Lord Lochinvar?"

" I long woo'd your daughter, my suit you denied;—
Love swells like the Solway, but ebbs like its tide;
And now am I come, with this lost love of mine
To lead but one measure, drink one cup of wine.

There are maidens in Scotland more lovely by far,
That would gladly be bride to the young Lochinvar!"

The bride kiss'd the goblet, the knight took it up,
He quaff'd off the wine and he threw down the cup;
She look'd down to blush, and she look'd up to sigh,
With a smile on her lips, and a tear in her eye.
He took her soft hand, ere her mother could bar,—
"Now tread we a measure!" said young Lochinvar.

So stately his form, and so lovely her face,
That never a hall such a galliard did grace;
While her mother did fret and her father did fume,
And the bridegroom stood dangling his bonnet and plume;
And the bride-maidens whisper'd, "'Twere better by far
To have match'd our fair cousin with young Lochinvar!"

One touch to her hand, and one word in her ear,
When they reach'd the hall-door; and the charger stood near;
So light to the croupe the fair lady he swung,
So light to the saddle before her he sprung!
"She is won! we are gone, over bank, bush and scaur!
They'll have fleet steeds that follow!" quoth young Lochinvar.

There was mounting 'mong Græmes of the Netherby clan;
Forsters, Fenwicks, and Musgraves, they rode and they ran;

There was racing and chasing on Cannobie lea;
But the lost bride of Netherby ne'er did they see.
—So daring in love, and so dauntless in war,
Have ye ere heard of gallant like young Lochinvar?

SCOTT.

WHEN THE WORLD IS BURNING.

(STANZAS FOR MUSIC.)

WHEN the world is burning,
    Fired within, yet turning
Round with face unscathed,—
Ere fierce flames, uprushing,
O'er all lands leap, crushing,
    Till earth fall, fire-swathed;
Up amidst the meadows,
Gently through the shadows,
    Gentle flames will glide,
Small and blue and golden:
Though by bard beholden
When in calm dreams folden,
    Calm his dreams will bide.

Where the dance is sweeping,
Through the greensward peeping
    Shall the soft lights start;
Laughing maids, unstaying,
Deeming it trick-playing,
High their robes upswaying,
    O'er the lights shall dart;
And the woodland haunter
Shall not cease to saunter

When, far down some glade,
Of the great world's burning
One soft flame upturning,
Seems, to his discerning,
Crocus in the shade.

   EBENEZER JONES.

MAY AND DEATH.

I WISH that when you died last May,
 Charles, there had died along with you
Three parts of Spring's delightful things;
 Aye, and for me, the fourth part too.

A foolish thought, and worse, perhaps!
 There must be many a pair of friends
Who, arm in arm, deserve the warm
 Moon's birth, and the long evening-ends.

So, for their sake, prove May still May!
 Let their new time, like mine of old,
Do all it did for me; I bid
 Sweet sights and sounds throng manifold.

Only, one little sight, one plant
 Woods have in May, that starts up green
Except a streak, which, so to speak
 Is Spring's blood, spilt its leaves between,—

That, they might spare: a certain wood
 Might lose the plant; their loss were small:
And I,—whene'er the plant is there
 Its drop comes from my heart, that's all.

   ROBERT BROWNING.

LINES TO AN INDIAN AIR.

I ARISE from dreams of thee,
   In the first sweet sleep of night,
     When the winds are breathing low,
   And the stars are shining bright.
I arise from dreams of thee,
   And a spirit in my feet
     Hath led me—who knows how?
   To thy chamber window, sweet!

The wandering airs they faint
   On the dark, the silent stream;
     And the champak odours pine
   Like sweet thoughts in a dream;
The nightingale's complaint
   It dies upon her heart;
     As I must die on thine,
   Oh! Beloved as thou art.

O lift me from the grass!
   I die, I faint, I fail!
     Let thy love in kisses rain
   On my lips and eyelids pale.
My cheek is cold and white, alas,
   My heart beats loud and fast;
     O press it to thine own again,
   Where it will break at last.

              SHELLEY.

THE DEATH OF THE OLD YEAR.

FULL knee-deep lies the winter snow,
    And the winter winds are wearily sighing:
Toll ye the church-bell sad and slow,
And tread softly and speak low,
  For the old year lies a-dying.
      Old year, you must not die;
      You came to us so readily,
      You lived with us so steadily,
      Old year, you shall not die.

He lieth still: he doth not move:
  He will not see the dawn of day.
He hath no other life above.
He gave me a friend and a true true-love,
  And the New Year will take 'em away.
      Old year, you must not go;
      So long as you have been with us,
      Such joy as you have seen with us,
      Old year, you shall not go.

He froth'd his bumpers to the brim;
  A jollier year we shall not see.
But though his eyes are waxing dim,
  He was a friend to me.
      Old year, you shall not die;
      We did so laugh and cry with you,
      I've half a mind to die with you,
      Old year, if you must die.

He was full of joke and jest,
  But all his merry quips are o'er,
To see him die, across the waste
His son and heir doth ride post-haste,
  But he'll be dead before.
    Every one for his own.
    The night is starry and cold, my friend,
    And the new year blithe and bold, my friend,
    Comes up to take his own.

How hard he breathes! over the snow
  I heard just now the crowing cock.
The shadows flicker to and fro:
The cricket chirps: the light burns low:
  'Tis nearly twelve o'clock.
    Shake hands, before you die.
    Old year, we'll dearly rue for you:
    What is it we can do for you?
    Speak out before you die.

His face is growing sharp and thin.
  Alack! our friend is gone.
Close up his eyes: tie up his chin:
Step from the corpse, and let him in
  That standeth there alone,
    And waiteth at the door.
    There's a new foot on the floor, my friend,
    And a new face at the door, my friend,
    A new face at the door.
              TENNYSON.

LYRICS FOR LEGACIES.

GOLD I've none, for use or show,
Neither silver to bestow
At my death; but thus much know,

That each lyric here shall be
Of my love a legacy,
Left to all posterity.

Gentle friends, then do but please
To accept such coins as these,
As my last remembrances.
HERRICK.

NOTES.

Note A. Dates.

	Born.	Died.
George Peele	1552?	1598?
John Lyly	1554?	
Sir Philip Sidney	1554	1586
Nicholas Breton	1555?	1624?
Robert Southwell	1560	1595
Michael Drayton	1563	1631
William Shakespeare	1564	1616
Christopher Marlowe	1563	1593
Sir Henry Wotton	1568	1639
Ben Jonson	1574	1637
John Fletcher	1576	1625
George Wither	1588	1667
Thomas Carew	1589	1639
Robert Herrick	1591	1674
Edmund Waller	1605	1687
John Milton	1608	1674
Richard Flecknoe		1678?
Sir John Suckling	1608?	1643?
Richard Lovelace	1618	1658
William Collins	1720	1756
William Cowper	1731	1800
John Logan	1748	1788
William Blake	1757	1828
Robert Burns	1759	1796
Lady Anne Lindsay	1750	1825
Joanna Baillie	1762	1851
William Wordsworth	1770	1850
Walter Scott	1771	1832
Samuel Taylor Coleridge	1772	1834
James Hogg	1772	1835

	Born.	Died.
Mary Boddington	1776?	18—
Thomas Campbell	1777	1844
Leigh Hunt	1784	1859
Richard Harris Barham	1788	1845
Percy Bysshe Shelley	1792	1822
Felicia Hemans	1794	1835
John Keats	1796	1821
Hartly Coleridge	1796	1849
Thomas Hood	1798	1845
Edgar A. Poe	1811?	1849

Note B. Page 5.

Sic Vita. Printed among the poems of Francis Beaumont,—and of Bishop King. Perhaps either of them may have put the lines into this shape, but neither originated them; for morallings to the same tune upon "Man's Mortalitie," were much in fashion about that time, and seem modelled upon some traditionary strain.

Note C. Page 7.

The Passionate Shepheard to his Love,—" that smooth song," as Izak Walton says, " which was made by Kit Marlowe," is taken from *England's Helicon*, A.D. 1600, a collection of short pieces in the pastoral form,—for there are fashions in themes as well as in styles. The phrase " passionate shepherd" itself was *à la mode*, and heads the only verses by Shakespeare (" On a day, alack the day!") which appear in that collection.

Note D. Page 13.

The Character of a Happy Life. " The variations in the different copies of these verses are unusually numerous; I have collated those of six," says Mr. Hannah, in his careful edition of " Poems by Wotton, Raleigh and others" (Pickering, 1845). In our version a few words (*humours* for *rumours*, *accusers* for *oppressors*, *well-chosen* for *religious*) differ, on good MS. authority, from the ordinary reading: see Hannah, as above, pages 29, 31.

Note E. Page 29.

At Hohenlinden, a forest and village about twenty English miles east of Munich, a French republican army, under Moreau, defeated the Austrians, Dec. 3rd, 1800. It was the first struggle of the winter campaign of that year, and resulted in an armistice favourable to the French. It has sometimes been stated that Campbell witnessed this battle, or that he visited the field soon after; but the poet had finally quitted Bavaria some six weeks before, and was then at Altona. The value of the lyric is from its general force, not its details, which are inexact.

Note F. Page 31.

Clerk Saunders. This wonderful old ballad was first printed in Scott's *Border Minstrelsy*, " from Mr. Herd's MSS. with several corrections from a shorter and more imperfect copy, in the same volume, and one or two conjectural emendations in the arrangement of the stanzas." This version here given is the fruit of further comparison and consideration.

The "clinking bell" was a hand-bell rung before the corpse at the funeral; those who heard it in its passing prayed for the soul of the deceased:—

" And as they sat, they heard a bell clinke
Biforn a corps, was caried to the grave."
Chaucer's *Pardonere's Tale.*

" Chrisom wand" is a conjectural emendation of the meaningless " chrystal wand," as hitherto printed.

The words " Old English and Scottish Ballads" awaken as single though complex an idea as if we spoke of Chaucer's Works, or Shakespeare's. Yet the Ballads, as we have them, are the work of a crowd of persons, belonging to different generations and various classes. Many of the versions are imperfect, many of the readings obviously spurious, and one may detect here and there the consequences of the unequal taste and skill, often arbitrarily applied, of the numerous transmitters and recorders. It seems possible, and very desirable, that an Editor, bringing special aptitude and diligence to the task, may sometime be found to bring part, at least, of this tangled heap of treasure into a shape more for the general benefit. The difficulties are not few, and the work, when finished, would need to be its own excuse and justification.

Note G. Page. 50.

To Mary in Heaven was written by Burns in September, 1789, on his farm of Ellisland, near Dumfries, he being then thirty years of age. His wife gave the following account, or at least the substance of it, according to Allan Cunningham's " Life of Burns:" " Robert, though ill of a cold, had busied himself all day long with his shearers in the field, and, as he had got much of the crop in, was in capital spirits. But when the gloaming came, he grew sad about something—he could not rest. He wandered first up the water-side, and then went to the barn-yard; and I followed him, begging him to come in, as he was ill, and the air was cold and sharp. He always promised, but still remained where he was, striding up and down, and looking at the clear sky, and particularly at a star that shone like another moon. He then threw himself down on some loose sheaves, still continuing to gaze at the star." When he came in he seemed deeply dejected, and sat down and wrote the first verse: " Thou lingering star," &c. The subject of his reverie was Mary Campbell, a peasant's daughter, who, when she captivated the Poet, some three or four years before the date given above, was dairy-maid in Coilsfield—" the Castle of Montgomery." One Sunday in May, the lovers met in a sequestered spot on the banks of the Ayr, to take farewell before Mary's departure, for a time, to her friends in the West Highlands. In parting they exchanged their Bibles, as trothplight, Burns having written in his, along with his name, the two texts, " And ye shall not swear by my name falsely—I am the Lord;" Levit. xix. 12.; and " Thou shalt not forswear thyself, but shalt perform unto the Lord thine oath;" Matthew, v. 33. This book is in existence, as well as a tress of Mary's hair, which is " very long, and very light and shining." It was the last meeting of the lovers; Mary died of fever in the following autumn.

NOTE II. PAGE 51.

The Northern Star. These lines, with another verse here omitted as inferior, are given in Hone's Table Book (1827), vol. i. page 657, with this preface: " Some years ago a Tynemouth vessel called ' The Northern Star' was lost, and the following ballad made on the occasion: the memory of a lady supplies the words." It is noticeable that strong natural feeling, in a mind where there is usually no poetic skill, can sometimes with success shape its experience into a simple poem.

Note I. Page 52.

Richard Lovelace, born 1618, eldest son of Sir William Lovelace, of Woolwich, Kent, was gentleman-commoner of Gloucester Hall, Oxford, 1634, served King Charles in Scotland as ensign, and afterwards captain, and " was accounted," says Wood, " the most amiable and beautiful person that ever eye beheld; of innate modesty, virtue, and courtly deportment." Staunch royalist, he presented to parliament the Kentish petition for the restoration of the King, and was therefore imprisoned for several months in the Gatehouse, Westminster, where he wrote his lyric " To Althea from Prison." After the surrender of Oxford, he commanded a regiment in the French King's service, and was wounded at Dunkirk; a false report of his death reaching Lucy Sacheverell, a lady whom he had long loved, and by whom most of his poems were inspired, she soon after was married to another. In 1648 he returned to London, and was again cast into prison, where he arranged his poems (many of them already separately published with music) for the press. The little volume (164 pages) appeared in 1649, under title " Lucasta: [i. e. *Lux Casta*, memorial of his Lucy] Epodes, Odes, Sonnets, Songs, &c., to which is added Araminta, a Pastorall, by Richard Lovelace, Esq.;" it contains three pretty pieces, which are often reprinted, " To Lucasta, going to the Warres," " The Grasse-hopper," and " To Althea." His losses in his King's cause, and generosity to all needy persons, ruined Lovelace's fortune, and, when set at liberty after the execution of Charles, " he grew very melancholy (which brought him into a consumption), became very poor in body and purse, was the object of charity, went in ragged clothes (whereas, when he was in his glory, he wore cloth of gold and silver) and mostly lodged in obscure and dirty places."—Wood. He expired in 1658, only forty years old, at very mean lodgings in Gunpowder Alley, near Shoe Lane, and was buried at the west end of St. Bride's Church. His portrait shows a long, shapely face, high, sweet, and pensive. His " Posthume Poems" were published by his brother in 1659. He also wrote two plays, never printed, " The Scholar," and " The Soldier."

Note J. Page 54.

William Blake was born November 28, 1757, the son of a hosier in Broad Street, Carnaby Market, which is now on the right-hand side of Regent Street, London. At the age of fourteen, having shown an early bent for pictorial design, he was apprenticed for seven years to Mr. Basire, engraver; and, besides learning his art, proceeded to make innumerable original sketches, and also to compose a vast quantity of wonderful verses. When twenty-six years old Blake's marriage with Katherine Boutcher took place—a real union, of mutual respect, perfect sympathy, tender affection. The quiet, brown-eyed Katherine had true taste for art, and gained skill enough to assist in colouring her husband's drawings; she copied with delight the strange verses he so often dictated; she honoured his painting, his poetry, his simplicity, and his mysticism. He now left his father's, and went to live in Green Street, Leicester Fields. In his thirtieth year, with the advice and assistance of John Flaxman, the sculptor, a volume of Blake's poems (seventy pages) was published, the style of which, incompact in thought and plan as they mostly are, reminds one, and in that sleepy hour of the English Muse, of our very highest men. Blake opened a print-shop, which did not succeed; and, during the last half of his life, gave his mornings to the graver, by which he earned a modest subsistence for himself and his wife, and his evenings to original drawing and poetry. "Were I to love money," he used to say, "I should lose all power of thought; desire of gain deadens the genius of man. My business is not to gather gold, but to make glorious shapes, expressing god-like sentiments." Music, too, we hear of his composing, but he wanted the art of noting it down, and no specimen remains. Most of Blake's engraved works are rare. His illustrations to "Job" are to be had,—to Blair's "Grave," and Young's "Night Thoughts" still more easily; but his own "Songs of Innocence and Experience," with sixty-four designs, or, as he calls them, "inventions," are scarcely ever publicly offered for sale; and as seldom, or more seldom, his "Urizen," twenty-seven inventions; and "Gates of Paradise," sixteen. The designs of the "Songs of Innocence and Experience" consist of a number of scenes, tinted in a sweet and peculiar manner, presenting, with a kind of spiritual exaltation, images of youth and manhood—of domestic sadness and fire-side joy—of the gaiety, the innocence and happiness of childhood; and each scene having its accompanying verses finely pencilled in colours, and curiously interwoven with the group or landscape.

Blake, as he grew older, grew poorer, but not less industrious or less cheerful; his habits became still more retired and inexpensive; he lived like a hermit in the wilderness of London, a hermit ministered to by an angel, who was his wife. A strange faculty which he had of *vision-seeing*, grew stronger and stronger; ideas of every sort took definite visible form, doubtless through large measure and over-activity of a power which we all possess—witness our dreams. It seems certain that the visual nerve may be stimulated from its internal or brain end with force equal, in some cases, to that exercised by external objects. One may note that while William Blake, a singular boy of fifteen, was busy learning engraving with Mr. Basire, and making sketches and verses, he may any day have met unwittingly in London streets, or walked beside, a placid, venerable, thin man of eighty-four, of erect figure and abstracted air, wearing a full-bottomed wig, a pair of long ruffles, and a curious-hilted sword, and carrying a gold-headed cane,—no Vision, still flesh and blood, but himself the greatest of modern Vision-Seers, Emanuel Swedenborg by name; who came from Amsterdam to London in August, 1771, and died, in No. 26, Great Bath Street, Coldbath Fields, on the 29th of March, 1772.

Blake was accustomed to paint the visionary faces and groups which appeared to him; and the ghosts, among whom were many historical personages, usually " sat " as steadily as could be wished. His verses, too, are always thoroughly *concrete* in their nature.

Blake spent the last year of his life in Fountain Court, Strand, which is nearly opposite Exeter Hall, and there died, 12th of August, 1828, aged seventy. His wife survived him some years. A memorial volume, selected from the abundant evidences of his genius, poetic and pictorial, which now lie scattered in several hands, and are mostly inaccessible to the world, would, if lovingly and liberally executed, be very charming and valuable, and, in truth, a national honour. Creative genius, in any department, is too rare and precious that we should be content " to lose a drop" of that immortal gift. But to produce adequate fac-similes of Blake's best engraved designs, and, in especial, of his curiously-tinted drawings, some of which are astoundingly fine, would be no jobber's work.

It remains to add that for the version of " The Tiger,"

here presented, differing somewhat from those hitherto published, use has been made of a MS. book of Blake's, belonging to a friend of the editor, full of the oddest chaos of verses, drawings, and memoranda.

NOTE K. PAGE 56.

Eugene Aram. In the summer of the year 1759, a human skeleton was accidentally turned up in a quarry near Knaresborough in Yorkshire, and was supposed to be that of one Daniel Clark, who had suddenly disappeared from the locality about thirteen years before. One Richard Houseman, being arrested on suspicion, exclaimed that the skeleton was not Clark's; and, losing his self-possession, at last directed a search to be made in St. Robert's Cave, where another skeleton was found which proved to be that of Clark. Further inquiry resulted in the arrest of Eugene Aram, formerly of Knaresborough, and now usher in a school at Lynn in Norfolk, a studious and learned man. He was tried at York Castle, on the 3rd of August, made an elaborate and ingenious—too ingenious defence (to be found in Kippis's *Biog. Britan.*), and was found guilty of the murder of Clark, who, with Houseman, had been his accomplice in several robberies. After confession of guilt, followed by an attempt at suicide, Eugene Aram was hanged at York, and his body suspended in chains in Knaresborough Forest.

NOTE L. PAGE 89.

Richard Harris Barham's best-known book is one of the comic order, entitled *The Ingoldsby Legends*, in which great cleverness is but poorly employed. These graver verses are said to have been the last he ever made.

NOTE M. PAGE 109.

I do confesse thou'rt smooth and faire, has been said, but not with certainty, to be by Sir Robert Ayton, a Scottish courtier of James I, and a friend of Ben Jonson.

NOTE N. PAGE 110.

Ned Bolton. The substance of what we have been able to learn regarding the author of this dashing buccaneer ballad, equal to Scott's best lyrics, is that he was a native of the north of Ireland, some time a newspaper writer, afterwards British Consul at Galveston in Texas, in which country he died, or, as some accounts say, was killed, about twenty years ago. We have seen a volume of his poems, entitled " Fitful Fancies," and published, we think, in 1826, which contains *Ned Bolton*, but nothing else near so good. We have an impression that he published another volume of verse, but have not been able to lay hands on it.

NOTE O. PAGE 120.

Ode to Evening. This poem is here printed with spacings that bring out both sense and sound more clearly than the usual arrangement, which is wholly superficial. Nothing is hereby lost, and much gained. The addition of four lines, enclosed with brackets, near the end, is less excusable—unless, with those readers to whom, after fit consideration, they may succeed in making their own excuse.

NOTE P. PAGE 134.

Auld Robin Gray was written by Lady Anne Lindsay, daughter of the Earl of Balcarras, born 1750; married to Sir A. Barnard, 1793; died, without issue, 1825, in Berkeley Square, London. She was pretty, vivacious, and agreeable. Writing shortly before her death to Sir Walter Scott, Lady Anne says: " *Robin Gray*, so called from its being the name of the old herd at Balcarras, was born soon after the close of the year 1771. My sister Margaret had married and accompanied her husband to London; I was melancholy, and endeavoured to amuse myself by attempting a few poetical trifles. There was an ancient Scottish melody of which I was passionately fond; [Miss Suff Johnstone], who lived before your day, used to sing it for us at Balcarras. She did not object to its having improper words, though I did. I longed to sing old Sophy's air to different words, and give to its plaintive tones some little history of virtuous distress in humble life, such as might suit it. . . . At our fireside and amongst our neighbours ' Auld Robin Gray' was always called for,—I was pleased in secret with the approbation it met with; but such was my dread of being suspected of writing anything, perceiving the shyness it created in those who could write nothing, that I carefully kept my own secret." It became a disputed question whether the ballad was ancient or modern, and a reward of twenty guineas was offered in the newspapers for decisive proof on the point. Mr. Jerningham, secretary to the Antiquarian Society, endeavoured to entrap the truth from Lady Anne in a manner which induced her to put him off unsatisfied, and the authorship was not made public until after her decease. (See Lockhart's Life of Scott, 1844, page 585, and note.) "It remains to be added, that although 'Auld Robin Gray' was originally written to the old tune of 'The Bridegroom greits when the sun gaes down,' it is now, with the exception of the first verse, which retains the old air, universally sung to a beautiful modern tune, composed by the Rev. William Leeves, rector of Wrington, who died in 1828, aged eighty."—Book of Scottish Song. (Blackie and Son. 1843.)

NOTE Q. PAGE 143.

The Laboratory. A study of the present lyric will throw some light upon the principles of this wonderful Poet's versification. Take this verse, for example, and emphasise the words given in italics:—

"*He* is with *her*; and they *know* that *I* know
Where they *are*, what they *do*: they believe *my tears* flow
While *they laugh*, laugh at *me*, at me fled to the drear
Empty church to pray God in for *them!*—I am *here*."

Emerson has frequently rhythms of a similar character, such as "*Tax not*," (two syllables to be dwelt on to the length of three):—

"*Tax not* my sloth that I
Fold my arms beside the brook."

And,

"*One* harvest from thy field
Homeward brought the oxen strong."

It is always delightful to recollect that both our Essayist (to be better known "after some time"), and our Biographer of Frederick (both *ours*, though one of them lives beyond sea) are admirable poets, with in each case certain peculiarities and limitations, very note-worthy, but not here to be expounded.

NOTE R. PAGE 169.

La Belle Dame sans Mercy. "Among the pieces printed at the end of Chaucer's works, and attributed to him, is a translation, under this title, of a poem of the celebrated Alain Chartier, secretary to Charles the Sixth and Seventh. It was the title which suggested to a friend the verses at the end of our present number."—Leigh Hunt's *Indicator,* for May 10th, 1820. The verses were there signed "*Caviare.*" In Mr. Milnes's "Life, &c. of Keats," II. 268, is a version beginning, "O what can ail thee, Knight-at-arms," transposing the fifth and sixth stanzas, and with a few other variations. It is dated 1819, and seems to be evidently an earlier form of the poem than that which is here given from the *Indicator.*

Note S. Page 178.

Fairy Song. Bishop Percy printed this in his "Reliques," under name *The Fairy Queen,* stating that it was "given, with some corrections by another copy, from a book entitled 'The Mysteries of Love and Eloquence, &c.'" London, 1658. 8vo. The verse which he gives as the sixth we have omitted; it runs:—

> "The brains of nightingales,
> With unctuous fat of snails,
> Between two cockles stew'd,
> Is meat that's easily chew'd;
> Tailes of wormes and marrow of mice
> Do make a dish that's wondrous nice."

Note T. Page 184.

The Lady's Grave is from certain "Poems, by Mrs. Boddington," (Longman, 1839,) which, though without substance enough to endure, have a delicate and tender strain of originality running through them, and drew the remark from a friend of ours, that "she must have been a delightful woman to know." A correspondent of "Willis's Current Notes," in May, 1852, has furnished the following information: "Mary Boddington was the daughter of Patrick Comerford, a Cork merchant, and niece of Sir William Glendowe Newcomen. She was born at Cork in 1776, and, having married, in 1803, Mr. Boddington, a West Indian merchant, left her native city. After the peace of 1815, Mrs. Boddington travelled much on the continent." She also published "The Gossip's Week," a collection of tales, "Sketches in the Pyrenees," and "Slight Reminiscences of the Rhine."

Note U. Page 186.

The Rev. William Barnes, a Church of England clergyman, residing at Dorchester, is author of several volumes of Poems, which, from being written in the dialect of his native Dorsetshire, have attracted less general notice than they deserve. A series of more genuine and delightful sketches, or *photographs* of rural character and scenery, cannot be found in English literature. The rustic dialect, come down, in our author's opinion, by independent descent from the Saxon dialect which our forefathers brought from the south of Denmark, is easy to master, and enhances the freshness and originality of these poems, which, soon or late, will infallibly be better known. Mr. Barnes has also published some works on Anglo-Saxon literature. John Russell Smith is his publisher.

Note V. Page 205.

[*Evening.*] These verses are from the "Poems; chiefly Lyrical," by Alfred Tennyson, published in 1830, wherein they are entitled " Elegiacs."

Note W. Page 218.

The wife of Usher's Well, hearing her three sons are lost at sea, passionately prays that the storm may never cease till they come back to her in flesh and blood. One night, at Martinmas, her three sons come home; the mother feasts all her house, then makes a wide bed for her three sons, and sits down by the bedside. But at cockcrow, when she has dropt asleep, these three, who are no living men, but spirits, strangely repossessed of their old bodies for a season, depart for ever from that house.

This Ballad was first published in Scott's " Border Minstrelsy:" two verses, " Lie still," &c., and " O, it's they've ta'en up," &c., are from Mr. Robert Chambers's version, recovered from recitation: one, " Our mother has nae mair," is now added, to complete the sense; and to the same end, the reading, " fish be in the flood " is put instead of " fishes in the flood"—Scott's, which he notes as obscure, and probably corrupted by reciters. Mr. Aytoun has " freshes in the flood ;" Mr. Lockhart suggested " *fashes*," i. e. troubles.

" Carline-wife" implies, here at least, a rustic woman, keeping a farm.

" Martinmas," the feast of St. Martin, 11th of November. One may remark that this, being the customary time to kill winter beef and pork, was a season of rustic feasting and jollity. " Birk" is birch. " Syke," a marshy bottom. "Sheugh," a small trench. "Channerin'," fretting (Scott). A large mantle used to be, and still is, in old-fashioned localities, perhaps the most important and indispensable article of every peasant woman's wardrobe. It served many uses, and lasted many years, a familiar and homely-sacred object to the children of a family.

Note X. Page 238.

Waly, waly was first published in Allan Ramsay's "Tea Table Miscellany," in 1724, and marked "Z," as an Old Song.

Note Y. Page 244.

Edward, Edward. This darkly terrible tragic ballad was first printed in "Percy's Reliques," "transmitted to the editor by Sir David Dalrymple, Bart., late Lord Hailes."

Note Z. Page 259.

This *Lyke-Wake* [i.e. Dead-Watch] *Dirge* is of the North of England, and is said to have been sung, in Yorkshire, over corpses, down to about 1624, (see Brand's "Pop. Antiq." 1841, II. 155.) Scott, publishing it in his *Border Minstrelsy*, noted: "The late Mr. Ritson found an illustration of this dirge in a MS. of the Cotton Library, containing an account of Cleveland, in Yorkshire, in the reign of Queen Elizabeth..... 'When any dieth, certaine women sing a song to the dead bodie, recyting the jorney that the partye deceased must goe; and they are of beliefe (such is their fondnesse) that, once in their lives, it is good to give a pair of new shoes to a poor man, forasmuch as, after this life, they are to pass barefoote through a great launde, full of thornes and furzen, except by the meryte of the almes aforesaid they have redeemed the forfeyte; for at the edge of the launde, an oulde man shall meet them with the same shoes that were given by the partye when he was lyving; and, after he hath shodde them, dismisseth them to go through thick and thin, without scratch or scalle.'—*Julius*, F. VI. 459."

"*The Bridge of Dread*, lying in our road when we pass from this world, is described," says Sir Walter, "in the legend of *Sir Owain*, No XL. in the MS. collection of Romances, W. XLI., Advocates' Library, Edinburgh." The Orientals have a similar fancy, of a narrow bridge over an abyss.

In the *Border Minstrelsy*, the second line is given, " Fire and sleet and candlelight," with the note that *sleet* seems to be corrupted from *selt*, i. e. salt, which it was customary to lay in a platter on the breast of the corpse. In Brand we have *fleet*, i. e. water (Anglo-Saxon), but the whole version there seems inferior. The sixth verse of the dirge is lost.

Note Z Z. Page 265.

Lines to an Indian Air. This exquisite song is here so given as to assist eye and mind in following the interwoven rhymes. Let us remark that hardly any great poet, certainly no modern one, has been so *inaccurately printed* as Shelley. Helps to the very necessary revision are in existence, and ought quickly to be used. The reading " pine," in the second verse, instead of " fail," must, for the present, rest on its own merits. We believe that the " fail," in the third verse, caused the same word to be slipt into the second, under the notion of making the iteration more exact; but such merely verbal and mechanical iteration is not in place here, and destroys the rhymic structure of the lyric in a very un-Shelleyan manner. The other slight variations from the usual version have come to the editor, through an eminent living poet, from a copy found in the pocket of Shelley's corpse We have inquired after the *Indian Air*, but, if there was one (and a friend of Shelley's thought there was), it seems untraceable.

INDEX OF FIRST LINES.

	Page
A CHIEFTAIN, to the Highlands bound	156
A flock of sheep that leisurely pass by	14
A jolly comrade in the port, a fearless mate at sea	110
A Spirit haunts the year's last hours	187
A sunny shaft did I behold	136
A weary lot is thine, fair maid	249
Abou Ben Adhem (may his tribe increase)	15
Ah, what can ail thee, wretched wight	169
Alexis calls me cruel	96
All thought, all passions, all delights	227
Among these latter busts we count by scores	64
As I lay a-thinking, a-thinking, a-thinking	89
As I was walking all alane	101
At me one night the angry moon	93
At the corner of Wood Street, when daylight appears	241
Because I breathe not love to everie one	173
Before my face the picture hangs	233
Being your slave, what should I do but tend	117
Beneath this starry arch	231
Between Nose and Eyes a strange contest arose	180
Bird of the wilderness	243
Blow, blow, thou winter wind	152
Break, break, break	94
Burly dozing humble-bee	132
By the moon we sport and play	205
Child, amidst the flowers at play	172
Clerk Saunders and may Margaret	31
Clouds, lingering yet, extend in solid bars	28
Come, follow, follow me	178
Come live with me, and be my Love	7
Come, see the Dolphin's anchor forged—'tis at a white heat now	125

INDEX OF FIRST LINES.

	Page
Come unto these yellow sands	103
Cyriack, this three years' day these eyes, though clear	177
Dear to the Loves, and to the Graces vow'd	137
Dishonour'd Rock and Ruin! that, by law	240
Dost thou idly ask to hear	27
Dost thou look back on what hath been	76
Down on the shore, on the sunny shore	254
Ere on my bed my limbs I lay	242
Ethereal minstrel! pilgrim of the sky	101
Fair daffodils, we weep to see	129
Faire, and faire, and twice so faire	181
False friend, wilt thou smile or weep	218
Flow down, cold rivulet, to the sea	53
From Stirling castle we had seen	97
From you I have been absent in the spring	95
Full fathom five thy father lies	107
Full knee-deep lies the winter-snow	266
Gather ye rose-buds while ye may	63
Get up our Anna dear, from the weary spinning-wheel	223
Give me a cell	227
Go, lovely rose	118
Gold, I've none, for use or show	268
Good-bye, proud world, I'm going home	113
Had I but plenty of money, money enough and to spare	163
Hail! beauteous stranger of the grove	18
Hail, Twilight, sovereign of one peaceful hour	54
Hark! hark! the lark at heaven's gate sings	217
Hast thou named all the birds without a gun	167
He is gone on the mountain	19
He that loves a rosie cheeke	134
Hear, sweet spirit, hear the spell	249
Hear the sledges with the bells	46
Hie upon Hielands	131
How do I love thee? let me count the ways	30
How happy is he born and taught	13
How long I sail'd and never took a thought	40
How strange it is to wake	221
How sweet it were, if without feeble fright	130

INDEX OF FIRST LINES.   285

	Page
I arise from dreams of thee	265
I cannot see the features right	199
I come from haunts of coot and hern	167
I do confess thou'rt smooth and faire	109
I dream'd a dream, what can it mean	235
I dream'd that, as I wander'd by the way	21
I heard a thousand blended notes	203
I heard the dogs howl in the moonlight night	16
I lov'd him not; and yet now he is gone	204
I remember, I remember	39
I shot an arrow into the air	158
I wander'd by the brook-side	66
I will not have the mad Clytie	88
I wish I were where Helen lies	252
I wish that when you died last May	264
If aught of oaten stop or pastoral song	120
In sober mornings, do not thou rehearse	260
In the greenest of our valleys	71
In the hour of my distress	188
In the merry month of May	211
In Xanadu did Kubla Kahn	160
Inland, within a hollow vale I stood	37
It fell about the Martinmas	206
It is not beautie I demand	20
It is the miller's daughter	11
It is the first mild day of March	174
It little profits that an idle king	105
Lady, wouldst thou heiress be	198
Lawrence, of virtuous father virtuous son	56
Let time and chance combine, combine	99
Like to the falling of a star	5
Look not thou on beauty's charming	16
Love me, sweet, with all thou art	91
Love, strong as death, is dead	194
Low-flowing breezes are roaming the broad valley dimm'd in the gloaming	205
Merry, merry sparrow	116
Much have I travell'd in the realms of gold	78
Music, when soft voices die	115
My heart aches, and a drowsy numbness pains	140
My heart is a-breaking, dear Tittie	119
No cloud, no relique of the sunken day	67

INDEX OF FIRST LINES.

	Page
No, no! go not to Lethe, neither twist	246
Now fades the last long streak of snow	189
Now hands to seed-sheet, boys	37
Now that I, tying thy glass mask tightly	143
Now the bright Morning-Star, day's harbinger	104
Now the hungry lion roars	250
Nuns fret not at their convent's narrow room	5
O blithe new-comer! I have heard	185
O give me, from this heartless scene released	137
O Maryanne, you pretty girl	196
O Mary, go and call the cattle home	139
O nightingale, that on yon bloomy spray	1
O saw ye not fair Ines	3
O Tibbie, I hae seen the day	79
O unknown Belov'd one! to the mellow season	115
O waly, waly, up the bank	238
O, where hae ye been, Lord Randal, my son	212
O whistle, and I'll come to you, my lad	158
O, young Lochinvar is come out of the west	261
Oh friend, whom glad or grave we seek	41
Oh, lovely Mary Donnelly, it's you I love the best	235
Once upon a midnight dreary, while I ponder'd, weak and weary	81
One more unfortunate	214
On Linden, when the sun was low	29
Orphan hours, the year is dead	102
Our bugles sang truce, for the night-cloud had lower'd	258
Over hill, over dale	138
Ov all the housen o' the pliace	186
Piping down the valleys wild	54
Poor Jenny were her Roberd's bride	146
Queen and huntress, chaste and fair	239
Rest! this little fountain runs	146
Season of mists and mellow fruitfulness	107
Seven daughters had Lord Archibald	9
Shall I wasting, in despair	256
She dwelt among the untrodden ways	162
Shepherds all, and maidens fair	72
She's up and gone, the graceless girl	248

INDEX OF FIRST LINES.

	Page
Sigh on, sad heart, for Love's eclipse	44
Since there's no help, come let us kiss and parte	179
So am I as the rich, whose blessed key	159
So here hath been dawning	8
Soldier, rest! thy warfare o'er	183
Still-born silence! thou that art	35
Surprised by joy—impatient as the wind	171
Sweet after showers, ambrosial air	213
Sweet, be not proud of those two eyes	46
Swifter far than summer's flight	124
Tall are the towers of O'Kennedy	151
Tears, idle tears, I know not what they mean	173
Tell me not, Sweet, I am unkinde	52
Tell me, thou star whose wings of light	24
That's my last Duchess painted on the wall	25
The dark green Summer with its massive hues	153
The might of one fair face sublimes my love	189
The mountain and the squirrel	89
The *Northern Star*	51
The skies they were ashen and sober	200
The swallow with summer	149
The warm sun is failing, the bleak wind is wailing	12
The waters are flashing	74
The year lies dying in this evening light	44
There is no architect can build	226
There lived a wife at Usher's Well	218
There was a jovial beggar	255
There's not a nook within this solemn Pass	247
They laid my lady in her grave	184
They shot him on the Nine-Stane Rig	23
Think me not unkind or rude	78
This ae nighte, this ae nighte	259
This Sycamore, oft musical with bees	2
Thou lingering star with lessening ray	50
Tiger, tiger, burning bright	95
'Twas in the prime of summer time	56
Two children in two neighbour villages	139
Under the greenwood tree	77
Up! quit thy bower, late wears the hour	2
Up the airy mountain	42
Up! up! ye dames, ye lasses gay	81
We are the sweet Flowers	190

We walk'd along, while bright and red	154
What pleasure have great Princes	251
When cats run home and light is come	55
When I consider how my light is spent	104
When, in disgrace with fortune and men's eyes	150
When the sheep are in the fauld, and the kye at hame	134
When the world is burning	263
Where Claribel low-lieth	36
Where is the grave of Sir Arthur o'Kellyn	220
Where shall the lover rest	148
Where the bee sucks, there suck I	198
Whither, 'midst falling dew	195
Why does your brand sae drap wi' blude	244
Why so pale and wan, fond lover	38
Why weep ye by the tide ladye	6
Ye mariners of England	176
"Yes" I answer'd you last night	123
Yonder to the kiosk beside the creek	114
You spotted snakes with double tongue	232
You thought my heart too far diseased	122
Your picture smiles as first it smiled	13

THE END.

CHISWICK PRESS:—PRINTED BY C. WHITTINGHAM,
TOOKS COURT, CHANCERY LANE.

186, Fleet Street,
June, 1863.

Messrs. BELL and DALDY'S
NEW AND STANDARD PUBLICATIONS.

New Books.

BRITISH Seaweeds. Drawn from Professor Harvey's "Phycologia Britannica," with Descriptions in popular language by Mrs. Alfred Gatty. 4to. 3*l*. 3*s*. [*Ready*.

This volume contains drawings of the British Seaweeds in 803 figures, with descriptions of each, including all the newly discovered species; an Introduction, an Amateur's Synopsis, Rules for preserving and laying out Seaweeds, and the Order of their arrangement in the Herbarium.

British Beetles. Transferred in 259 plates from Curtis's "British Entomology;" with Descriptions by E. W. Janson, Esq., Secretary of the Entomological Society. 4to. 18*s*. Coloured, 1*l*. 11*s*. 6*d*. [*Ready*.

British Moths and Butterflies. Transferred in 195 plates from Curtis's "British Entomology;" with Descriptions by E. W. Janson, Esq., Secretary of the Entomological Society. 4to. [*In the press*.

Jerusalem Explored; being a Description of the Ancient and Modern City, with upwards of One Hundred Illustrations, consisting of Views, Ground-plans, and Sections. By Dr. Ermete Pierotti, Architect-Engineer to His Excellency Soorraya Pasha of Jerusalem, and Architect of the Holy Land. [*In the press*.

Plan de Jerusalem Ancienne et Moderne. Par le Docteur Ermete Pierotti. On a large sheet, 41 in. by 29 in.; with numerous details. Price 10*s*. [*Ready*.

Life, Law, and Literature; Essays on Various Subjects. By W. G. T. Barter. Fcap. 8vo. *[In the press.*

Hymns of Love and Praise for the Church's Year. By the Rev. J. S. B. Monsell, LL.D. Fcap. 8vo. 5s. *[Ready.*

A Manual for Communion Classes and Communicant Meetings. Addressed specially to the Parish Priests and Deacons of the Church of England. By C. Pickering Clarke, M.A., Author of "The Acts and Writings of the Apostles." Fcap. 8vo. 3s. 6d. *[Ready.*

Ballads and Songs. By Bessie Rayner Parkes. Fcap. 8vo. 5s. *[Ready.*

The Story of Queen Isabel, and other Verses. By M. S. Fcap. 8vo. 3s. 6d. *[Ready.*

Love and Mammon, and other Poems. By F. S. Wyvill, Author of "Pansies." Fcap. 8vo. 5s. *[Ready.*

The Odes and Carmen Sæculare of Horace. Translated into English Verse by John Conington, M.A., Corpus Professor of Latin in the University of Oxford. Fcap. 8vo. Roxburgh binding, 5s. 6d. *[Ready.*

The Book of Common Prayer. Ornamented with Head-pieces and Initial Letters specially designed for this edition. Printed in red and black at the Cambridge University Press. 24mo. Best morocco. 10s. 6d. Also in ornamental bindings, at various prices. *[Ready.*

Also a large paper Edition, crown 8vo. Best morocco, 18s. Also in ornamental bindings, at various prices. *[Ready.*

Memoir of a French New Testament, in which the Mass and Purgatory are found in the Sacred Text; together with Bishop Kidder's "Reflections" on the same. By Henry Cotton, D.C.L., Archdeacon of Cashel. *Second Edition, enlarged.* 8vo. 3s. 6d. *[Ready.*

The Divine Authority of the Pentateuch. By Daniel Moore, M.A., Incumbent of Camden Church, Camberwell. Cr. 8vo. 6s. 6d. *[Ready.*

Colenso's Examination of the Pentateuch Examined. By the Rev. G. S. Drew, Author of "Scripture Lands," "Reasons of Faith." Crown 8vo. 3s. 6d. *[Ready.*

The Redeemer: a Series of Sermons on Certain Aspects of the Person and Work of our Lord Jesus Christ. By W. R. Clark, M.A., Vicar of Taunton. Fcap. 8vo. 5s. *[Ready.*

The Fulness of the Manifestation of Jesus Christ: being a Course of Epiphany Lectures. By Hilkiah Bedford Hall, B.C.L. Afternoon Lecturer of the Parish Church, Halifax, Author of "A Companion to the Authorised Version of the New Testament." Fcap. 8vo. 2s. *[Ready.*

The Argument of St. Paul's Epistles to the Churches in Rome Traced and Illustrated: being Twenty-six Sermons with Appendices. By the Rev. C. P. Shepherd, M.A., Magdalen College, Cambridge. Vol. I. Part I, containing Chapters I. to VIII. 8vo. 10s. *[Ready.*

The Bishop of Worcester's Primary Charge, August, 1862. 8vo. 2s. *[Ready.*

A Commentary on the Gospels for the Sundays and other Holy Days of the Christian Year. By the Rev. W. Denton, A.M., Worcester College, Oxford; and Incumbent of St. Bartholomew's Cripplegate. Vol. III. *[In the press.*

Denise. By the Author of "Mademoiselle Mori." 2 vols. Fcap. 8vo. 10s. [Ready.

Legend of the Lintel and the Ley. By W. C. Dendy, Esq. Crown 8vo. 9s. [Ready.

The Adventures of a Little French Boy. With 50 Illustrations. Crown 8vo. Uniform with "Andersen's Tales," and "Robinson Crusoe." [Immediately.

Katie; or the Simple Heart. By D. Richmond, Author of "Annie Maitland." Illustrated by M. I. Booth. Crown 8vo. 6s. [Ready.

Glimpses into Petland. By the Rev. J. G. Wood, M. A. with Frontispiece by Crane. Fcap. 8vo. 3s. 6d. [Ready.

Mildred's Last Night; or, the Franklyns. By the Author of "Aggesden Vicarage." Fcap. 8vo. 4s. 6d. [Ready.

The Leadbeater Papers: a Selection from the MSS. and Correspondence of Mary Leadbeater, containing her Annals of Ballitore, with a Memoir of the Author; Unpublished Letters of Edmund Burke; and the Correspondence of Mrs. R. Trench and Rev. G. Crabbe. *Second Edition.* 2 vols. crown 8vo. 14s. [Ready.

Servia and the Servians By the Rev. W. Denton, M.A. With Illustrations. Crown 8vo. 9s. 6d. [Ready.

An Old Man's Thoughts about Many Things. Being Essays on Schools, Riches, Statues, Books, Place and Power, The Final Cause, &c. Crown 8vo. 7s. 6d. [Ready.

Hints for Pedestrians, Practical and Medical. By G. C. Watson, M.D. *Third Edition, enlarged.* Fcap. 8vo. 2s. 6d. [Ready.

Church Stories. Edited by the Rev. J. E. Clarke. Crown 8vo. 2s. 6d. [Ready.

Karl and the Six Little Dwarfs. By Julia Goddard. Illustrated. 16mo. 2s. 6d. [Ready.

The Thoughts of the Emperor M. Aurelius Antoninus. Translated by George Long. Fcap. 8vo. 6s. [Ready.

The Schole Master. By Roger Ascham. Edited, with copious Notes and a Glossary, by the Rev. J. E. B. Mayor, M.A. Fcap. 8vo. 6s. [Ready.

Charades, Enigmas, and Riddles. Collected by a Cantab. *Fourth Edition, enlarged.* Illustrated. Fcap. 8vo. 2s. 6d. [Ready.

The Book of Psalms; a New Translation, with Introductions and Notes, Critical and Explanatory. By the Rev. J. J. Stewart Perowne, B.D., Fellow of C. C. College, Cambridge, and Examining Chaplain to the Lord Bishop of Norwich. 8vo. [In the Press.

Analecta Graeca Minora. With Introductory Sentences, English Notes, and a Dictionary. By the Rev. P. Frost, late Fellow of St. John's College, Cambridge. Fcap. 8vo. 3s. 6d. [Ready.

Dual Arithmetic, A New Art, by Oliver Byrne, formerly Professor of Mathematics at the late College of Civil Engineers, Putney. 8vo. 10s. 6d. [Ready.

Bell and Daldy's Pocket Volumes. A Series of Select Works of Favourite Authors, adapted for general reading, moderate in price, compact and elegant in form, and executed in a style fitting them to be permanently preserved. Imperial 32mo.

Now Ready.

Sea Songs and Ballads. By Charles Dibdin and others. 2s. 6d.
Burns's Poems. 2s. 6d.
Walton's Complete Angler. Illustrated. 2s. 6d.
White's Natural History of Selborne. 3s.
Coleridge's Poems. 2s. 6d.
The Robin Hood Ballads. 2s. 6d.
The Midshipman.—Autobiographical Sketches of his own early Career, by Capt. Basil Hall, R.N., F.R.S. From his "Fragments of Voyages and Travels." 3s.
The Lieutenant and Commander. By the same Author. 3s.
Southey's Life of Nelson. 2s. 6d.
George Herbert's Poems. 2s.
George Herbert's Works. 3s.

Longfellow's Poems. 2s. 6d.
Lamb's Tales from Shakspeare. 2s.6d.
Milton's Paradise Lost. 2s. 6d.
Milton's Paradise Regained and other Poems. 2s. 6d.

Preparing.

Burns's Songs.
The Conquest of India. By Capt. Basil Hall, R.N.
Walton's Lives of Donne, Wotton, Hooker, &c.
Gray's Poems.
Goldsmith's Poems.
Goldsmith's Vicar of Wakefield.
Henry Vaughan's Poems.
And others.

In cloth, top edge gilt, at 6d. per volume extra; in half morocco, Roxburgh style, at 1s. extra; in antique or best plain morocco (Hayday) at 4s. extra.

DR. RICHARDSON'S New Dictionary of the English Language. Combining Explanation with Etymology, and copiously illustrated by Quotations from the best authorities. *New Edition,* with a Supplement containing additional Words and further Illustrations. In Two Vols. 4to. 4*l*. 14s. 6d. Half bound in russia, 5*l*. 15s. 6d. Russia, 6*l*. 12s.

The Words—with those of the same Family—are traced to their Origin.

The Explanations are deduced from the Primitive Meaning through the various Usages.

The Quotations are arranged Chronologically, from the Earliest Period to the Present Time.

⁎⁎ The Supplement separately, 4to. 12s.

Also, AN EDITION TO BE COMPLETED in 20 Monthly Parts. Price 4s. 6d. each. Parts 1 to 5 *now ready.*

An 8vo. Edition, without the Quotations, 15s. Half-russia, 20s. Russia, 24s.

"It is an admirable addition to our Lexicography, supplying a great desideratum, as exhibiting the biography of each word—its birth, parentage and education, the changes that have befallen it, the company it has kept, and the connexions it has formed—by rich series of quotations, all in chronological order. This is such a Dictionary as perhaps no other language could ever boast."—*Quarterly Review.*

Dr. Richardson on the Study of Language: an Exposition of Horne Tooke's Diversions of Purley. Fcap. 8vo. 4s. 6d.

The Library of English Worthies.

A Series of reprints of the best Authors carefully edited and collated with the Early Copies, and handsomely printed by Whittingham in Octavo.

GOWER'S Confessio Amantis, with Life by Dr. Pauli, and a Glossary. 3 vols. 2*l*. 2*s*. Antique calf, 3*l*. 6*s*. Only a limited number of Copies printed.

This important work is so scarce that it can seldom be met with even in large libraries. It is wanting in nearly every collection of English Poetry.

Spenser's Complete Works; with Life, Notes, and Glossary, by John Payne Collier, Esq., F.S.A. 5 vols. 8vo. 3*l*. 15*s*. Antique calf, 6*l*. 6*s*.

Bishop Butler's Analogy of Religion; with Analytical Index, by the Rev. Edward Steere, LL.D. 8vo. 12*s*. Antique calf, 1*l*. 1*s*.
"The present edition has been furnished with an Index of the Texts of Scripture quoted, and an Index of Words and Things considerably fuller than any hitherto published."—*Editor's Preface.*

Bishop Jeremy Taylor's Rule and Exercises of Holy Living and Dying. 2 vols. 8vo. 1*l*. 1*s*. Morocco, antique calf or morocco, 2*l*. 2*s*.

Herbert's Poems and Remains; with S. T. Coleridge's Notes, and Life by Izaak Walton. Revised, with additional Notes, by Mr. J. Yeowell. 2 vols. 8vo. 1*l*. 1*s*. Morocco, antique calf or morocco, 2*l*. 2*s*.

Uniform with the above.

The Physical Theory of Another Life. By Isaac Taylor, Esq. Author of "Logic in Theology," "Ultimate Civilization, &c." *New Edition.* 10*s*. 6*d*. Antique calf, 21*s*.

HISTORY of England, from the Invasion of Julius Cæsar to the end of the Reign of George II., by Hume and Smollett. With the Continuation, to the Accession of Queen Victoria, by the Rev. T. S. Hughes, B.D. late Canon of Peterborough. *New Edition,* containing Historical Illustrations, Autographs, and Portraits, copious Notes, and the Author's last Corrections and Improvements. In 18 vols. crown 8vo. 4*s*. each.

Vols. I. to VI. (Hume's portion), 1*l*. 4*s*.
Vols. VII. to X. (Smollett's ditto), 16*s*.
Vols. XI. to XVIII. (Hughes's ditto), 1*l*. 12*s*.

History of England, from the Accession of George III. to the Accession of Queen Victoria. By the Rev. T. S. Hughes, B.D. *New Edition,* almost entirely re-written. In 7 vols. 8vo. 3*l*. 13*s*. 6*d*.

The Aldine Edition of the British Poets.

The Publishers have been induced, by the scarcity and increasing value of this admired Series of the Poets, to prepare a New Edition, very carefully corrected, and improved by such additions as recent literary research has placed within their reach.

The general principle of Editing which has been adopted is *to give the entire Poems of each author in strict conformity with the Edition which received his final revision, to prefix a Memoir,* and *to add such notes as may be necessary to elucidate the sense of obsolete words or explain obscure allusions.* Each author will be placed in the hands of a competent editor specially acquainted with the literature and bibliography of the period.

Externally this new edition will resemble the former, but with some improvements. It will be elegantly printed by Whittingham, on toned paper manufactured expressly for it; and a highly-finished portrait of each author will be given.

The *Aldine Edition of the British Poets* has hitherto been the favourite Series with the admirers of choice books, and every effort will be made to increase its claims as a comprehensive and faithful mirror of the poetic genius of the nation.

AKENSIDE'S Poetical Works, with Memoir by the Rev. A. Dyce, and additional Letters, carefully revised. 5s. Morocco, or antique morocco, 10s. 6d.

Collins's Poems, with Memoir and Notes by W. Moy Thomas, Esq. 3s. 6d. Morocco, or antique morocco, 8s. 6d.

Gray's Poetical Works, with Notes and Memoir by the Rev. John Mitford. 5s. Morocco, or antique morocco, 10s. 6d.

Kirke White's Poems, with Memoir by Sir H. Nicolas, and additional notes. Carefully revised. 5s. Morocco, or antique morocco, 10s. 6d.

Shakespeare's Poems, with Memoir by the Rev. A. Dyce. 5s. Morocco, or antique morocco, 10s. 6d.

Young's Poems, with Memoir by the Rev. John Mitford, and additional Poems. 2 vols. 10s. Morocco, or antique morocco, 1l. 1s.

Thomson's Poems, with Memoir by Sir H. Nicolas, annotated by Peter Cunningham, Esq., F.S.A., and additional Poems, carefully revised. 2 vols. 10s. Morocco, or antique morocco, 1l. 1s.

Thomson's Seasons, and Castle of Indolence, with Memoir. 6s. Morocco, or antique morocco, 11s. 6d.

Dryden's Poetical Works, with Memoir by the Rev. R. Hooper, F.S.A. Carefully revised. [*In the Press.*

Cowper's Poetical Works, including his Translations. Edited, with Memoir, by John Bruce, Esq., F.S.A. [*In the Press.*

Uniform with the Aldine Edition of the Poets.

The Works of Gray, edited by the Rev. John Mitford. With his Correspondence with Mr. Chute and others, Journal kept at Rome, Criticism on the Sculptures, &c. New Edition. 5 vols. 1*l*. 5*s*.

The Temple and other Poems. By George Herbert, with Coleridge's Notes. New Edition. Fcap. 8vo. 5*s*. Morocco, antique calf or morocco, 10*s*. 6*d*.

Vaughan's Sacred Poems and Pious Ejaculations, with Memoir by the Rev. H. F. Lyte. New Edition. Fcap. 8vo. 5*s*. Antique calf or morocco, 10*s*. 6*d*. Large Paper, 7*s*. 6*d*. Antique calf, 14*s*. Antique morocco, 15*s*.

"Preserving all the piety of George Herbert, they have less of his quaint and fantastic turns, with a much larger infusion of poetic feeling and expression."—*Lyte.*

Bishop Jeremy Taylor's Rule and Exercises of Holy Living and Holy Dying. 2 vols. 2*s*. 6*d*. each. Morocco, antique calf or morocco, 7*s*. 6*d*. each. In one volume, 5*s*. Morocco, antique calf or morocco, 10*s*. 6*d*.

Bishop Butler's Analogy of Religion; with Analytical Introduction and copious Index, by the Rev. Dr. Steere. 6*s*. Antique calf, 11*s*. 6*d*.

Bishop Butler's Sermons and Remains; with Memoir, by the Rev. E. Steere, LL.D. 6*s*.

*** This volume contains some additional remains, which are copyright, and render it the most complete edition extant.

Bishop Butler's Complete Works; with Memoir by the Rev. Dr. Steere. 2 vols. 12*s*.

Bacon's Advancement of Learning. Edited, with short Notes, by the Rev. G. W. Kitchin, M.A., Christ Church, Oxford. 6*s*.; antique calf, 11*s*. 6*d*.

Bacon's Essays; or, Counsels Civil and Moral, with the Wisdom of the Ancients. With References and Notes by S. W. Singer, F.S.A. 5*s*. Morocco, or antique calf, 10*s*. 6*d*.

Bacon's Novum Organum. Newly translated, with short Notes, by the Rev. Andrew Johnson, M.A. 6*s*. Antique calf, 11*s*. 6*d*.

Locke on the Conduct of the Human Understanding; edited by Bolton Corney, Esq., M. R. S. L. 3*s*. 6*d*. Antique calf, 8*s*. 6*d*.

"I cannot think any parent or instructor justified in neglecting to put this little treatise into the hands of a boy about the time when the reasoning faculties become developed."—*Hallam.*

Ultimate Civilization. By Isaac Taylor, Esq. 6*s*.

Logic in Theology, and other Essays. By Isaac Taylor, Esq. 6*s*.

The Physical Theory of Another Life. By Isaac Taylor, Esq., Author of the "Natural History of Enthusiasm," "Restoration of Belief," &c. New Edition. 6*s*. Antique calf, 11*s*. 6*d*.

DOMESTIC Life in Palestine. By M. E. Rogers. Post 8vo. *Second Edition.* 10s. 6d.

By-Roads and Battle Fields in Picardy: with Incidents and Gatherings by the Way between Ambleteuse and Ham; including Agincourt and Crécy. By G. M. Musgrave, M.A., Illustrated. Super-royal 8vo. 16s.

The Boat and the Caravan. A Family Tour through Egypt and Syria. *New and cheaper Edition.* Fcap. 8vo. 5s. 6d.

Fragments of Voyages and Travels. By Captain Basil Hall, R.N. 1st, 2nd, and 3rd Series in 1 vol. complete. Royal 8vo. 10s. 6d.

Frederick Lucas. A Biography. By C. J. Riethmüller, author of " Teuton," a Poem. Crown 8vo. 4s. 6d.

Adventures of Baron Wenceslas Wratislaw of Mitrowitz; what he saw in the Turkish Metropolis, Constantinople, experienced in his Captivity, and, after his happy return to his country, committed to writing, in the year of our Lord, 1599. Literally translated from the original Bohemian by A. H. Wratislaw, M.A. Crown 8vo. 6s. 6d.

The Gem of Thorney Island; or, The Historical Associations of Westminster Abbey. By the Rev. J. Ridgway, M.A. Crown 8vo. 7s. 6d.

Gifts and Graces. A new Tale, by the Author of "The Rose and the Lotus." Post 8vo. 7s. 6d.

Childhood and Youth. By Count Nicola Tolstoi. Translated from the Russian by Malwida von Meysenbug. Post 8vo. 8s. 6d.

Baronscliffe; or, the Deed of other Days. By Mrs. P. M. Latham, Author of "The Wayfarers." Crown 8vo. 6s.

The Wayfarers: or, Toil and Rest. By Mrs. Latham. Fcap. 5s.

The Manse of Mastland. Sketches: Serious and Humorous, in the Life of a Village Pastor in the Netherlands. Translated from the Dutch by Thomas Keightley, M.A. Post 8vo. 9s.

The Home Life of English Ladies in the Seventeenth Century. By the Author of "Magdalen Stafford." *Second Edition, enlarged.* Fcap. 8vo. 6s. Calf, 9s. 6d.

The Romance and its Hero. By the Author of "Magdalen Stafford." 2 vols. Fcap. 8vo. 12s.

Magdalen Stafford. A Tale. Fcap. 8vo. 5s.

Claude de Vesci; or, the Lost Inheritance. 2 vols. Fcap. 8vo. 9s.

Maud Bingley. By Frederica Graham. 2 vols. Fcap. 8vo. 14s.

BY THE LATE MRS. WOODROOFFE.

COTTAGE Dialogues. *New Edition.* 12mo. 4s. 6d.

Shades of Character; or, the Infant Pilgrim. 7*th Edition*. 2 vols. 12mo. 12s.

Michael Kemp, the Happy Farmer's Lad. 8*th Edition*. 12mo. 4s.

A Sequel to Michael Kemp. *New Edition.* 12mo. 6s. 6d.

Mrs. Alfred Gatty's Popular Works.

"We should not be doing justice to the highest class of juvenile fiction, were we to omit, as particularly worthy of attention at this season, the whole series of Mrs. Gatty's admirable books. They are quite *sui generis*, and deserve the widest possible circulation."—*Literary Churchman*.

PARABLES from Nature; with Notes on the Natural History. Illustrated by W. Holman Hunt, Otto Speckter, C. W. Cope, R. A., E. Warren, W. Millais, G. Thomas, and H. Calderon. 8vo. Ornamental cloth, 10s. 6d. Antique morocco elegant, 1l. 1s.

Parables from Nature. 16mo. with Illustrations. *Tenth Edition*. 3s. 6d. Separately: First Series, 1s. 6d.; Second Series, 2s.

Red Snow, and other Parables from Nature. With Illustrations. Third Series. *Second Edition*. 16mo. 2s.

Worlds not Realized. 16mo. *Third Edition*. 2s.

Proverbs Illustrated. 16mo. with Illustrations. *3rd Edition*. 2s.

*** *These little works have been found useful for Sunday reading in the family circle, and instructive and interesting to school children.*

The Human Face Divine, and other Tales. With Illustrations by C. S. Lane. Fcap. 8vo. 3s. 6d.

The Fairy Godmothers and other Tales. *Third Edition*. Fcap. 8vo. with Frontispiece. 2s. 6d.

Legendary Tales. With Illustrations by Phiz. Fcap. 8vo. 5s.

The Poor Incumbent. Fcap. 8vo. Sewed, 1s. Cloth, 1s. 6d.

The Old Folks from Home; or, a Holiday in Ireland in 1861. *Second Edition*. Post 8vo. 7s. 6d.

Aunt Judy's Tales. Illustrated by Clara S. Lane. Fcap. 8vo. *Third Edition*. 3s. 6d.

Aunt Judy's Letters. Illustrated by Clara S. Lane. Fcap. 8vo. 3s. 6d.

Melchior's Dream, and other Tales. By J. H G. Edited by Mrs. Gatty. Illustrated. Fcap. 8vo. 3s. 6d.

THE Life and Adventures of Robinson Crusoe. By Daniel Defoe. With 100 Illustrations by E. H. Wehnert. Uniform with "Andersen's Tales." Small 8vo. Cloth, gilt edges, 7s. 6d.

Andersen's Tales for Children. Translated by A. Wehnert. With 105 Illustrations by E. H. Wehnert, W. Thomas, and others. Small 8vo. Cloth, gilt edges, 7s. 6d.

Among the Tartar Tents; or, the Lost Fathers. A Tale By Anne Bowman, Author of "Esperanza," "The Boy Voyagers," &c. With Illustrations. Crown 8vo. 5s.

Little Maggie and her Brother. By Mrs. G. Hooper, Author of "Recollections of Mrs. Anderson's School," "Arbell," &c. With a Frontispiece. Fcap. 8vo. 2s. 6d.

Guessing Stories; or, the Surprising Adventures of the Man with the Extra Pair of Eyes. A Book for Young People. By a Country Parson. Imperial 16mo. Cloth, gilt edges, 3s.

Cavaliers and Round Heads. By J. G. Edgar, Author of "Sea Kings and Naval Heroes." Illustrated by Amy Butts. Fcap. 8vo. 5s.

Sea-Kings and Naval Heroes. A Book for Boys. By J. G. Edgar. With Illustrations by C. K. Johnson and C. Keene. Fcap. 8vo. 5s.

The Life of Christopher Columbus, in Short Words. By Sarah Crompton. Crown 8vo. 2s. 6d. Also an Edition for Schools, 1s.

The Life of Martin Luther, in Short Words. By the same Author. Crown 8vo. 1s. 6d. Stiff cover, 1s.

Nursery Tales. By Mrs. Motherly. With Illustrations by C. S. Lane. Imperial 16mo. 2s. 6d. Coloured, gilt edges, 3s. 6d.

Nursery Poetry. By Mrs. Motherly. With Eight Illustrations by C. S. Lane. Imperial 16mo. 2s. 6d. Coloured, gilt edges, 3s. 6d.

Nursery Carols. Illustrated with 120 Pictures. By Ludwig Riether and Oscar Pletsch. Imperial 16mo. Ornamental Binding. 3s. 6d. coloured, 6s.

Poetry for Play-Hours. By Gerda Fay. With Eight large Illustrations. Imperial 16mo. 3s. 6d. Coloured, gilt edges, 4s. 6d.

Very Little Tales for Very Little Children In single Syllables of *Four* and *Five* letters. New Edition. Illustrated. 2 vols. 16mo. 1s. 6d. each, or in 1 vol. 3s.

Progressive Tales for Little Children. In words of *One* and *Two* Syllables. Forming the sequel to "Very Little Tales." New Edition. Illustrated. 2 vols. 16mo. 1s. 6d. each, or in 1 vol. 3s.

The White Lady and Undine, translated from the German by the Hon. C. L. Lyttelton. With numerous Illustrations. Fcap. 8vo. 5s. Or, separately, 2s. 6d. each.

The Lights of the Will o' the Wisp. Translated by Lady Maxwell Wallace. With a coloured Frontispiece. Imperial 16mo. Cloth, gilt edges, 5s.

Voices from the Greenwood. Adapted from the Original. By Lady Maxwell Wallace. With Illustrations. Imperial 16mo. 2s. 6d.

Princess Ilse: a Legend, translated from the German. By Lady Maxwell Wallace. With Illustrations. Imperial 16mo. 2s. 6d.

A Poetry Book for Children. Illustrated with Thirty-seven highly-finished Engravings, by C. W. Cope, R. A., Helmsley, Palmer, Skill, Thomas, and H. Weir. New Edition. Crown 8vo. 2s. 6d.

The Children's Picture Book Series.

Written expressly for Young People, super-royal 16mo.

Cloth, gilt edges, price 5s. each.

BIBLE Picture Book. Eighty Illustrations. (Coloured, 9s.)

Scripture Parables and Bible Miracles. Thirty-two Illustrations. (Coloured, 7s. 6d.)

English History. Sixty Illustrations. (Coloured, 9s.)

Good and Great Men. Fifty Illustrations. (Coloured, 9s.)

Useful Knowledge. One Hundred and Thirty Figures.

Cloth, red edges, price 2s. 6d. each. (*Coloured, gilt edges, 3s. 6d.*)

Scripture Parables. By Rev. J. E. Clarke. 16 Illustrations.

Bible Miracles. By Rev. J. E. Clarke, M.A. 16 Illustrations.

The Life of Joseph. Sixteen Illustrations.

Bunyan's Pilgrim's Progress. Sixteen Illustrations.

CLARK'S Introduction to Heraldry.—Containing Rules for Blazoning and Marshalling Coats of Armour—Dictionary of Terms—Orders of Knighthood explained—Degrees of the Nobility and Gentry—Tables of Precedency; 48 Engravings, including upwards of 1,000 Examples, and the Arms of numerous Families. *Sixteenth Edition improved.* Small 8vo. 7s. 6d. Coloured, 18s.

Book of Family Crests and Mottoes, with *Four Thousand Engravings* of the Crests of the Peers, Baronets, and Gentry of England and Wales, and Scotland and Ireland. A Dictionary of Mottos, &c. *Tenth Edition, enlarged.* 2 vols. small 8vo. 1l. 4s.

"Perhaps the best recommendation to its utility and correctness (in the main) is, that it has been used as a work of reference in the Heralds College. No wonder it sells."—*Spectator.*

A Handbook of Mottoes borne by the Nobility, Gentry, Cities, Public Companies, &c. Translated and Illustrated, with Notes and Quotations, by C. N. Elvin, M.A. Small 8vo. 6s.

Gothic Ornaments; being a Series of Examples of enriched Details and Accessories of the Architecture of Great Britain. Drawn from existing Authorities. By J. K. Colling, Architect. Royal 4to. Vol. I. 3l. 13s. 6d. Vol. II. 3l. 16s. 6d.

Details of Gothic Architecture, Measured and Drawn from existing Examples. By J. K. Colling, Architect. Royal 4to. 2 vols. 5l. 5s.

The Architectural History of Chichester Cathedral, with an Introductory Essay on the Fall of the Tower and Spire. By the Rev. R. Willis, M.A., F.R.S., &c., Jacksonian Professor in the University of Cambridge.—Of Boxgrove Priory, by the Rev. J. L. Petit, M.A., F.S.A. —And of Shoreham Collegiate Church, together with the Collective Architectural History of the foregoing buildings, as indicated by their mouldings, by Edmund Sharpe, M.A., F.R.I B.A. Illustrated by one hundred Plates, Diagrams, Plans and Woodcuts. Super-royal 4to. 1l. 10s.

Architectural Studies in France. By the Rev. J. L. Petit, M.A., F.S.A. With Illustrations from Drawings by the Author and P. H. Delamotte. Imp. 8vo. 2l. 2s.

Remarks on Church Architecture. With Illustrations. By the Rev. J. L. Petit, M.A. 2 vols. 8vo. 1l. 1s.

A Few Notes on the Temple Organ. By Edmund Macrory, M.A. Second Edition. Super-royal 16mo. Half morocco, Roxburgh, 3s. 6d.

Scudamore Organs, or Practical Hints respecting Organs for Village Churches and small Chancels, on improved principles. By the Rev. John Baron, M.A., Rector of Upton Scudamore, Wilts. With Designs by George Edmund Street, F.S.A. *Second Edition, revised and enlarged.* 8vo. 6s.

The Bell; its Origin, History, and Uses. By Rev. A. Gatty. 3s.

Practical Remarks on Belfries and Ringers. By the Rev. H. T. Ellacombe, M.A., F.A.S., Rector of Clyst St. George, Devonshire. *Second Edition*, with an Appendix on Chiming. Illustrated. 8vo. 3s.

Engravings of Unedited or Rare Greek Coins. With Descriptions. By General C. R. Fox. 4to. Part I, Europe. Part II, Asia and Africa. 7s. 6d. each.

Proceedings of the Archæological Institute at Newcastle, in 1853. With Numerous Engravings. 2 vols. 8vo. 2l. 2s.

History of the Parish of Ecclesfield, in the County of York. By the Rev. J. Eastwood, M.A., Incumbent of Hope, Staffordshire, formerly Curate of Ecclesfield. 8vo. 16s.

A Handbook for Visitors to Cambridge. By Norris Deck. Illustrated by 8 Steel Engravings, 97 Woodcuts, and a Map. Crown 8vo. 5s.

Canterbury in the Olden Time: from the Municipal Archives and other Sources. By John Brent, F.S.A. With Illustrations. 5s.

Whirlwinds and Dust-Storms of India. With numerous Illustrations drawn from Nature, bound separately; and an Addendum on Sanitary Measures required for European Soldiers in India. By P. F. H. Baddeley, Surgeon, Bengal Army, Retired List. Large 8vo. With Illustrations, 8s. 6d.; without Illustrations, 3s.
    Two Transparent Wind Cards in Horn, adapted to the Northern and Southern Hemispheres, for the use of Sailors. 2s.

The Addresses of the Hungarian Diet of 1861, to H. I. M. the Emperor of Austria, with the Imperial Rescript and other Documents. Translated for presentation to Members of both Houses of the British Parliament. By J. Horne Payne, Esq., M.A., Lond., of the Inner Temple. Royal 8vo. 2s. 6d.

EBSTER'S Complete Dictionary of the English Language. *New Edition*, revised and greatly enlarged, by CHAUNCEY A. GOODRICH, Professor in Yale College. 4to. (1624 pp.) 1*l*. 11*s*. 6*d*.; half calf, 2*l*.; calf, or half russia, 2*l*. 2*s*.; russia, 2*l*. 10*s*.

Though the circulation of Dr. Webster's celebrated Dictionary, in its various forms, in the United States, in England, and in every country where the English Language is spoken, may be counted by hundreds of thousands, it is believed that there are many persons to whom the book is yet unknown, and who, if seeking for a Dictionary which should supply all reasonable wants, would be at a loss to select one from the numerous competitors in the field.

In announcing this New Edition, the Proprietors desire to call attention to the features which distinguish it, and to put before those who are in want of such a book, the points in which it excels all other Dictionaries, and which render it the best that has as yet been issued for the practical purposes of daily use:—

1. Accuracy of Definition. 2. Pronunciation intelligibly marked. 3. Completeness. 4. Etymology. 5. Obsolete Words. 6. Uniformity in the Mode of Spelling. 7. Quotations. 8. Cheapness.

With the determination that the superiority of the work shall be fully maintained, and that it shall keep pace with the requirements of the age and the universal increase of education, the Proprietors have added to this New Edition, under the editorship of Professor Goodrich.—

A Table of Synonyms. An Appendix of New Words. Table of Quotations, Words, Phrases, &c.

Tables of Interest, enlarged and Improved; calculated at Five per Cent.; Showing at one view the Interest of any Sum, from £1 to £365: they are also carried on by hundreds to £1,000, and by thousands to £10,000. from one day to 365 days. To which are added, Tables of Interest, from one to 12 months, and from two to 13 years. Also Tables for calculating Commission on Sales of Goods or Banking Accounts, from ¼ to 5 per Cent., with several useful additions, among which are Tables for calculating Interest on large sums for 1 day, at the several rates of 4 and 5 per Cent. to £100.000,000. By Joseph King, of Liverpool. 24*th Edition*. With a Table showing the number of days from any one day to any other day in the Year. 8vo. 1*l*. 1*s*.

The Housekeeping Book, or Family Ledger. An Improved Principle, by which an exact Account can be kept of Income and Expenditure; suitable for any Year, and may be begun at any time. With Hints on Household Management, Receipts, &c. By Mrs. Hamilton. 8vo. Cloth, 1*s*. 6*d* sewed, 1*s*.

The Executor's Account Book, with short Practical Instructions for the guidance of Executors. By a Solicitor. Folio. 4*s*.

EGENDS and Lyrics, by Adelaide Anne Procter. 7*th Edition*. Fcap. 5*s*. Antique or best plain morocco, 10*s*. 6*d*.

—— Second Series. *Third Edition.* Fcap. 8vo. 5*s*.; antique or best plain morocco, 10*s*. 6*d*.

The Legend of the Golden Prayers, and other Poems. By C. F. Alexander, Author of "Moral Songs," &c. Fcap. 8vo. 5*s*.; antique or best plain morocco, 10*s*. 6*d*.

Verses for Holy Seasons. By the Same Author. Edited by the Very Rev. W. F. Hook, D.D. 4*th Edition*. Fcap. 3*s*. 6*d*.; morocco, antique calf or morocco, 8*s*. 6*d*.

Nightingale Valley; a Collection of Choice Lyrics and Short Poems. From the time of Shakespeare to the present day. Edited by William Allingham. Fcap. 8vo. 5s.; mor., antique calf or mor., 10s.6d.

Latin Translations of English Hymns. By Charles Buchanan Pearson, M.A., Prebendary of Sarum, and Rector of Knebworth. Fcap. 8vo. 5s.

The Frithiof Saga. A Poem. Translated from the Norwegian. By the Rev. R. Mucklestone, M.A., Rector of Dinedor, Herefordshire; late Fellow and Tutor of Worcester Coll. Oxford. Cr. 8vo. 7s. 6d.

Saul, a Dramatic Poem; Elizabeth, an Historical Ode; and other Poems. By William Fulford, M.A. Fcap. 8vo. 5s.

Lays and Poems on Italy. By F. A. Mackay. Fcap. 8vo. 5s.

Poems from the German. By Richard Garnett, Author of "Io in Egypt, and other Poems." Fcap. 8vo. 3s. 6d.

Io in Egypt, and other Poems. By R. Garnett. Fcap. 8vo. 5s.

The Monks of Kilcrea, and other Poems. *Third Edition.* Post 8vo. 7s. 6d.

Christopheros, and other Poems. By the Ven. W. B. Mant, Archdeacon of Down. Crown 8vo. 6s.

Teuton. A Poem. By C. J. Riethmüller. Crown 8vo. 7s. 6d.

Dryope, and other Poems. By T. Ashe. Fcap. 8vo. 6s.

Wild Thyme. By E. M. Mitchell. Fcap. 8vo. 5s.

Lyrics and Idylls. By Gerda Fay. Fcap. 8vo. 4s.

The Defence of Guenevere, and other Poems. By W. Morris. 5s.

David Mallet's Poems. With Notes and Illustrations by F. Dinsdale, LL.D., F.S.A. *New Edition.* Post 8vo. 10s. 6d.

Ballads and Songs of Yorkshire. Transcribed from private MSS., rare Broadsides, and scarce Publications; with Notes and a Glossary. By C. J. D. Ingledew, M.A., Ph.D., F.G.H.S., author of "The History of North Allerton." Fcap. 8vo. 6s.

Percy's Reliques of Ancient English Poetry. 3 vols. sm. 8vo. 15s. Half-bound, 18s. Antique calf, or morocco, 1l. 11s. 6d.

Ellis's Specimens of Early English Poetry. 3 vols. sm. 8vo. 15s. Half-bound, 18s. Antique calf, or morocco, 1l. 11s. 6d.

The Book of Ancient Ballad Poetry of Great Britain. Historical, Traditional and Romantic: with Modern Imitations, Translations, Notes and Glossary, &c. Edited by J. S. Moore. *New and Improved Edition*, 8vo. Half-bound, 14s. Antique morocco, 21s.

The Promises of Jesus Christ. Illuminated by Albert H. Warren, *Second Edition.* Ornamental cloth, 15s. Antique morocco elegant, 21s.

Christmas with the Poets: a Collection of English Poetry relating to the Festival of Christmas. Illustrated by Birket Foster, and with numerous initial letters and borders beautifully printed in gold and colours by Edmund Evans. *New and improved Edition.* Super royal 8vo. Ornamental binding, 21s. Antique morocco, 31s. 6d.

ATHENÆ Cantabrigienses. By C. H. Cooper, F.S.A., and Thompson Cooper. Volume I. 1500—1585. 8vo. 18s. Vol. II. 1586—1609. 8vo. 18s.

This work, in illustration of the biography of notable and eminent men who have been members of the University of Cambridge, comprehends notices of:—1. Authors. 2. Cardinals, archbishops, bishops, abbots, heads of religious houses and other church dignitaries. 3. Statesmen, diplomatists, military and naval commanders. 4. Judges and eminent practitioners of the civil or common law. 5. Sufferers for religious or political opinions. 6. Persons distinguished for success in tuition. 7. Eminent physicians and medical practitioners. 8. Artists, musicians, and heralds. 9. Heads of colleges, professors, and principal officers of the university. 10. Benefactors to the university and colleges, or to the public at large.

The Early and Middle Ages of England. By C. H. Pearson, M.A., Fellow of Oriel College, Oxford, and Professor of Modern History, King's College, London. 8vo. 12s.

Choice Notes from "Notes and Queries," by the Editor. Fcap. 8vo. 5s. each.
  Vol. I.—History.   Vol. II.—Folk Lore.

Master Wace's Chronicle of the Conquest of England. Translated from the Norman by Sir Alexander Malet, Bart., H.B.M. Plenipotentiary, Frankfort. With Photograph Illustrations of the Bayeaux Tapestry. Medium 4to. Half-morocco, Roxburgh, 2l. 2s.

The Prince Consort's Addresses on Different Public Occasions. Beautifully printed by Whittingham. 4to. 10s. 6d.

Life and Books; or, Records of Thought and Reading. By J. F. Boyes, M.A. Fcap. 8vo. 5s.; calf, 8s. 6d.

Life's Problems. By Sir Rutherford Alcock, K.C.B. *Second Edition*, revised and enlarged. Fcap. 5s.

Parliamentary Short-Hand (Official System). By Thompson Cooper. Fcap. 8vo. 2s. 6d.

This is the system *universally practised by the Government Official Reporters*. It has many advantages over the system ordinarily adopted, and has hitherto been inaccessible, except in a high-priced volume.

English Retraced; or, Remarks, Critical and Philological, founded on a Comparison of the Breeches Bible with the English of the present day. Crown 8vo. 5s.

The Pleasures of Literature. By R. Aris Willmott, Incumbent of Bear-Wood. *Fifth Edition*, enlarged. Fcap. 8vo. 5s. Morocco, 10s. 6d.

Hints and Helps for Youths leaving School. By the Rev. J. S. Gilderdale, M.A. Fcap. 8vo. 5s. Calf, 8s. 6d.

Hints to Maid Servants in Small Households, on Manners, Dress, and Duties. By Mrs. Motherly. Fcap. 8vo. 1s. 6d.

A Wife's Home Duties; containing Hints to inexperienced Housekeepers. Fcap. 8vo. 2s. 6d.

Geology in the Garden: or, The Fossils in the Flint Pebbles. With 106 Illustrations. By the Rev. Henry Eley, M.A. Fcap. 8vo. 6s.

Halcyon: or Rod-Fishing in Clear Waters. By Henry Wade, Secretary to the Weardale Angling Association. With Coloured representations of the principal Flies, and other Illustrations. Cr. 8vo. 7s. 6d.

A Handy Book of the Chemistry of Soils: Explanatory of their Composition, and the Influence of Manures in ameliorating them, with Outlines of the various Processes of Agricultural Analysis. By John Scoffern, M.B. Crown 8vo. 4s. 6d.

Flax and its Products in Ireland. By William Charley, J. P., Juror and Reporter Class XIV, Great Exhibition 1851; also appointed in 1862 for Class XIX. With a Frontispiece. Crown 8vo. 5s.

SERMONS.

PARISH SERMONS. By the Rev. M. F. Sadler, M.A., Vicar of Bridgwater. Author of the "Sacrament of Responsibility," and "The Second Adam and the New Birth." Fcap. 8vo. Vol. I, Advent to Trinity; Vol. II, Trinity to Advent. 7s. 6d. each.

Twenty-four Sermons on Christian Doctrine and Practice, and on the Church. By C. J. Blomfield, D.D., late Lord Bishop of London. (*Hitherto unpublished.*) 8vo. 10s. 6d.

King's College Sermons. By the Rev. E. H. Plumptre, M.A., Divinity Professor. Fcap. 8vo. 2s. 6d.

Sermons preached in Westminster. By the Rev. C. F. Secretan, M.A., Incumbent of Holy Trinity, Vauxhall-Bridge Road. Fcap. 8vo. 6s.

Sermons. By the Rev. A. Gatty, D.D., Vicar of Ecclesfield. 12mo. 8s.

Twenty Plain Sermons for Country Congregations and Family Reading. By the Rev. A. Gatty, D.D., Vicar of Ecclesfield. Fcap. 5s.

Sermons to a Country Congregation—Advent to Trinity. By the Rev. Hastings Gordon, M.A. 12mo 6s.

Sermons on Popular Subjects, preached in the Collegiate Church, Wolverhampton. By the Rev. Julius Lloyd, M.A. 8vo. 4s. 6d.

Gospel Truths in Parochial Sermons for the Great Festivals. By the Rev. J. Townson, M.A. Fcap. 8vo. 2s. 6d.

Four Sermons on the "Comfortable Words" in the Office for the Holy Communion. By Alexander Goalen, B.A. Fcap. 8vo. 2s.

The Prodigal Son. Sermons by W. R. Clark, M.A., Vicar of Taunton, S. Mary Magdalene. Fcap. 8vo. 2s. 6d.

The Redeemer: a Series of Sermons on Certain Aspects of the Person and Work of our Lord Jesus Christ. By W. R. Clark, M.A., Vicar of Taunton. Fcap. 8vo. 5s.

The Fulness of the Manifestation of Jesus Christ; being a Course of Epiphany Lectures. By Hilkiah Bedford Hall, B.C.L., Afternoon Lecturer of the Parish Church, Halifax, Author of " A Companion to the Authorized Version of the New Testament. Fcap. 8vo. 2s.

Parochial Sermons. By the Rev. D. G. Stacy, Vicar of Hornchurch, Essex. Fcap. 8vo. 5s.

Sermons Suggested by the Miracles of our Lord and Saviour Jesus Christ. By the Very Rev. Dean Hook. 2 vols. Fcap. 8vo. 12s.

Five Sermons Preached before the University of Oxford. By the Very Rev. W. F. Hook, D.D., Dean of Chichester. *Third Edition.* 3s.

Plain Parochial Sermons. By the Rev. C. F. C. Pigott, B.A., late Curate of St. Michael's, Handsworth. Fcap. 8vo. 6s.

Our Privileges, Responsibilities, and Trials. By the Rev. E. Phillips, M.A. Fcap. 8vo. 5s.

Sermons, chiefly Practical. By the Rev. T. Nunns, M.A. Edited by the Very Rev. W. F. Hook, D.D., Dean of Chichester. Fcap. 8vo. 6s.

Sermons, Preached in the Parish Church of Godalming, Surrey, by the Rev. E. J. Boyce, M.A., Vicar. *Second Edition.* Fcap. 8vo. 6s.

Life in Christ. By the Rev. J. Llewellyn Davies, M.A., Rector of Christ Church, Marylebone. Fcap. 8vo. 5s.

The Church of England; its Constitution, Mission, and Trials. By the Rt. Rev. Bishop Broughton. Edited, with a Prefatory Memoir, by the Ven. Archdeacon Harrison. 8vo. 10s. 6d.

Plain Sermons, Addressed to a Country Congregation. By the late E. Blencowe, M.A. 1st and 3rd Series, fcap. 8vo. 7s. 6d. each.

Occasional Sermons. By a Member of the Church of England. Fcap. 8vo. 2s. 6d.

Missionary Sermons preached at Hagley. Fcap. 3s. 6d.

The Sufficiency of Christ. Sermons preached during the Reading Lenten Mission of 1860. Fcap. 8vo. 2s. 6d.

Westminster Abbey Sermons for the Working Classes. Fcap. *Authorized Edition.* 1858. 2s.; 1859. 2s. 6d.

Sermons preached at St. Paul's Cathedral. *Authorized Edition.* 1859. Fcap. 8vo. 2s. 6d.

AILY Readings for a Year, on the Life of Our Lord and Saviour Jesus Christ. By the Rev. Peter Young, M.A. *Second Edition,* improved. 2 vols. Crown 8vo. 1l. 1s. Antique calf, 1l. 16s. Morocco, Hayday, 2l.

Short Sunday Evening Readings, Selected and Abridged from various Authors by the Dowager Countess of Cawdor. In large type. 8vo. 5s.

A Commentary on the Gospels for the Sundays and other Holy Days of the Christian Year. By the Rev. W. Denton, A.M., Worcester College, Oxford, and Incumbent of St. Bartholomew's, Cripplegate. 8vo. Vol. 1. Advent to Easter, 15s. Vol. II. Easter to the Sixteenth Sunday after Trinity, 14s.

Lights of the Morning: or, Meditations for every Day in the Year. From the German of Frederic Arndt. With a Preface by the Rev. W. C. Magee, D.D. Fcap. 8vo. Advent to Whitsuntide, 5s. 6d. Trinity, 5s. 6d.

The Second Adam, and the New Birth; or, the Doctrine of Baptism as contained in Holy Scripture. By the Rev. M. F. Sadler, M.A. Vicar of Bridgewater, Author of "The Sacrament of Responsibility." *Third Edition*, greatly enlarged. Fcap. 8vo. 4s. 6d.

The Sacrament of Responsibility; or, Testimony of the Scripture to the teaching of the Church on Holy Baptism, with especial reference to the Cases of Infants, and Answers to Objections. *Sixth Edition.* 6d.

Popular Illustrations of some Remarkable Events recorded in the Old Testament. By the Rev. J. F. Dawson, LL.B., Rector of Toynton. Post 8vo. 8s. 6d.

The Acts and Writings of the Apostles. By C. Pickering Clarke, M.A., late Curate of Teddington. Post 8vo. Vol. I., with Map., 7s. 6d.

The Spirit of the Hebrew Poetry. By Isaac Taylor, Esq., Author of "The Natural History of Enthusiasm," "Ultimate Civilization," &c. 8vo. 10s. 6d.

The Wisdom of the Son of David: an Exposition of the First Nine Chapters of the Book of Proverbs. Fcap. 8vo. 5s.

A Companion to the Authorized Version of the New Testament: being Explanatory Notes, together with Explanatory Observations and an Introduction. By the Rev. H. B. Hall, B.C.L. *Second and cheaper Edition*, revised and enlarged. Fcap. 8vo. 3s. 6d.

A History of the Church of England from the Accession of James II. to the Rise of the Bangorian Controversy in 1717. By the Rev. T. Debary, M.A. 8vo. 14s.

A Treatise on Metaphysics in Connection with Revealed Religion. By the Rev. J. H. MacMahon. 8vo. 14s.

Aids to Pastoral Visitation, selected and arranged by the Rev. H. B. Browning, M.A., Curate of St. George, Stamford. *Second Edition.* Fcap. 8vo. 3s. 6d.

Remarks on Certain Offices of the Church of England, popularly termed the Occasional Services. By the Rev. W. J. Dampier. 12mo. 5s.

The Sympathy of Christ. Six Readings for the Sundays in Lent, or for the Days of the Holy Week. By the Rev. W. J. Dampier, M.A., Vicar of Coggeshall. *Second Edition.* 18mo. 2s. 6d.

Reasons of Faith; or, the Order of the Christian Argument developed and explained. By the Rev. G. S. Drew, M.A. Fcap. 8vo. 4s. 6d.

Charles and Josiah; or, Friendly Conversations between a Churchman and a Quaker. Crown 8vo. 5s.

Papers on Preaching and Public Speaking. By a Wykehamist. Fcap. 8vo. 5s.
> This volume is an enlargement and extension, with corrections, of the Papers which appeared in the "Guardian" in 1858-9.

The Speaker at Home. Chapters on Public Speaking and Reading aloud, by the Rev. J. J. Halcombe, M.A., and on the Physiology of Speech, by W. H. Stone, M.A., M.B. *Second Edition.* Fcap. 8vo. 3s. 6d.

The English Churchman's Signal. By the Writer of "A Plain Word to the Wise in Heart." Fcap. 8vo. 2s. 6d.

A Plain Word to the Wise in Heart on our Duties at Church, and on our Prayer Book. *Fourth Edition.* Sewed, 1s. 6d.

Readings on the Morning and Evening Prayer and the Litany. By J. S. Blunt. *Second Edition, enlarged.* Fcap. 8vo. 3s. 6d.

Confirmation. By J. S. Blunt, Author of "Readings on the Morning and Evening Prayer," &c. Fcap. 8vo. 3s. 6d.

Life after Confirmation. By the same Author. 18mo. 1s.

The Book of Psalms (Prayer Book Version). With Short Headings and Explanatory Notes. By the Rev. Ernest Hawkins, B.D., Prebendary of St. Paul's. *Second and cheaper Edition, revised and enlarged,* Fcap. 8vo., cloth limp, red edges, 2s. 6d.

Family Prayers:—containing Psalms, Lessons, and Prayers, for every Morning and Evening in the Week. By the Rev. Ernest Hawkins, B.D., Prebendary of St. Paul's. *Eighth Edition.* Fcap. 8vo. 1s.; sewed, 9d.

Household Prayers on Scriptural Subjects, for Four Weeks. With Forms for various occasions. By a Member of the Church of England. *Second Edition, enlarged.* 8vo. 4s. 6d.

Forms of Prayer adapted to each Day of the Week. For use in Families or Households. By the Rev. John Jebb, D.D., 8vo. 2s. 6d.

Walton's Lives of Donne, Wotton, Hooker, Herbert, and Sanderson. A New Edition, to which is now added a Memoir of Mr. Isaac Walton, by William Dowling, Esq. of the Inner Temple, Barrister-at-Law. With Illustrative Notes, numerous Portraits, and other Engravings, Index, &c. Crown 8vo. 10s. 6d. Calf antique, 15s. Morocco, 18s.

The Life of Martin Luther. By H. Worsley, M.A., Rector of Easton, Suffolk. 2 vols. 8vo. 1l. 4s.

Civilization considered as a Science in Relation to its Essence, its Elements, and its End. By George Harris, F.S.A., of the Middle Temple, Barrister at Law, Author of "The Life of Lord Chancellor Hardwicke." 8vo. 12s.

The Church Hymnal, (with or without Psalms.) 12mo. Large Type, 1s. 6d. 18mo. 1s. 32mo. for Parochial Schools, 6d.
This book is now in use in every English Diocese, and is the *Authorized* Book in some of the Colonial Dioceses.

Three Lectures on Archbishop Cranmer. By the Rev. C. J. Burton, M.A., Chancellor of Carlisle. 12mo. 3s.

Church Reading: according to the method advised by Thomas Sheridan. By the Rev. J. J. Halcombe, M.A. 8vo. 3s. 6d.

The Kafir, the Hottentot, and the Frontier Farmer. Passages of Missionary Life from the Journals of the Ven. Archdeacon Merriman. Illustrated. Fcap. 8vo. 3s. 6d.

Lectures on the Tinnevelly Missions. By the Rev. Dr. Caldwell, of Edeyenkoody. Crown 8vo. 2s. 6d.

The "Cruise of the Beacon." A Narrative of a Visit to the Islands in Bass's Straits. By the Right Rev. the Bishop of Tasmania. With Illustrations. Crown 8vo. 5s.

*** Messrs. Bell and Daldy are agents for all the other Publications of the Society for the Propagation of the Gospel in Foreign Parts.

Authentic Memoirs of the Christian Church in China. By John Laurence de Mosheim, Chancellor of the University of Göttingen. Translated from the German. Edited, with an Introduction and notes, by Richard Gibbings, B.D., Rector of Tessauran, and Vicar of Ferbane, in the Diocese of Meath. 3s. 6d.

Giles Witherne; or, The Reward of Disobedience. A Village Tale for the Young. By the Rev. J. P. Parkinson, D.C.L. *Sixth Edition.* Illustrated by the Rev. F. W. Mann. Super-royal 16mo. 1s. Cloth, gilt edges, 2s. 6d.

The Disorderly Family; or, the Village of R****. A Tale for Young Persons. In Two Parts. By a Father. 6d.; Cloth, gilt edges, 1s.

The Offertory: the most excellent way of contributing Money for Christian Purposes. By J. H. Markland, D.C.L., F.R.S., S.A. *Second Edition, enlarged,* 2d.

By the Rev. J. ERSKINE CLARKE, *of Derby.*

HEART Music, for the Hearth-Ring; the Street-Walk; the Country Stroll; the Work-Hours; the Rest-Day; the Trouble-Time. *New Edition.* 1s. paper; 1s. 6d. cloth limp.

The Giant's Arrows. A Book for the Children of Working People. 16mo. 6d.; cloth, 1s.

Children at Church. Twelve Simple Sermons. 2 vols. 1s. each; 1s. 6d. cloth, gilt; or together in 1 vol. cloth gilt, 2s. 6d.

Plain Papers on the Social Economy of the People. Fcap. 8vo. 2s. 6d.
No. 1. Recreations of the People.—No. 2. Penny Banks.—No. 3. Labourers' Clubs and Working Men's Refreshment Rooms.—No. 4. Children of the People. 6d. each.

The Devotional Library.

Edited by the Very Rev. W. F. HOOK, D.D., Dean of Chichester.

A Series of Works, original or selected from well-known Church of England Divines, published at the lowest price, and suitable, from their practical character and cheapness, for Parochial distribution.

SHORT Meditations for Every Day in the Year. 2 vols. (1260 pages,) 32mo. Cloth, 5s.; calf, gilt edges, 9s. Calf antique, 12s.

In Separate Parts.

ADVENT to LENT, cloth, 1s.; limp calf, gilt edges, 2s. 6d.; LENT, cloth, 9d.: calf. 2s. 3d. EASTER, cloth, 9d.; calf, 2s. 3d. TRINITY, Part I. 1s.; calf, 2s. 6d. TRINITY, Part II. 1s.; calf, 2s. 6d.

*** *Large Paper Edition,* 4 vols. fcap. 8vo. large type. 14s. Morocco, 30s.

The Christian taught by the Church's Services. (490 pages), royal 32mo. Cloth, 2s. 6d.; calf, gilt edges, 4s. 6d. Calf antique, 6s.

In Separate Parts.

ADVENT TO TRINITY, cloth, 1s.; limp calf, gilt edges, 2s. 6d. TRINITY, cloth, 8d.; calf, 2s. 2d. MINOR FESTIVALS, 8d.; calf, 2s. 2d.

*** *Large Paper Edition,* Fcap. 8vo. large type. 6s. 6d. Calf antique, or morocco, 11s. 6d.

Devotions for Domestic Use. 32mo. cloth, 2s.; calf, gilt edges, 4s. Calf antique, 5s. 6d. Containing:—

    The Common Prayer Book the best Companion in the Family as well as in the Temple. 3d.
    Litanies for Domestic Use, 2d.
    Family Prayers; or, Morning and Evening Services for every Day in the Week. By the Bishop of Salisbury; cloth, 6d.; calf, 2s.
    Bishop Hall's Sacred Aphorisms. Selected and arranged with the Texts to which they refer. By the Rev. R. B. Exton, M.A.; cloth, 9d.

*** These are arranged together as being suitable for Domestic Use; but they may be had separately at the prices affixed.

Aids to a Holy Life. First Series. 32mo. Cloth, 1s. 6d.; calf, gilt edges, 3s. 6d. Calf antique, 5s. Containing:—

    Prayers for the Young. By Dr. Hook, ½d.
    Pastoral Address to a Young Communicant. By Dr. Hook, ½d.
    Helps to Self-Examination. By W. F. Hook, D.D., ½d.
    Directions for Spending One Day Well. By Archbishop Synge, ½d.
    Rules for the Conduct of Human Life. By Archbishop Synge. 1d.
    The Sum of Christianity, wherein a short and plain Account is given of the Christian Faith; Christian's Duty; Christian Prayer; Christian Sacrament. By C. Ellis, 1d.
    Ejaculatory Prayer; or, the Duty of Offering up Short Prayers to God on all Occasions. By R. Cook. 2d.
    Prayers for a Week. From J. Sorocold, 2d.
    Companion to the Altar; being Prayers, Thanksgivings, and Meditations. Edited by Dr. Hook. Cloth, 6d.

*** Any of the above may be had for distribution at the prices affixed; they are arranged together as being suitable for Young Persons and for Private Devotion.

The Devotional Library continued.

Aids to a Holy Life. Second Series. 32mo. Cloth, 2s.; calf, gilt edges, 4s. Calf antique, 5s. 6d. Containing:—
   Holy Thoughts and Prayers, arranged for Daily Use on each Day in the Week, 3d.
   The Retired Christian exercised on Divine Thoughts and Heavenly Meditations. By Bishop Ken. 3d.
   Penitential Reflections for the Holy Season of Lent, and other Days of Fasting and Abstinence during the Year. 6d.
   The Crucified Jesus; a Devotional Commentary on the XXII and XXIII Chapters of St. Luke. By A. Horneck, D.D. 3d.
   Short Reflections for every Morning and Evening during the Week. By N. Spinckes, 2d.
   The Sick Man Visited; or, Meditations and Prayers for the Sick Room. By N. Spinckes, 3d.

** These are arranged together as being suitable for Private Meditation and Prayer: they may be had separately at the prices affixed.

Helps to Daily Devotion. 32mo. Cloth, 8d. Containing:—
   The Sum of Christianity, 1d.
   Directions for spending One Day Well, ½d.
   Helps to Self-Examination, ½d.
   Short Reflections for Morning and Evening, 2d.
   Prayers for a Week, 2d.

The History of our Lord and Saviour Jesus Christ; in Three Parts, with suitable Meditations and Prayers. By W. Reading, M.A. 32mo. Cloth, 2s.; calf, gilt edges, 4s. Calf antique, 5s. 6d.

Hall's Sacred Aphorisms. Selected and arranged with the Texts to which they refer, by the Rev. R. B. Exton, M.A. 32mo. cloth, 9d.; limp calf, gilt edges, 2s. 3d.

Devout Musings on the Book of Psalms. 2 vols. 32mo. Cloth, 5s.; calf, gilt edges, 9s.; calf antique, 12s. Or, in four parts, price 1s. each; limp calf, gilt edges, 2s. 6d.

The Church Sunday School Hymn Book. 32mo. cloth, 8d.; calf, gilt edges, 2s. 6d.

** A *Large Paper Edition* for Prizes, &c. 1s. 6d.; calf, gilt edges, 3s. 6d.

SHORT Meditations for Every Day in the Year. Edited by the Very Rev. W. F. Hook, D.D. *New Edition.* 4 vols. fcap. 8vo., large type, 14s.; morocco, 30s.

The Christian taught by the Church's Services. Edited by the Very Rev. W. F. Hook, D.D. *New Edition*, fcap. 8vo. large type. 6s. 6d. Antique calf, or morocco, 11s. 6d.

Holy Thoughts and Prayers, arranged for Daily Use on each Day of the Week, according to the stated Hours of Prayer. *Fifth Edition,* with additions. 16mo. Cloth, red edges, 2s.; calf, gilt edges, 3s.

A Companion to the Altar. Being Prayers, Thanksgivings, and Meditations, and the Office of the Holy Communion. Edited by the Very Rev. W. F. Hook, D.D. *Second Edition.* Handsomely printed in red and black. 32mo. Cloth, red edges, 2s. Morocco, 3s. 6d.

The Church Sunday School Hymn Book. Edited by W. F. Hook, D.D. *Large paper.* Cloth, 1s. 6d.; calf, gilt edges, 3s. 6d.

** For cheap editions of the above Five Books, see List of the Devotional Library.

EDUCATIONAL BOOKS.

Bibliotheca Classica.

A Series of Greek and Latin Authors. With English Notes. 8vo. Edited by various Scholars, under the direction of G. Long, Esq., M.A., Classical Lecturer of Brighton College: and the late Rev. A. J. Macleane, M.A, Head Master of King Edward's School, Bath.

ÆSCHYLUS. By F. A. Paley, M.A. 18s.

    Cicero's Orations. Edited by G. Long, M.A. 4 vols.
    Vol. I. 16s.; Vol. II. 14s; Vol. III. 16s.; Vol. IV. 18s.

Demosthenes. By R. Whiston, M.A., Head Master of Rochester Grammar School. Vol. I. 16s. Vol. II. *preparing.*

Euripides. By F. A. Paley, M.A. 3 vols. 16s. each.

Herodotus. By J. W. Blakesley, B.D., late Fellow and Tutor of Trinity College, Cambridge. 2 vols. 32s.

Hesiod. By F. A. Paley, M.A. 10s. 6d.

Homer. By F. A. Paley, M. A. Vol. I. [*Preparing.*

Horace. By A. J. Macleane, M.A. 18s.

Juvenal and Persius. By A. J. Macleane, M.A. 14s.

Plato. By W. H. Thompson, M.A. Vol. I. [*Preparing.*

Sophocles. By F. H. Blaydes, M.A. Vol. I. 18s. Vol. II. *preparing.*

Terence. By E. St. J. Parry, M.A., Balliol College, Oxford. 18s.

Virgil. By J. Conington, M.A., Professor of Latin at Oxford.
    Vol. I. containing the Bucolics and Georgics. 12s. Vol. II. containing the Æneid, Books I. to VI. 14s.

Grammar-School Classics.

A Series of Greek and Latin Authors. Newly Edited, with English Notes for Schools. Fcap. 8vo.

CAESARIS Commentarii de Bello Gallico. *Second Edition.* By G. Long, M.A. 5s. 6d.

    Caesar de Bello Gallico, Books 1 to 3. With English Notes for Junior Classes. By G. Long, M A. 2s. 6d.

M. Tullii Ciceronis Cato Major, Sive de Senectute, Laelius, Sive de Amicitia, et Epistolae Selectae. By G. Long, M.A. 4s. 6d.

Quinti Horatii Flacci Opera Omnia. By A. J. Macleane, 6s. 6d.

Juvenalis Satirae XVI. By H. Prior, M.A. (Expurgated Edition). 4s. 6d.

Grammar-School Classics continued.

P. Ovidii Nasonis Fastorum Libri Sex. By F. A. Paley. 5s.

C. Sallustii Crispi Catilina et Jugurtha. By G. Long, M.A. 5s.

Taciti Germania et Agricola. By P. Frost, M.A. 3s. 6d.

Xenophontis Anabasis, with Introduction; Geographical and other Notes, Itinerary, and Three Maps compiled from recent surveys. By J. F. Macmichael, B.A. *New Edition.* 5s.

Xenophontis Cyropaedia. By G. M. Gorham, M.A., late Fellow of Trinity College, Cambridge. 6s.

Uniform with the above.

The New Testament in Greek. With English Notes and Prefaces by J. F. Macmichael, B.A. 730 pages. 7s. 6d.

Cambridge Greek and Latin Texts.

THIS series is intended to supply for the use of Schools and Students cheap and accurate editions of the Classics, which shall be superior in mechanical execution to the small German editions now current in this country, and more convenient in form.

The texts of the *Bibliotheca Classica* and *Grammar School Classics*, so far as they have been published, will be adopted. These editions have taken their place amongst scholars as valuable contributions to the Classical Literature of this country, and are admitted to be good examples of the judicious and practical nature of English scholarship; and as the editors have formed their texts from a careful examination of the best editions extant, it is believed that no texts better for general use can be found.

The volumes will be well printed at the Cambridge University Press, in a 16mo. size, and will be issued at short intervals.

AESCHYLUS, ex novissima recensione F. A. Paley. 3s.

Caesar de Bello Gallico, recensuit G. Long, A.M. 2s.

Cicero de Senectute et de Amicitia et Epistolae Selectae, recensuit G. Long, A.M. 1s. 6d.

Euripides, ex recensione F. A. Paley, A. M. 3 vols. 3s. 6d. each.

Herodotus, recensuit J. W. Blakesley, S.T.B. 2 vols. 7s.

Horatius, ex recensione A. J. Macleane, A.M. 2s. 6d.

Lucretius, recognovit H. A. J. Munro, A.M. 2s. 6d.

Sallusti Crispi Catilina et Jugurtha, recognovit G. Long, A.M. 1s. 6d.

Thucydides, recensuit J. G. Donaldson, S.T.P. 2 vols. 7s.

Vergilius, ex recensione J. Conington, A.M. 3s. 6d.

Xenophontis Anabasis recensuit J. F. Macmichael, A.B. 2s. 6d.

Novum Testamentum Graecum Textus Stephanici, 1550. Accedunt variae Lectiones editionum Bezae, Elzeviri, Lachmanni, Tischendorfii, Tregellesii, curante F. H. Scrivener, A.M. 4s. 6d.

Also, on 4to. writing paper, for MSS. notes. Half bound, gilt top, 12s.

Foreign Classics.

With English Notes for Schools. Uniform with the GRAMMAR SCHOOL CLASSICS. Fcap. 8vo.

AVENTURES de Télémaque, par Fénelon. Edited by C. J. Delille. *Second Edition, revised.* 4s. 6d.

Histoire de Charles XII. par Voltaire. Edited by L. Direy. *Second Edition, revised.* 3s. 6d.

Select Fables of La Fontaine. *Third Edition, revised.* Edited by F. Gasc, M.A. 3s.

" None need now be afraid to introduce this eminently French author, either on account of the difficulty of translating him, or the occasional licence of thought and expression in which he indulges. The renderings of idiomatic passages are unusually good, and the purity of English perfect."—*Athenæum.*

Picciola, by X. B. Saintine. Edited by Dr. Dubuc. 3s. 6d.

This interesting story has been selected with the intention of providing for schools and young persons a good specimen of contemporary French literature, free from the solecisms which are frequently met with in writers of a past age.

Schiller's Wallenstein, complete Text. Edited by Dr. A. Buchheim. 6s 6d.

German Ballads from Uhland, Goethe, and Schiller Edited by C. L. Bielefield, of the Forest School, Walthamstow. [*In the press.*

Classical Tables. 8vo.

NOTABILIA Quædam: or, the principal tenses of such Irregular Greek Verbs and such elementary Greek, Latin, and French Constructions as are of constant occurrence. 1s. 6d.

Greek Accidence. By the Rev. P. Frost, M.A. 1s.

Latin Accidence. By the Rev. P. Frost, M.A. 1s.

Latin Versification. 1s.

The Principles of Latin Syntax. 1s.

Homeric Dialect: its leading Forms and Peculiarities. By J. S. Baird, T.C.D. 1s. 6d.

A Catalogue of Greek Verbs, Irregular and Defective; their leading formations, tenses in use, and dialectic inflexions; with a copious Appendix, containing Paradigms for conjugation, Rules for formation of tenses, &c. &c. By J. S. Baird, T.C.D. *New Edition, revised.* 3s. 6d.

Richmond Rules to form the Ovidian Distich, &c. By J. Tate, M.A. *New Edition, revised.* 1s. 6d.

AN Atlas of Classical Geography, containing 24 Maps; constructed by W. Hughes, and edited by G. Long. *New Edition*, with coloured outlines, and an Index of Places. 12s. 6d.

A Grammar School Atlas of Classical Geography. The Maps constructed by W. Hughes, and edited by G. Long. Imp. 8vo. 5s.

First Classical Maps, with Chronological Tables of Grecian and Roman History, Tables of Jewish Chronology, and a Map of Palestine. By the Rev. J. Tate, M.A. *Third Edition.* Imp. 8vo. 7s. 6d.

The Choephorae of Æschylus and its Scholia. Revised and interpreted by J. F. Davies, Esq., B.A., Trin. Coll., Dublin. 8vo. 7s. 6d.

Homer and English Metre. An Essay on the Translating of the Iliad and Odyssey. With a Literal Rendering in the Spenserian Stanza of the First Book of the Odyssey, and Specimens of the Iliad. William G. T. Barter, Esq., Author of " A Literal Translation, in Spenserian Stanza, of the Iliad of Homer." Crown 8vo. 6s. 6d.

Auxilia Graeca : containing Forms of Parsing and Greek Trees, the Greek Prepositions, Rules of Accentuation, Greek Idioms, &c. &c. By the Rev. H. Fowler, M.A. 12mo. 3s. 6d.

A Latin Grammar. By T. Hewitt Key, M.A., F.R.S., Professor of Comparative Grammar, and Head Master of the Junior School, in University College. *Third Edition, revised.* Post 8vo. 8s.

A Short Latin Grammar, for Schools. By T. H. Key, M.A., F.R.S. *Third Edition.* Post 8vo. 3s. 6d.

Latin Accidence. Consisting of the Forms, and intended to prepare boys for Key's Short Latin Grammar. Post 8vo. 2s.

A First Cheque Book for Latin Verse Makers. By the Rev. F. Gretton, Stamford Free Grammar School. 1s. 6d. Key, 2s. 6d.

Reddenda; or Passages with Parallel Hints for translation into Latin Prose and Verse. By the Rev. F. E. Gretton. Crown 8vo. 4s. 6d.

Rules for the Genders of Latin Nouns, and the Perfects and Supines of Verbs; with hints on Construing, &c. By H. Haines, M.A. 1s. 6d.

Latin Prose Lessons. By the Rev. A. Church, M.A., one of the Masters of Merchant Taylors' School. Fcap. 8vo. 2s. 6d.

Materials for Latin Prose Composition. By the Rev. P. Frost, M.A., St. John's College, Cambridge. *Second Edition.* 12mo. 2s. 6d. Key, 4s.

Materials for Greek Prose Composition. By the Rev. P. Frost, M.A. Fcap. 8vo. 3s. 6d. Key to ditto. 5s.

The Works of Virgil, closely rendered into English Rhythm, and illustrated from British Poets of the 16th, 17th, and 18th Centuries. By the Rev. R. C. Singleton, M.A. 2 vols. post 8vo. 18s.

Quintus Horatius Flaccus. Illustrated with 50 Engravings from the Antique. Fcap. 8vo. 5s. Morocco, 9s.

Selections from Ovid : Amores, Tristia, Heroides, Metamorphoses. With English Notes, by the Rev. A. J. Macleane, M.A. Fcap. 8vo. 3s. 6d.

Sabrinae Corolla in hortulis Reginae Scholae Salopiensis contexuerunt tres viri floribus legendis. *Editio Altera.* 8vo. 12s. Morocco, 21s.

Dual Arithmetic, a New Art, by Oliver Byrne, formerly Professor of Mathematics at the late College of Civil Engineers, Putney. 8vo. 10s. 6d.

A Graduated Series of Exercises in Elementary Algebra, with an Appendix containing Papers of Miscellaneous Examples. Designed for the Use of Schools. By the Rev. G. F. Wright, M.A., Mathematical Master at Wellington College. Crown 8vo. 3s. 6d.

The Elements of Euclid. Books I.—VI. XI. 1—21; XII. 1, 2; a new text, based on that of Simson, with Exercises. Edited by H. J Hose, late Mathematical Master of Westminster School. Fcap. 4s. 6d.

A Graduated Series of Exercises on the Elements of Euclid: Books I.—VI.; XI. 1—21; XII. 1, 2. Selected and arranged by Henry J. Hose, M.A. 12mo. 1s.

The Enunciations and Figures belonging to the Propositions in the First Six and part of the Eleventh Books of Euclid's Elements, (usually read in the Universities,) prepared for Students in Geometry. By the Rev. J. Brasse, D.D. *New Edition.* Fcap. 8vo. 1s. On cards, in case, 5s. 6d.; without the Figures, 6d.

A Compendium of Facts and Formulæ in Pure and Mixed Mathematics. For the use of Mathematical Students. By G. R. Smalley, B.A., F.R.A.S. Fcap. 8vo. 3s. 6d.

A Table of Anti-Logarithms; containing to seven places of decimals, natural numbers, answering to all Logarithms from ·00001 to ·99999; and an improved table of Gauss' Logarithms, by which may be found the Logarithm of the sum or difference of two quantities. With an Appendix, containing a Table of Annuities for three Joint Lives at 3 per cent. Carlisle. By H. E. Filipowski. *Third Edition.* 8vo. 15s.

Handbook of the Slide Rule: showing its applicability to Arithmetic, including Interest and Annuities; Mensuration, including Land Surveying. With numerous Examples and useful Tables. By W. H. Bayley, H. M. East India Civil Service. 12mo. 6s.

The Mechanics of Construction; including the Theories on the Strength of Materials, Roofs, Arches, and Suspension Bridges. With numerous Examples. By Stephen Fenwick, Esq., of the Royal Military Academy, Woolwich. 8vo. 12s.

A NEW FRENCH COURSE, BY MONS. F. E. A. GASC, M.A.

French Master at Brighton College.

FIRST French Book; being a New, Practical, and Easy Method of Learning the Elements of the French Language. New Edition. Fcap. 8vo. 1s. 6d.

French Fables, for Beginners, in Prose, with an Index of all the words at the end of the work. Fcap. 8vo. 2s.

Second French Book; being a Grammar and Exercise Book, on a new and practical plan, exhibiting the chief peculiarities of the French Language, as compared with the English, and intended as a sequel to the "First French Book." Fcap. 8vo. 2s. 6d.

A Key to the First and Second French Books. Fcap. 8vo. 3s. 6d.

Histoires Amusantes et Instructives; or, Selections of Complete Stories from the best French Authors, who have written for the Young. With English Notes. *New Edition.* Fcap. 8vo. 2s. 6d.

Practical Guide to Modern French Conversation: containing:— I. The most current and useful Phrases in Every-Day Talk; II. Everybody's Necessary Questions and Answers in Travel-Talk. Fcap. 2s. 6d.

French Poetry for the Young. With English Notes, and preceded by a few plain Rules of French Prosody. Fcap. 8vo. 2s.

Materials for French Prose Composition; or, Selections from the best English Prose Writers. With copious Foot Notes, and Hints for Idiomatic Renderings. *New Edition.* Fcap. 8vo. 4s. 6d. Key, 6s.

Le Petit Compagnon: a French Talk-book for Little Children. With 52 Illustrations. 16mo. 2s. 6d.

THE French Drama; being a Selection of the best Tragedies and Comedies of Molière, Racine, P. Corneille, T. Corneille, and Voltaire. With Arguments in English at the head of each scene, and Notes, Critical and Explanatory, by A. Gombert. 18mo. Sold separately at 1s. each. Half-bound, 1s. 6d. each.

COMEDIES BY MOLIERE.

Le Misanthrope.
L'Avare.
Le Bourgeois Gentilhomme.
Le Tartuffe.
Le Malade Imaginaire.
Les Femmes Savantes.
Les Fourberies de Scapin.

Les Précieuses Ridicules.
L'Ecole des Femmes.
L'Ecole des Maris.
Le Médecin Malgré Lui.
M. de Pouceaugnac.
Amphitryon.

TRAGEDIES, &c. BY RACINE.

La Thébaïde, ou les Frères Ennemis.
Alexandre le Grand.
Andromaque.
Les Plaideurs, (Com.)
Britannicus.
Bérénice.

Bajazet.
Mithridate.
Iphigénie.
Phèdre.
Esther.
Athalie.

TRAGEDIES, &c. BY P. CORNEILLE.

Le Cid.
Horace.
Cinna.
Polyeucte.

Pompée.

BY T. CORNEILLE.
Ariane.

PLAYS BY VOLTAIRE.

Brutus.
Zaire.
Alzire.
Orestes.

Le Fanatisme.
Mérope.
La Mort de César.
Semiramis.

Le Nouveau Trésor: or, French Student's Companion: designed to facilitate the Translation of English into French at Sight. *Thirteenth Edition*, with Additions. By M. E*** S*****. 12mo. Roan, 3s. 6d.

A Test-Book for Students: Examination Papers for Students preparing for the Universities or for Appointments in the Army and Civil Service, and arranged for General Use in Schools. By the Rev. Thomas Stantial, M.A., Head Master of the Grammar School, Bridgwater. Part I.—History and Geography. 2s. 6d. Part II.—Language and Literature. 2s. 6d. Part III.—Mathematical Science. 2s. 6d. Part IV.—Physical Science. 1s. 6d. Or in 1 vol., Crown 8vo., 7s. 6d.

Tables of Comparative Chronology, illustrating the division of Universal History into Ancient, Mediæval, and Modern History; and containing a System of Combinations, distinguished by a particular type, to assist the Memory in retaining Dates. By W. E. Bickmore and the Rev. C. Bickmore, M.A. *Third Edition*. 4to. 5s.

A Course of Historical and Chronological Instruction. By W. E. Bickmore. 2 Parts. 12mo. 3s. 6d. each.

A Practical Synopsis of English History: or, A General Summary of Dates and Events for the use of Schools, and Candidates for Public Examinations. By Arthur Bowes. *Third Edition*, enlarged. 8vo. 2s.

Educational Books.

Under Government: an Official Key to the Civil Service, and
Guide for Candidates seeking Appointments under the Crown. By J. C. Parkinson, Inland Revenue, Somerset House. *New Edition.* Cr. 8vo. 3s. 6d.

Government Examinations; being a Companion to "Under Government," and a Guide to the Civil Service Examinations. By J. C. Parkinson. Crown 8vo. 2s. 6d.

The Student's Text-Book of English and General History, from B.C. 100 to the present time. With Genealogical Tables, and a Sketch of the English Constitution. By D. Beale. *Sixth Edition.* Post 8vo. Sewed, 2s. Cloth, 2s. 6d.
"This is very much in advance of most works we have seen devoted to similar purposes. We can award very high praise to a volume which may prove invaluable to teachers and taught."—*Athenæum.*

The Elements of the English Language for Schools and Colleges. By Ernest Adams, Ph. D. University College School. *New Edition, enlarged, and improved.* Crown 8vo. 4s. 6d.

The Geographical Text-Book; a Practical Geography, calculated to facilitate the study of that useful science, by a constant reference to the Blank Maps. By M. E... S..... 12mo. 2s.
II. The Blank Maps done up separately. 4to. 2s. coloured.

The Manual of Book-keeping; by an Experienced Clerk. 12mo. *Eighth Edition.* 4s.

Double Entry Elucidated. By B. W. Foster. 4to. 8s. 6d.

Penmanship, Theoretical and Practical, Illustrated and Explained. By B. F. Foster. 12mo. *New Edition.* 2s. 6d.

Goldsmith's (J.) Copy Books: five sorts, large, text, round, small, and mixed. Post 4to. on fine paper. 6s. per dozen.

The Young Ladies' School Record: or, Register of Studies and conduct. 12mo. 6d.

Welchman on the Thirty-nine Articles of the Church of England, with Scriptural Proofs, &c. 18mo. 2s. or interleaved for Students, 3s.

Bishop Jewel's Apology for the Church of England, with his famous Epistle on the Council of Trent, and a Memoir. 32mo. 2s.

A Short Explanation of the Epistles and Gospels of the Christian Year, with Questions for Schools. Royal 32mo. 2s. 6d.; calf, 4s. 6d.

Manual of Astronomy: a Popular Treatise on Descriptive, Physical, and Practical Astronomy. By John Drew, F.R.A.S. *Second Edition.* Fcap. 8vo. 5s.

The First Book of Botany. Being a Plain and Brief Introduction to that Science for Schools and Young Persons. By Mrs. Loudon. Illustrated with 36 Wood Engravings. *Second Edition.* 18mo. 1s.

English Poetry for Classical Schools; or, Florilegium Poeticum Anglicanum. 12mo. 1s. 6d.

BELL AND DALDY'S ILLUSTRATED SCHOOL BOOKS.
Royal 16mo.

SCHOOL Primer. 6d.

School Reader. 1s. [*Shortly*.

Poetry Book for Schools. 1s.

COURSE OF INSTRUCTION FOR THE YOUNG, BY HORACE GRANT.

EXERCISES for the Improvement of the Senses; for Young Children. 18mo. 1s. 6d.

Geography for Young Children. *New Edition*. 18mo. 2s.

Arithmetic for Young Children. *New Edition*. 18mo. 1s. 6d.

Arithmetic. Second Stage. *New Edition*. 18mo. 3s.

PERIODICALS.

NOTES and Queries: a Medium of Intercommunication for Literary Men, Artists, Antiquaries, Geneulogists, &c. Published every Saturday. 4to. 4d., stamped, 5d. Vols. I. to XII. Second Series, and Vols. I. and II. Third Series, now ready, 10s. 6d. each.
*** General Index to the First Series, 5s.
——————— Second Series. Sewed 5s.; cloth 5s. 6d.

The Parish Magazine. Edited by J. Erskine Clarke, M.A., Derby. Monthly, price 1d. Volumes for 1859, 1860, 1861, and 1862, 1s. 6d. and 2s. each.

The Mission Field: a Monthly Record of the Proceedings of the Society for the Propagation of the Gospel. Vols. II. to VII. post 8vo. 3s. each. (Vol. I. is out of print.) Continued in Numbers, 2d. each.

The Gospel Missionary. Published for the Society for the Propagation of the Gospel in Foreign Parts. Monthly at ½d. Vols. II. to XII. in cloth, 1s. each. (Vol. I. is out of print.)

Missions to the Heathen; being Records of the Progress of the Efforts made by the Society for the Propagation of the Gospel in Foreign Parts for the Conversion of the Heathen Published occasionally in a cheap form for distribution, at prices varying from 1d. to 1s. 6d. each. Nos. 1 to 43 are already published.

Church in the Colonies, consisting chiefly of Journals by the Colonial Bishops of their Progress and Special Visitations. Published occasionally at prices varying from 2d. to 1s. 6d. each. Nos. 1 to 37 are already published.

CLARKE'S COMMERCIAL COPY-BOOKS.
Price 4d. A liberal allowance to Schools and Colleges.

The FIRST COPY-BOOK contains *elementary turns*, with a broad mark like a T, which divides a well-formed turn into two equal parts. This exercise enables the learner to judge of *form, distance, and proportion.*

The SECOND contains *large-hand letters*, and the means by which such letters may be properly combined; the joinings in writing being probably as difficult to learn as the form of each character. This book also gives the whole alphabet, not in separate letters, but rather as one *word;* and, at the end of the alphabet, the difficult letters are repeated so as to render the writing of the pupil more thorough and *uniform.*

The THIRD contains additional *large-hand practice.*

The FOURTH contains *large-hand words*, commencing with *unflourished* capitals; and the words being short, the capitals in question receive the attention they demand. As Large, and Extra Large-text, to which the fingers of the learner are not equal, have been dispensed with in this series, the popular objection of having *too many Copy-books* for the pupil to drudge through, is now fairly met. When letters are very large, the scholar cannot compass them without stopping to change the position of his hand, which *destroys* the *freedom* which such writing is intended to promote.

The FIFTH contains the essentials of a useful kind of *small-hand.* There are first, as in large-hand, five easy letters of the alphabet, forming four copies, which of course are repeated. Then follows the remainder of the alphabet, with the difficult characters alluded to. The letters in this hand, especially the *a, c, d, g, o,* and *q*, are so formed that when the learner will have to correspond, his writing will not appear stiff. The copies in this book are not *mere Large-hand reduced.*

The SIXTH contains *small-hand copies*, with instructions as to the manner in which the pupil should hold his pen, so that when he leaves school he may not merely have some facility in copying, but really possess the information on the subject of writing which he may need at any future time.

The SEVENTH contains the foundation for a style of *small-hand*, adapted to females, *moderately pointed.*

The EIGHTH contains copies for females; and the holding of the pen is, of course, the subject to which they specially relate.

This Series is specially adapted for those who are preparing for a commercial life. It is generally found when a boy leaves school that his writing is of such a character that it is some months before it is available for book-keeping or accounts. The special object of this Series of Copy-Books is to form his writing in such a style that he may be put to the work of a counting-house at once. By following this course from the first the writing is kept free and legible, whilst it avoids unnecessary flourishing.

Specimens of hand-writing after a short course may be seen on application to the Publishers.

BELL AND DALDY'S
Pocket Volumes.
A SERIES OF SELECT WORKS OF FAVOURITE AUTHORS.

THE intention of the Publishers is to produce a Series of Volumes adapted for general reading, moderate in price, compact and elegant in form, and executed in a style fitting them to be permanently preserved.

They do not profess to compete with the so-called cheap volumes. They believe that a cheapness which is attained by the use of inferior type and paper, and absence of editorial care, and which results in volumes that no one cares to keep, is a false cheapness. They desire rather to produce books superior in quality, and relatively as cheap.

Each volume will be carefully revised by a competent editor, and printed at the Chiswick Press, on fine paper, with new type and ornaments and initial letters specially designed for the series.

The *Pocket Volumes* will include all classes of Literature, both copyright and non-copyright ;—Biography, History, Voyages, Travels, Poetry, sacred and secular, Books of Adventure and Fiction. They will include Translations of Foreign Books, and also such American Literature as may be considered worthy of adoption.

The Publishers desire to respect the moral claims of authors who cannot secure legal copyright in this country, and to remunerate equitably those whose works they may reprint.

The books will be issued at short intervals, in paper covers, at various prices, from 1s. to 3s. 6d., and in cloth, top edge gilt, at 6d. per volume extra, in half morocco, Roxburgh style, at 1s. extra, in antique or best plain morocco (Hayday), at 4s. extra.

Now Ready.

White's Natural History of Selborne. 3s.
Coleridge's Poems. 2s. 6d.
The Robin Hood Ballads. 2s. 6d.
The Midshipman. By Capt. Basil Hall, R.N. 3s.
The Lieutenant and Commander. By the same Author. 3s.
Southey's Life of Nelson. 2s. 6d.
George Herbert's Poems. 2s.
George Herbert's Works. 3s.
Longfellow's Poems. 2s. 6d.
Lamb's Tales from Shakspeare. 2s. 6d.
Milton's Paradise Lost. 2s. 6d.
Milton's Paradise Regained and other Poems. 2s. 6d.

Sea Songs and Ballads. By Charles Dibdin, and others. 2s. 6d.
Burns's Poems. 2s. 6d.
Walton's Complete Angler. Illustrated. 2s. 6d.

Preparing.

Burns's Songs.
The Conquest of India. By Capt. Basil Hall, R.N.
Walton's Lives of Donne, Wotton Hooker, &c.
Gray's Poems.
Goldsmith's Poems.
Goldsmith's Vicar of Wakefield.
Henry Vaughan's Poems.
And others.

CHISWICK PRESS :—PRINTED BY WHITTINGHAM AND WILKINS, TOOKS COURT, CHANCERY LANE.

www.ingramcontent.com/pod-product-compliance
Lightning Source LLC
Chambersburg PA
CBHW030003240426
43672CB00007B/805